THE ARTIST'S GUIDE TO PEN AND INK

Take Your Drawings to the Next Level with Gorgeous Shading Techniques

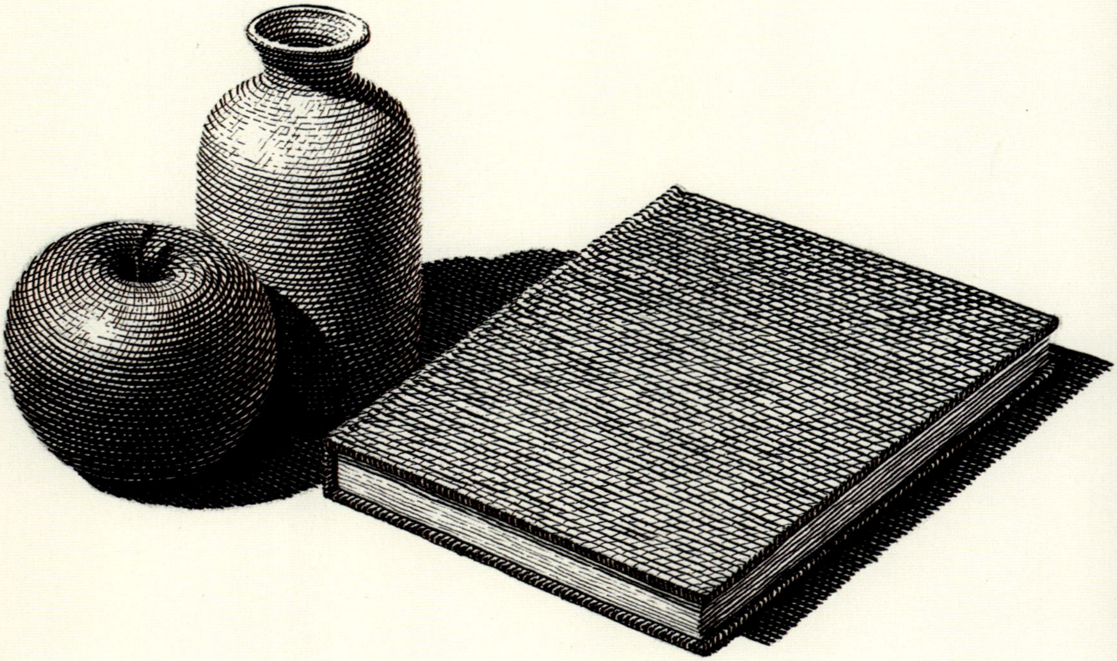

THE ARTIST'S GUIDE TO PEN AND INK

Take Your Drawings to the Next Level with Gorgeous Shading Techniques

From Basic Strokes to Full Compositions

TRI LE

PAGE STREET
PUBLISHING CO.

PAGE STREET
PUBLISHING CO.

First published in 2025 by
Page Street Publishing Co.
27 Congress Street, Suite 1511
Salem, MA 01970
www.pagestreetpublishing.com

Distributed by Macmillan, sales in Canada by The Canadian Manda Group.

29 28 27 26 25 1 2 3 4 5

ISBN-13: 979-8-89003-180-8

Library of Congress Control Number: 2024933690

Edited by Franny Donington-Ayad and Sarah Monroe
Cover and book design by Tri Le and Molly Kate Young for Page Street Publishing Co.
Illustrations by Tri Le

Printed and bound in China

To my beloved mother, Thuy Nguyen, father, Thanh Le, and brother,
Tai Le, where I remain forever a child.

To my wife, Trang Cao, who sees the truth in the passions I dedicate myself to.

To my son, Du Le, the glowing light in the heart of winter.

To Tho Nguyen, Nam Nguyen, Hung Le, Trong Nguyen, and all my dear friends,
where laughter and joy abound.

To Ngoc Sy Luong and Anh Tuan Do, I always dream of us wandering like young souls.

To my editor Franny, and the entire team at Page Street, who guided me
in bringing this book to life.

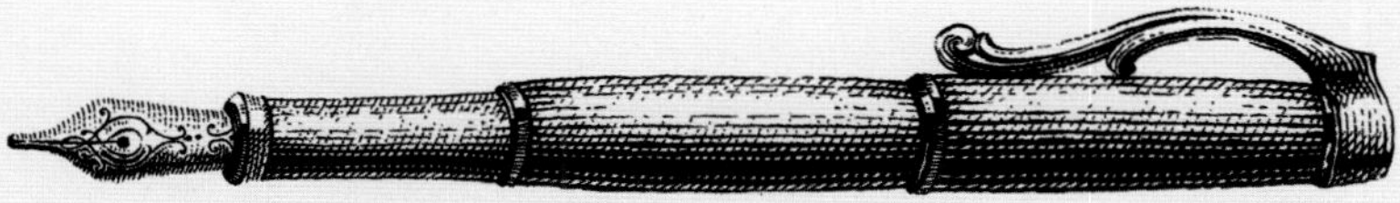

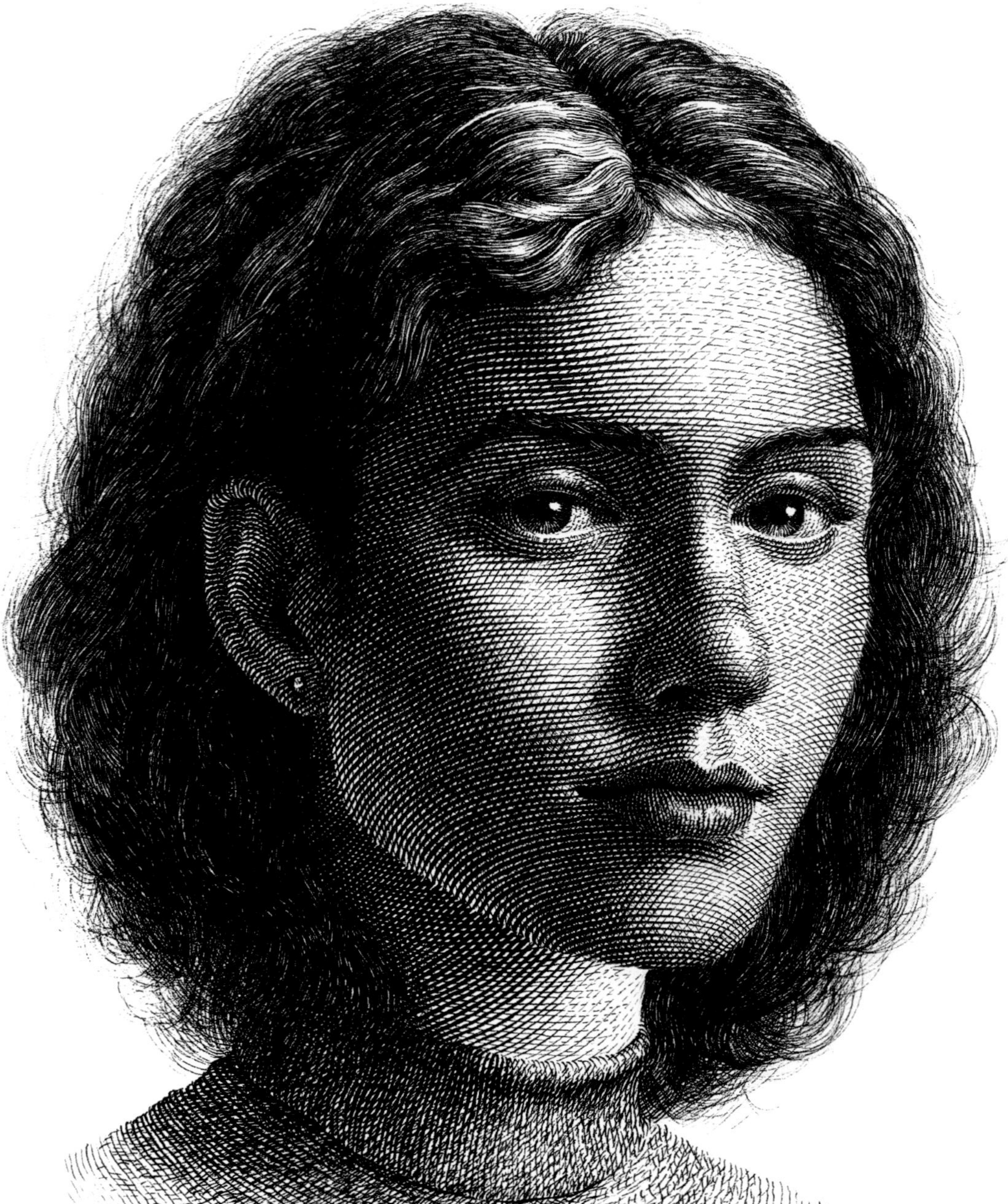

CONTENTS

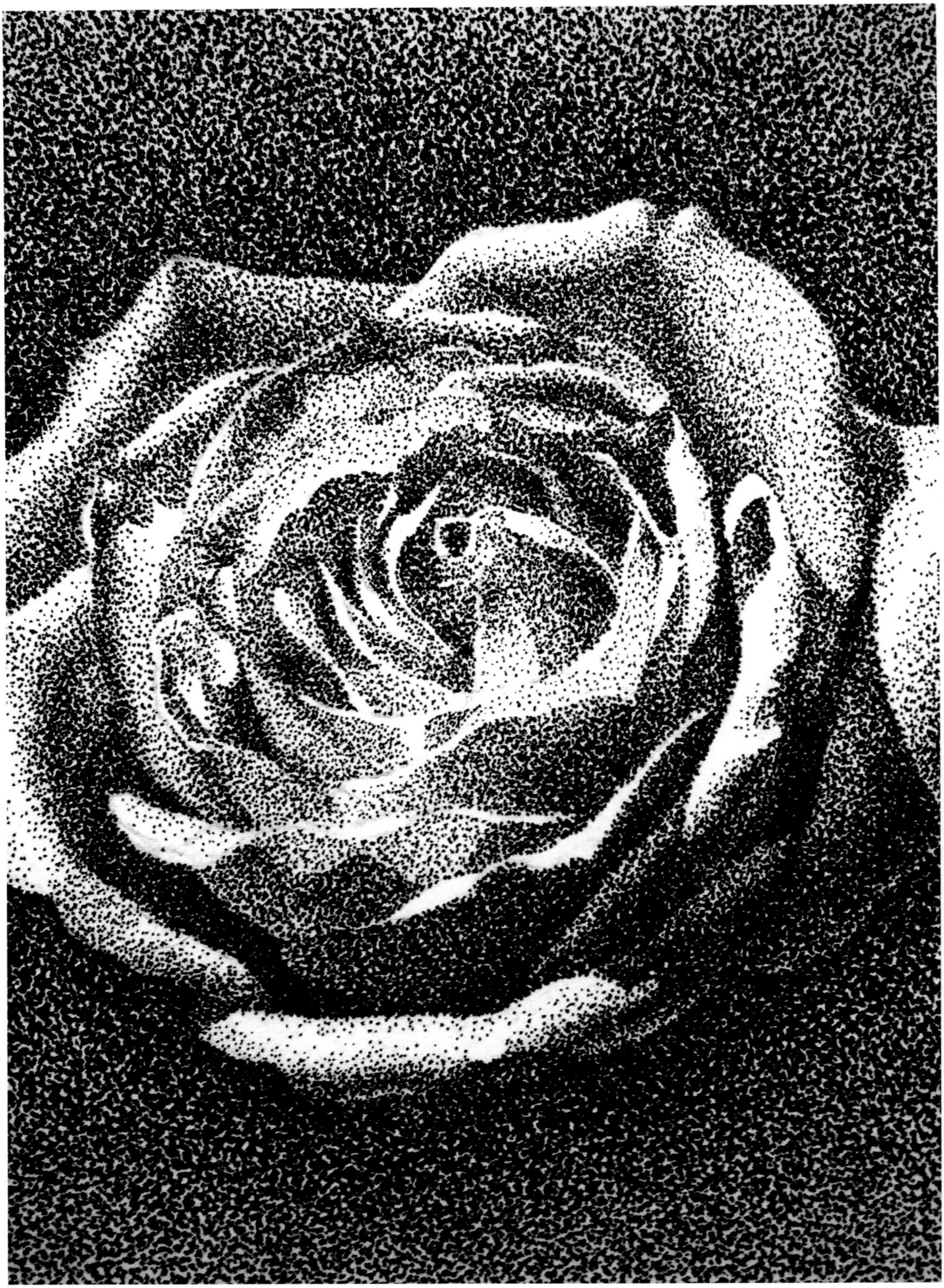

Introduction

Welcome to the journey of exploring the art of pen and ink! My name is Tri Le, and I'm an artist currently based in Canada. It's been years since my artistic journey began, especially with pen and ink. I'm honored to share my experience in this type of art with you. Whether you're a beginner or looking to refine your existing skills, my goal is not only to help you practice specific and detailed techniques but also to help you discover your own artistic identity and uniqueness through the art of pen and ink.

To me, art is not just about showcasing visual beauty; it's a way to tell stories and communicate. I've had a passion for art since I was a kid, and self-study has been my "best friend" along the way, helping me refine my skills. I have had the opportunity to work on book illustration projects, participate in exhibitions, and teach art classes over the years. This has given me a solid foundation to dive deep into, synthesize, and share with you valuable information about the art of pen and ink.

After spending years immersed in the world of pen and ink, I wrote this book to share with you everything I have learned and experienced, with the hope of contributing to the community of art lovers and helping you build a strong foundation as you begin your journey into this visual art medium.

Throughout the following pages, we'll discuss and learn pen-and-ink drawing in depth. We'll start with the most fundamental concepts and move on to more specific techniques through practical exercises with detailed step-by-step descriptions that you can follow and practice along with. From there, your learning journey will go beyond just pen strokes, leading to a deeper understanding of the art foundation, concepts, and creativity.

Today, art materials are more diverse than ever, and pen and ink are among the earliest developed mediums still widely used by art enthusiasts. With pen and ink, you have the freedom to express not only the visual beauty of your artwork but also your thoughts, ideas, stories, and creativity.

Pen-and-ink drawing emphasizes the expression of light by creating monochromatic works. Through specific techniques like hatching, crosshatching, and stippling, the way you depict your artwork becomes incredibly varied and flexible, allowing you to convey the subject's appearance and your ideas and emotions within your art. As you progress through this book, I hope that you will not only gain practical knowledge but also find inspiration to express your own artistic creations.

Let's head to the first station on our pen-and-ink art journey!

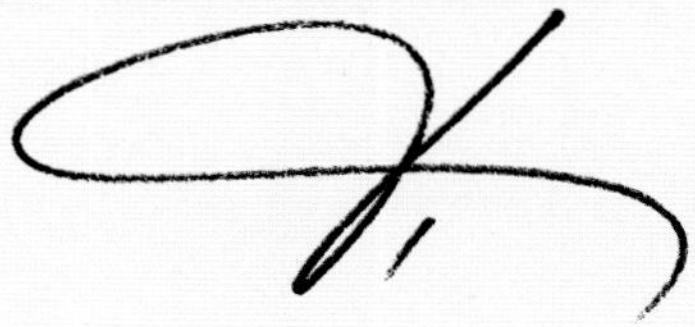

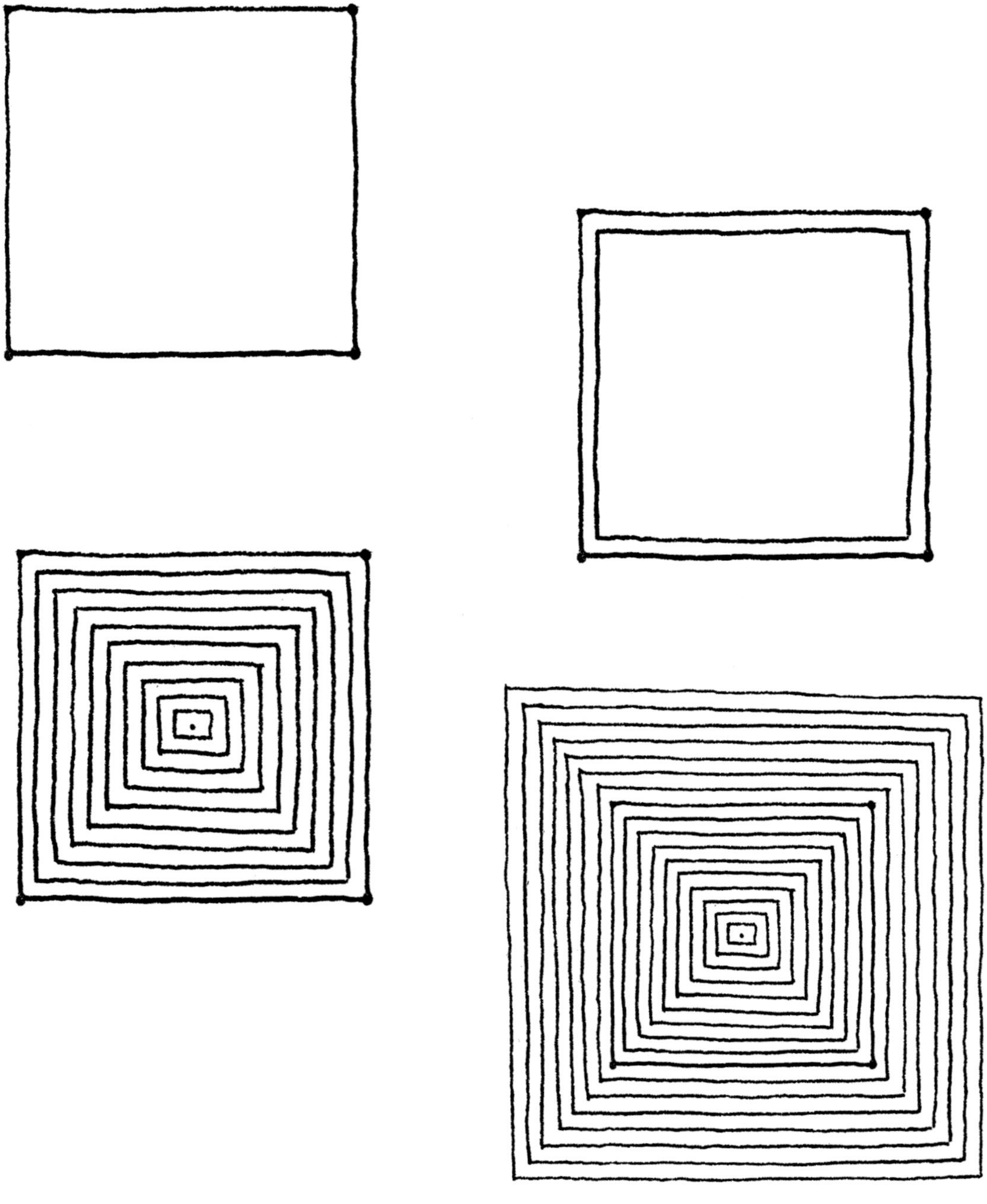

CHAPTER 1
YOUR DRAWING KIT ESSENTIALS

Materials and tools are your companions throughout your practice and creative process. Choosing the right tools and materials will closely support your drawing journey, helping you create more effective practice exercises and artworks that fully express your thoughts.

In the realm of pen-and-ink drawing, we have a wide range of supplies available to us. In this section, let's explore the world of pen-and-ink materials and tools and learn how to choose the ones that are just right for you.

Choosing the Right Pens

Drawing pens come in all shapes and sizes, from technical pens to fancy fountain pens and the beloved fineliners. Fineliners are popular choices because they are easy to use, are affordable, and have a variety of nib sizes. Fineliners are perfect for sketching, outlining, or adding small details to your work.

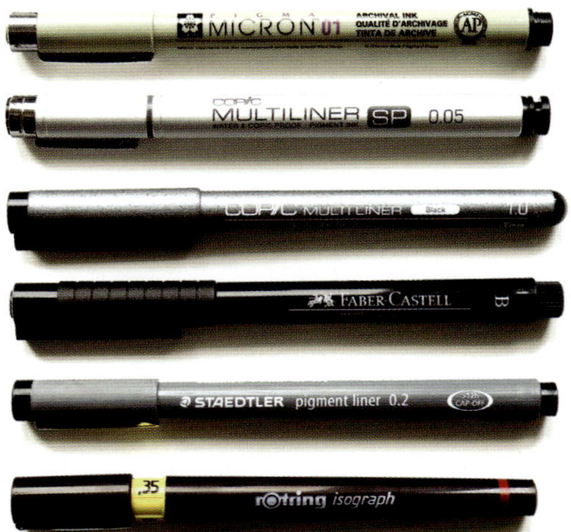

Popular brands and options like **Sakura Pigma Micron®**, **Copic® Multiliner**, **Faber-Castell Pitt Artist Pen (or Ecco Pigment)**, and **STAEDTLER Pigment Liner** offer a variety of nib sizes, from superfine 003 to broader 1.0, and brush tips. Moreover, if you enjoy using technical pens with steel nibs and liquid ink cartridges, you might want to try out **rOtring Isograph** pens. They're known for delivering incredibly precise lines, making them a great option for detailed work.

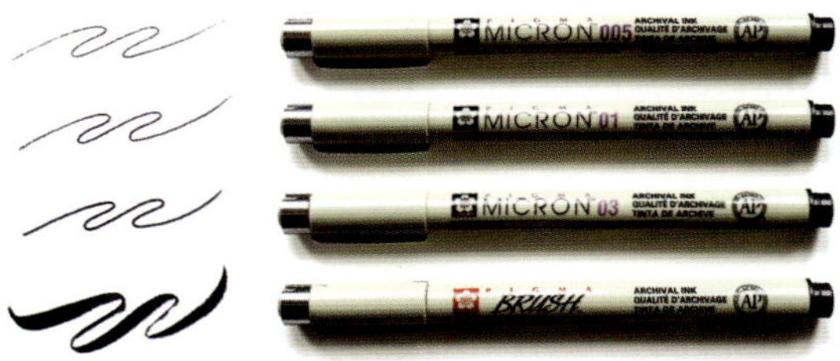

Trying out different nib sizes lets you play around with your drawing style and add various levels of detail to your artwork. To begin and practice the exercises in this book, I recommend using three pen tip sizes:

- **005** for very fine and delicate lines
- **01** for medium lines when outlining or shading
- **03** for bolder strokes when shading the dark tone
- **BR** (Brush) for shading solid black areas (optional)

Among all these options, my favorite is **Sakura Pigma Micron**, which offers consistent pricing, standard quality, sharp lines, and rich ink tones.

FINDING YOUR PERFECT PAPER

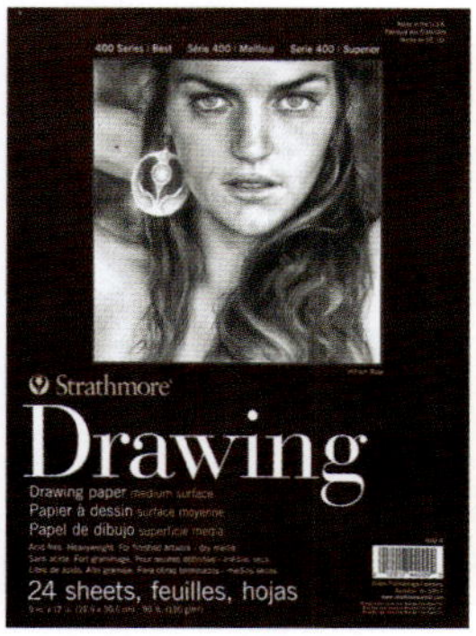

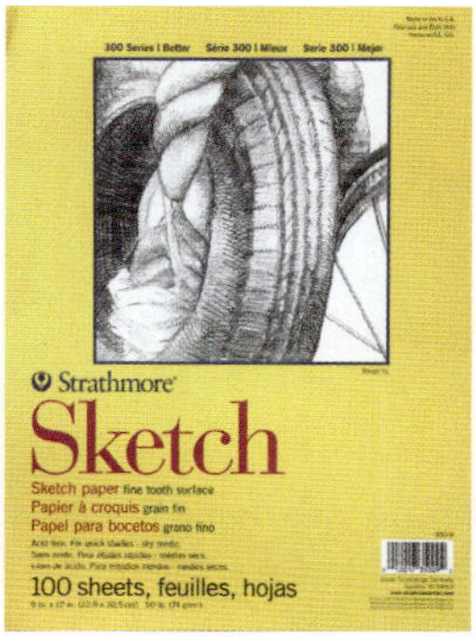

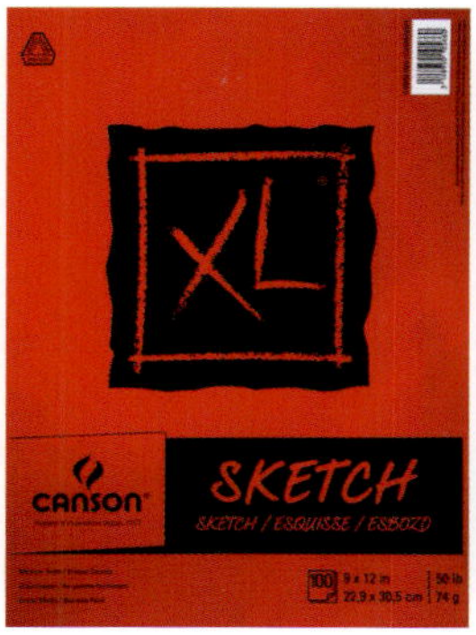

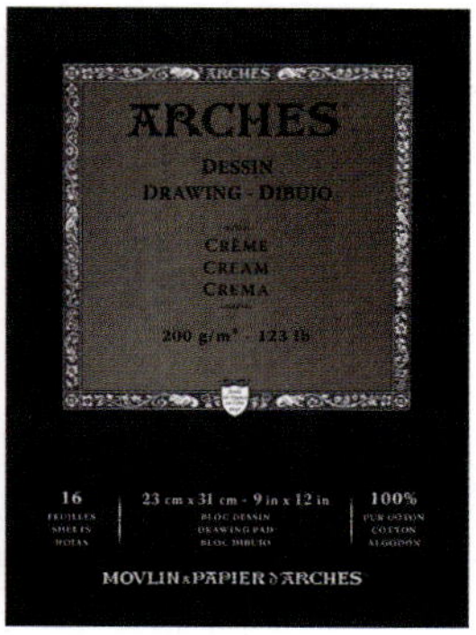

Paper is our trusty sidekick, specially crafted to pair perfectly with pen-and-ink drawing. The type of paper we choose depends on the pen-and-ink techniques we will be using. For drawings with fineliners, choosing a paper is easy since this type of pen works well with most art papers. However, if you are interested in exploring ink wash techniques beyond this book, where you mix water and liquid ink for drawing, the paper used will have some specific differences.

One of the most popular brands is **Strathmore®**, particularly their **Series 400 Drawing**, offering excellent compatibility with pen and ink. If you're looking for a more affordable paper for practice, Strathmore offers the **300 Series Drawing** and **300 Series Sketching**, which feature thinner paper and come in larger quantities. Despite being more budget-friendly, the quality remains very stable.

Another top choice is **Canson® XL® Sketch, or Arches® Drawing Sketchbook** (professional quality), known for their high-quality paper products. In addition, you can also explore the individual paper section at your local art supply store; you never know what hidden gems you might find to experiment with from various manufacturers.

Must-Have Drawing Tools

In addition to the materials and tools for pen-and-ink drawing, we will also need some basic tools for practicing, measuring, and sketching throughout the drawing process. Following are my tips for selecting each of these tools.

Pencils

Pencils are an essential tool when it comes to brainstorming and sketching. There are many options available, with **STAEDTLER** pencils being the most popular due to their standard quality and affordable price. Another brand that I personally love is **Faber-Castell**, known for its high quality, durability, and impressive drawing results.

When it comes to pencils, you'll often notice letters and numbers like HB, 2B, 6B, etc., on the end of the pencil. These symbols indicate the hardness or softness of the pencil, as well as the darkness. You can categorize them as follows:

- **H** (Hard): These are hard, light pencils. The higher the number, the lighter the pencil, such as 4H, 2H, etc. These are typically used for sketching and drawing faint lines.
- **B** (Black): These pencils are soft and dark, ranging from HB (Hard-Black) to 8B or 10B. The higher the number, the darker the pencil, and these are usually used for shading and drawing darker areas.
- **F** (Fine): In addition to H and B, F is a specific pencil designed for finer, more detailed lines, and it doesn't usually come with a number.

For this book, I recommend using the following three types of pencils:

- **H or HB:** For sketching.
- **2B or 3B:** For practicing basic shading with moderate darkness.
- **6B or 8B:** For practicing very dark and shaded areas.

Rulers and Erasers

A ruler may not be an essential tool used frequently in the exercises (since we will be practicing more freehand drawing), but it can be very useful in certain situations when we need to measure and create guidelines. For rulers, you can use any type you find at art supply stores.

An eraser is a valuable tool when sketching with pencils. It allows you to easily correct your sketches and improve your drawings. My two favorite erasers are **Faber-Castell** and **Tombow MONO**. Additionally, you can use a small-sized eraser, like the **Tombow MONO Eraser Pen**, for erasing more detailed areas in your drawings.

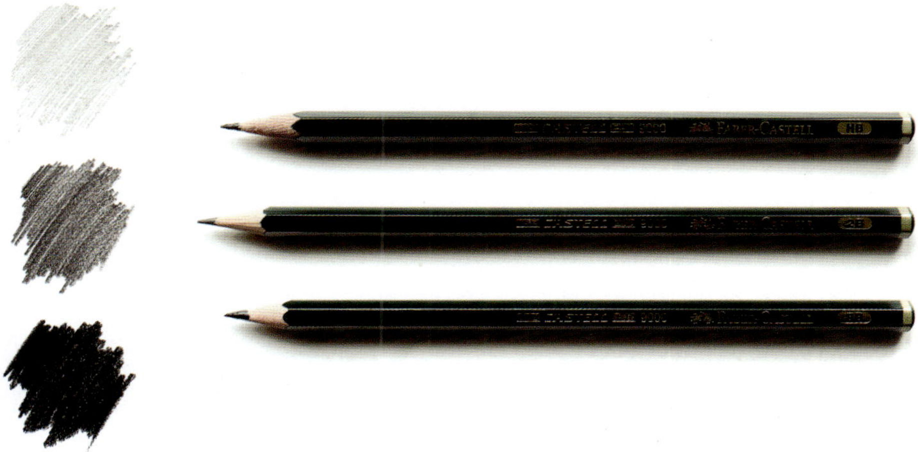

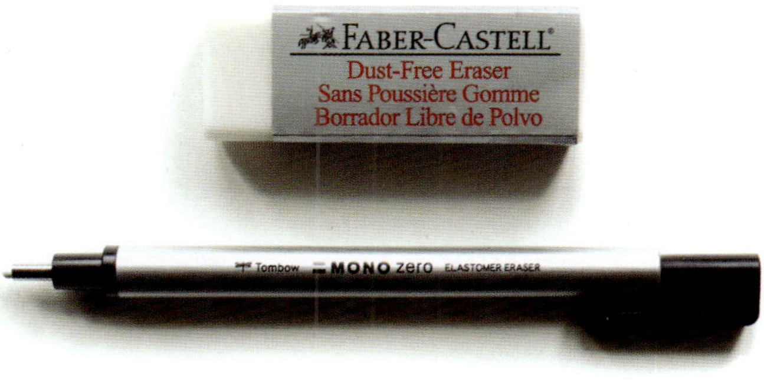

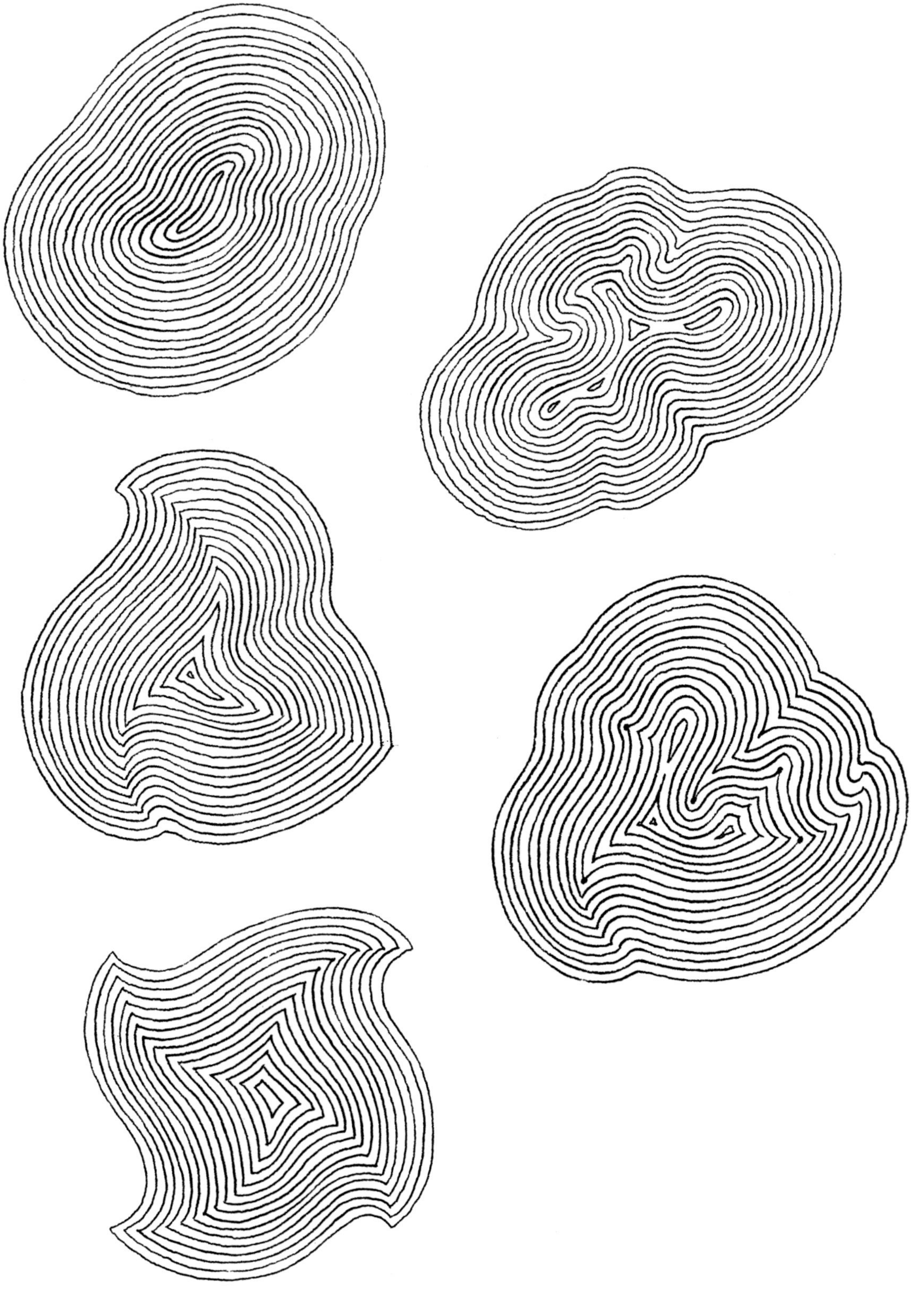

CHAPTER 2
LET'S WARM UP!

Warming up is just as important as creating the actual artwork. In pen-and-ink drawing, warming up helps us get used to the drawing tools and have a better "feeling" in the art expression. It's like stretching before playing a sport—this practice gets us ready to dive in with enthusiasm and creativity!

Warm-up exercises always help you achieve the best results, whether you're in a practice session or working on a complete art piece. Take about 10 to 15 minutes to warm up before you start drawing. Not only will it help relax your hand, but it also enhances your sensitivity, making your strokes more refined and precise.

These warm-up exercises can be done regularly to enhance the skills needed in pen-and-ink drawing. Furthermore, I encourage you to diversify your warm-up routines by exploring additional resources and creating new methods, making the process more enjoyable and exciting.

Playing with Pens

Let's start with some simple exercises to help you get used to drawing lines using fineliners. From basic straight and curved lines to random shapes and drawings, these exercises will serve as a great starting point to improve your pen control and enhance your hand's "feeling." In these warm-up exercises, you can use any fineliner nib size you prefer. However, to achieve clearer and more manageable strokes, I recommend using a nib size of around 01 to 03.

Drawing with Basic Lines

Step 1: Let's start by drawing some random simple lines in a horizontal direction, such as straight lines, zigzag lines, curved lines, wavy lines, and dashed lines about 1 inch (2.5 cm) in length.

Step 2: Repeat these lines below so that the new lines have the same shape and are parallel to the previous ones.

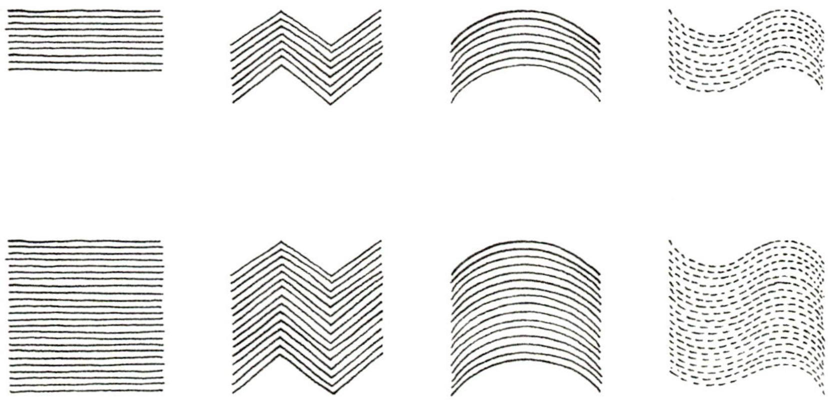

Step 3: Continue the exercise by drawing some small basic geometric shapes (about 1 inch [2.5 cm] in size) like circles, squares, triangles, ovals, or any random shapes you can think of. In this exercise, it's recommended to draw freehand and not use a ruler. These shapes don't need to be perfect; they're just for you to get comfortable with controlling your lines while drawing.

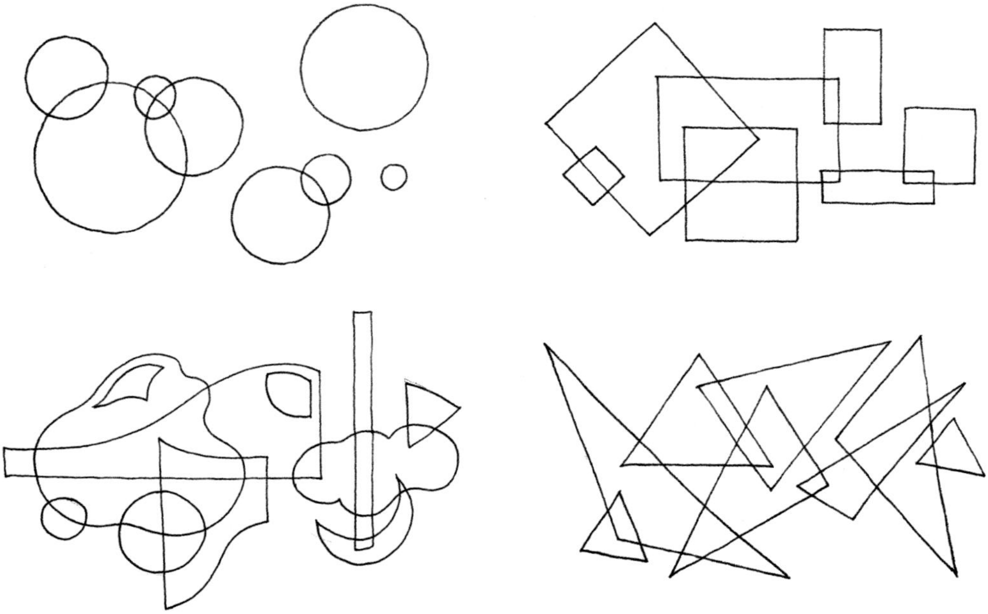

Step 4: After completing some basic shapes, be like a child and draw some simple, specific subjects like a tree, a house, or a face by combining different lines and shapes. Whatever comes to your mind, just draw it! Try adding more details to the drawings you just created. Draw branches and leaves on the tree. Add bricks, wood beams, and details to the house, or additional elements to the mini portrait, like a hat or earrings.

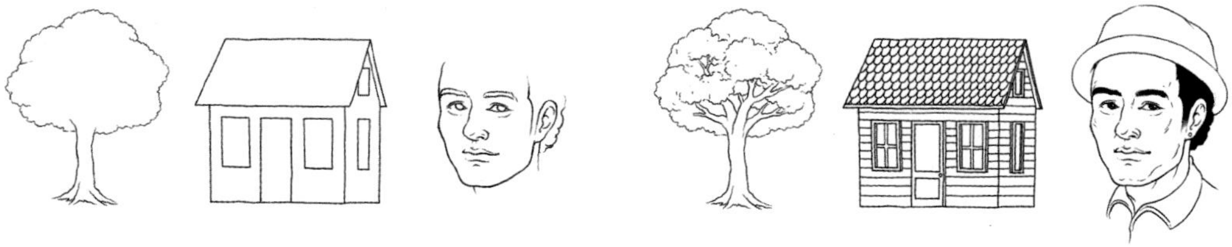

Drawing Lines in Different Lengths

Step 1: Start by drawing a simple straight horizontal line about 1 inch (2.5 cm) in length. Below that, draw simple lines at different angles. Draw one diagonal line, one curved line, and one zigzag line.

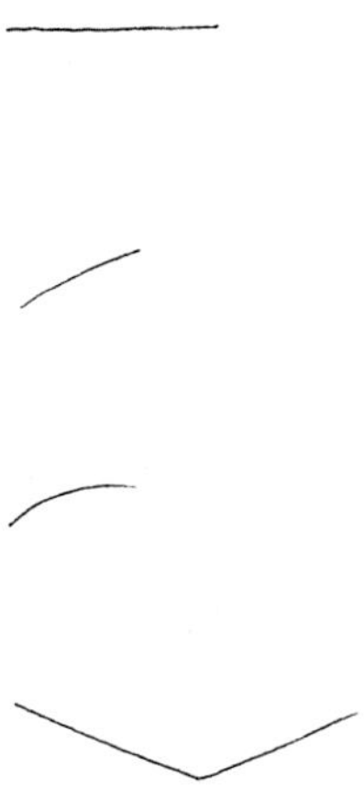

Step 2: Draw another line parallel to the first line, but increase the length to 2 inches (5 cm). Do this for the remaining lines, following each one's shape.

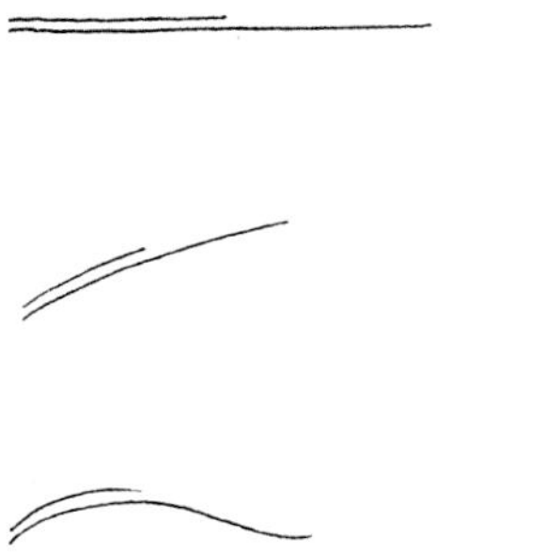

Step 3: Following this method, gradually increase the length of each line until you can draw across the entire width of the paper or sketchbook. To draw longer lines more easily and comfortably, you can lift the edge of your hand off the paper and only use your ring finger and pinky as the points of contact with the surface while your hand moves. Draw at a moderate speed, and try to make each stroke smooth and uninterrupted. Don't worry if you make a mistake—that's one of the best ways to improve your skills.

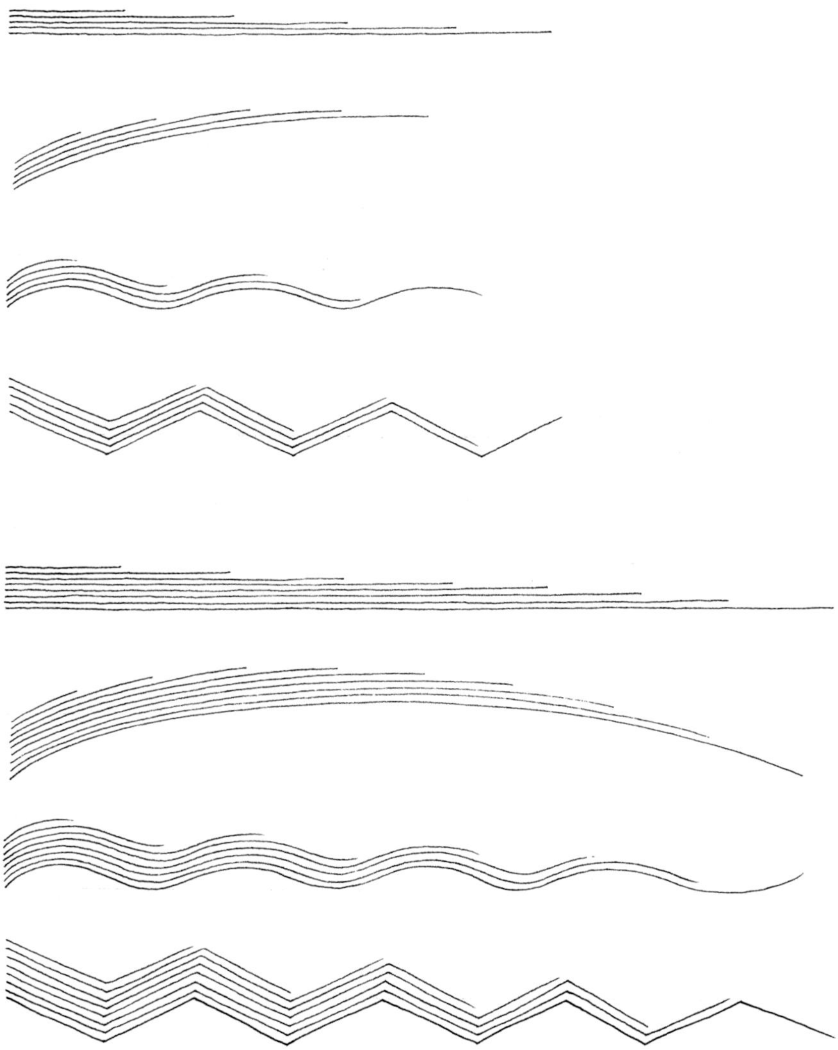

Step 4: After warming up with lines of varying lengths, why not try drawing the space around you? Temporarily set aside thoughts of accuracy or specific techniques, and focus on enjoying the process and the comfort of your hand while drawing. Combine short and long lines with a variety of strokes to capture the space and subjects around you.

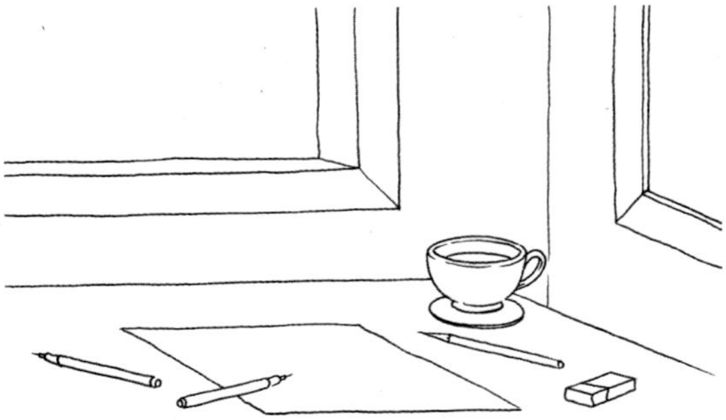

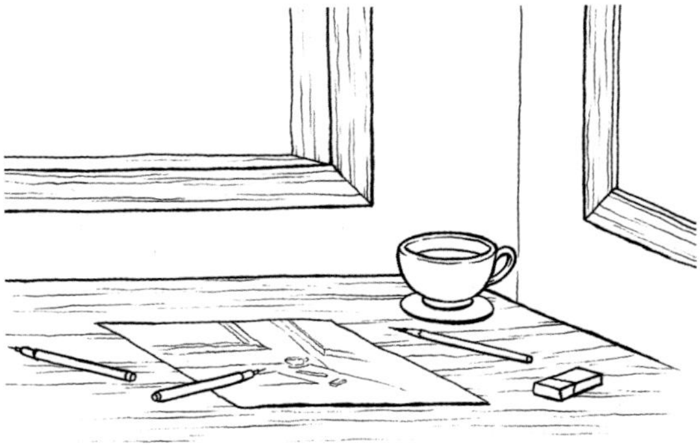

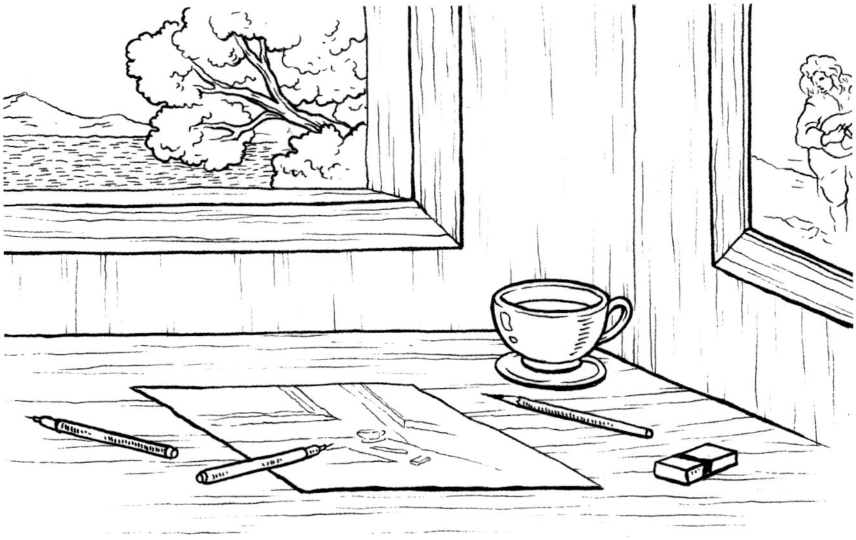

Experimental Pen-and-Ink Shading

Step 1: Use a fineliner with a pen tip size of around 01. Position your fingers holding the pen farther away from the nib, approximately in the middle of the pen's body. Scratch the pen on the paper in a horizontal line about 2 inches (5 cm) long, ensuring the strokes are continuous and without lifting the pen off the paper. As you scratch, move your hand slowly from top to bottom.

Step 2: At this point, you should see a layer of gray ink on the paper. Using the same technique, apply another layer over this gray, but only draw on either the left or right side with strokes about 1 inch (2.5 cm) long. Once completed, you should notice one side is a lighter gray and the other is a darker gray.

Step 3: Use a similar scratching technique to blend these two parts together, creating a smooth transition from the darker to the lighter shade. This exercise is a warm-up for experimenting with shading, helping you convey light and the three-dimensional space of subjects.

1

2

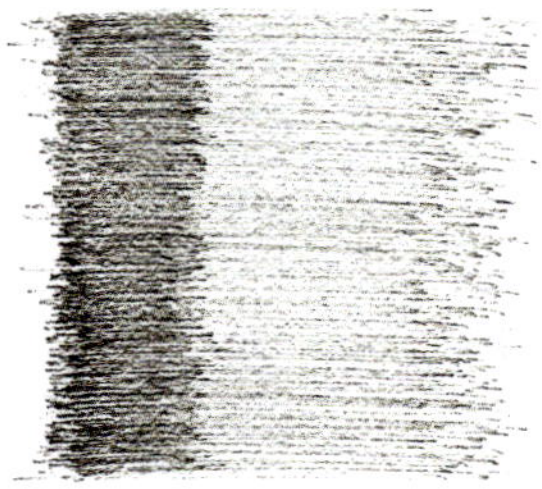

3

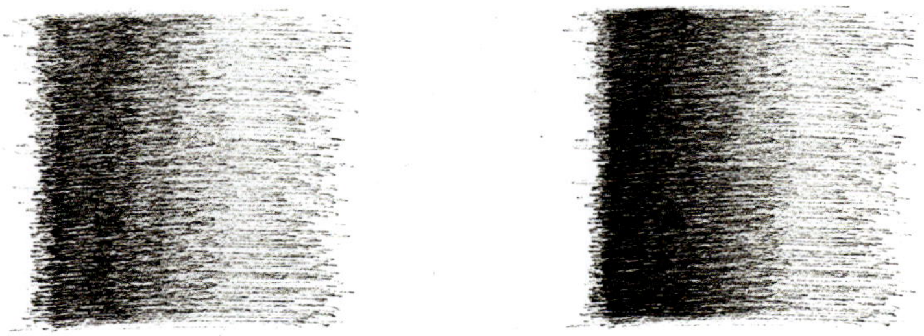

Step 4: Draw a simple subject from your surroundings, or you can revisit Step 4 of Drawing with Basic Lines, where you drew simple shapes like a house or a tree. Divide the subject into two parts: light and dark. Then use the scratching technique you just practiced, making one part lighter and the other part darker. For subjects with curved forms, blend these shading areas smoothly together. Don't worry about perfection right now; just do your best. We will fine-tune our skills in the sections to come.

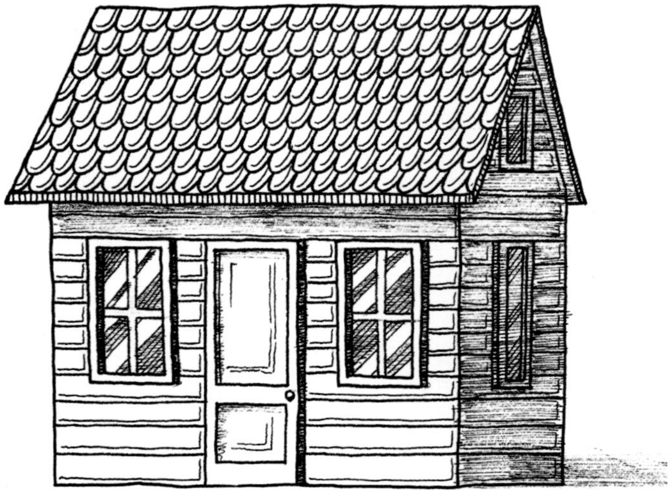

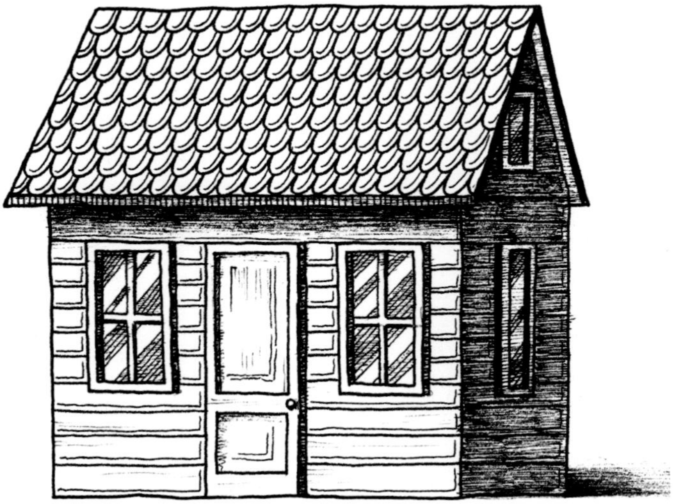

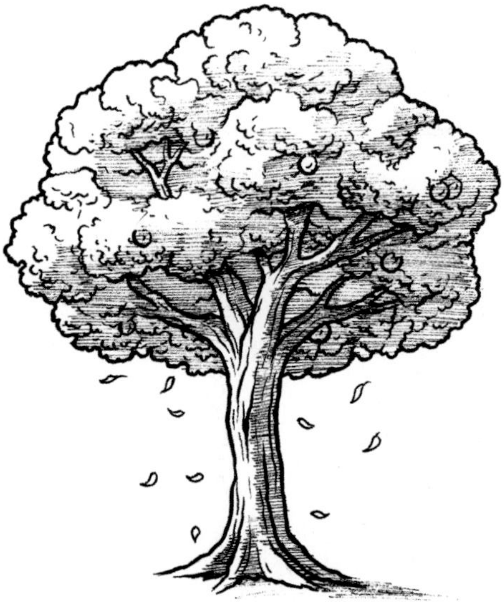

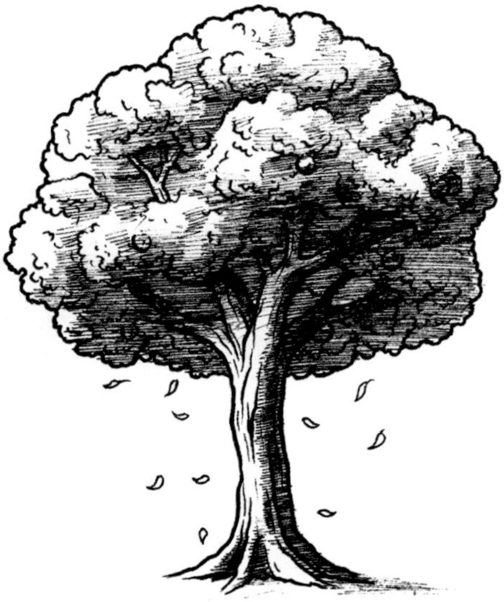

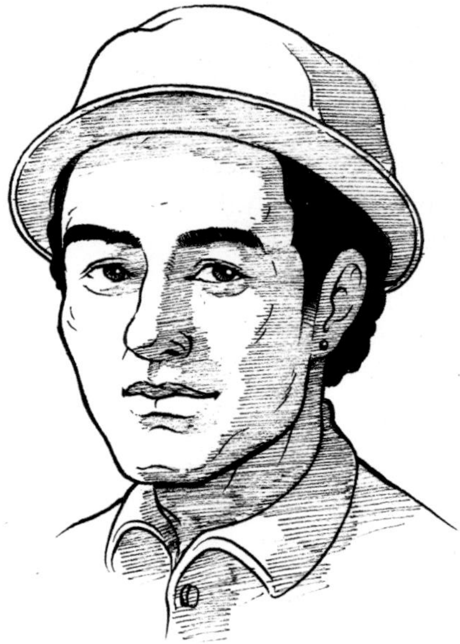

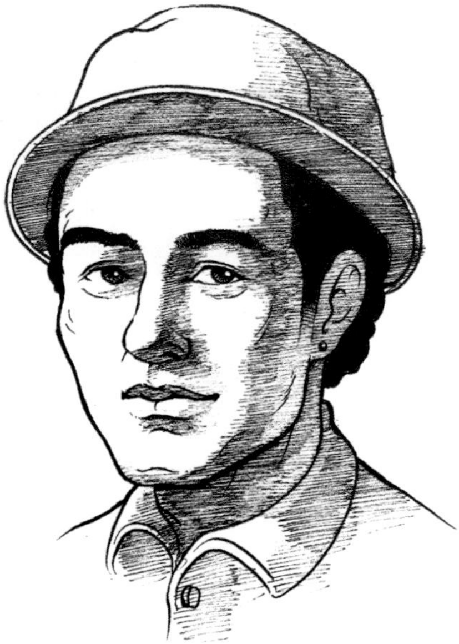

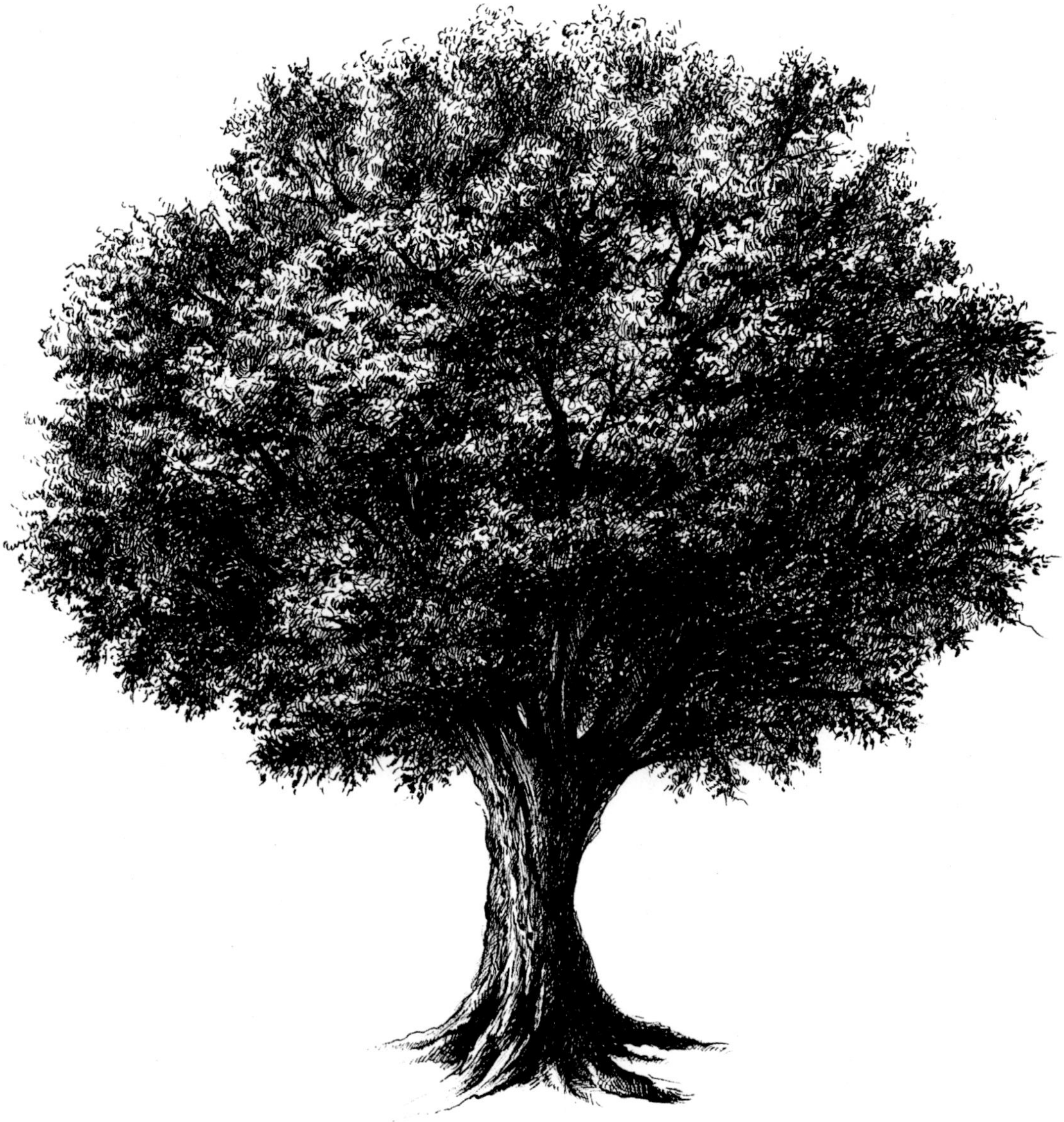

Chapter 3
First Steps in Pen-and-Ink Techniques

These pen-and-ink drawing techniques are some of the most powerful skills for creating complete works of art. From drawing simple strokes and basic shapes to sketching techniques, these elements serve as a solid foundation for building other skills in the following chapters.

In this chapter, we'll practice and refine the control of straight and curved lines, as well as depict basic shapes and forms using pen and ink. We'll also touch on constructive sketching, a method that helps accurately depict your desired composition, along with basic linear perspective to convey depth and three-dimensional space in your work.

Exploring Lines, Shapes, and Forms

In the art of ink drawing, detailed artworks created with skillful techniques and unique ideas are impressive, and sometimes we might say, *"How can they do that? It seems so hard to create that drawing!"* However, did you know that complex pen-and-ink pieces all began with basic and simple techniques? In this section, we will learn how to draw lines, shapes, and forms, the most essential concepts in pen-and-ink drawing.

Lines, shapes, and forms are the foundations of representing the subject's three-dimensional structure, shape, and textures. By practicing these elements, we not only master the basics and improve the hand movement, but we also develop the ability to express the shading techniques (that we will learn in the next chapters), and enhance our drawing skills. Let's kick things off with lines!

Lines

In pen-and-ink drawing, lines do more than just outline shapes; they're the foundation for shading techniques and adding fine details. Practicing simple straight lines can help you draw a magnificent building, curved lines can create romantic human eyes, and wavy lines can depict the ocean at sunset. These basic line exercises might seem repetitive at times, but once mastered, they'll open up a rich world of artistic expression for you.

In this exercise, feel free to use any tools you like. However, fineliners are recommended for their convenience and ease of use. A fineliner with a size of 01 or 03 is ideal for practice. Follow the illustrations below and start practicing!

Drawing Straight Lines: Exercise 1

In the first exercises, we'll start by drawing straight lines. While this is considered a basic and simple exercise, straight lines can sometimes be challenging. Practicing straight lines will help you improve control over your strokes and refine your hand-movement skills. In this exercise, combine finger movements for shorter lines and wrist movements for longer strokes. Let's get started!

Step 1: Draw horizontal lines about 1–2 inches (2.5–5 cm) long. Repeat these lines below, aiming to keep them parallel and evenly spaced (about 1 mm apart). Alternate between different drawing directions, from left to right and vice versa. Try to maintain a moderate hand speed—too slow may cause shaky lines, while too fast may lead to less precise lines.

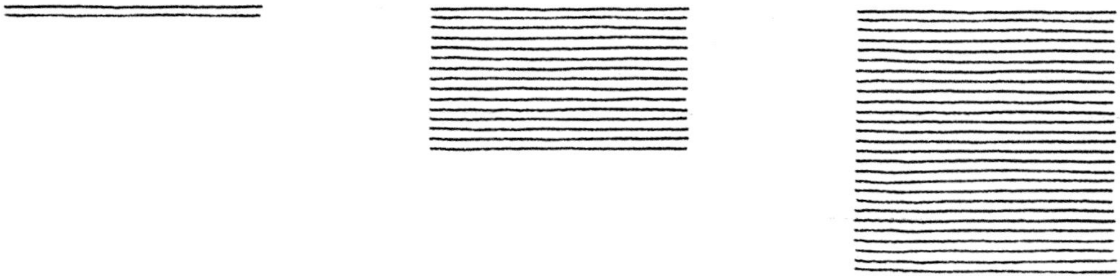

Step 2: Repeat the same practice from Step 1, but experiment with different line directions, such as vertical, diagonal, or any random direction you choose.

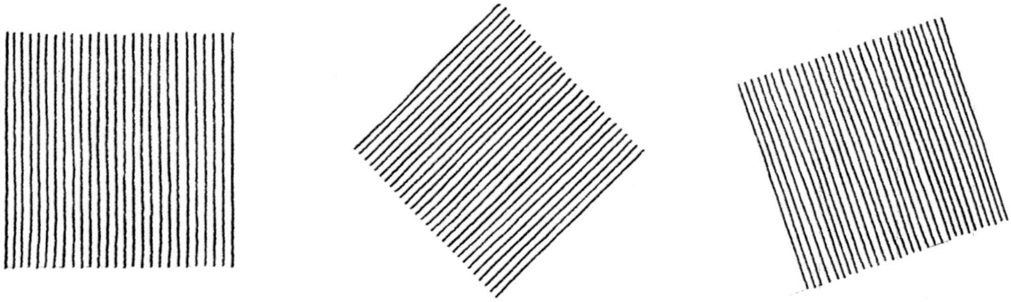

Drawing Straight Lines: Exercise 2

Step 1: Just like in the first exercise, draw a straight horizontal line about 1 inch (2.5 cm) long.

Step 2: Draw additional parallel lines, gradually increasing their length while maintaining a consistent 1-mm gap between them. Draw each line in one continuous motion without lifting your pen from the paper, continuing until the line extends beyond your comfortable hand-movement range.

Step 3: To draw longer lines seamlessly, lift the side of your hand off the paper, using only your ring finger and pinky to lightly guide your hand on the surface. This technique allows for a broader range of motion, enabling you to draw longer, uninterrupted lines.

Step 4: Continue this exercise with lines in various directions to improve the flexibility of your hand movements.

1

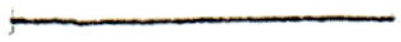

2

3

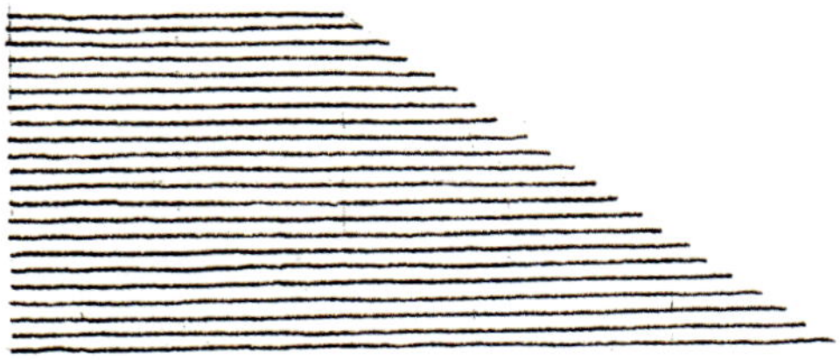

4

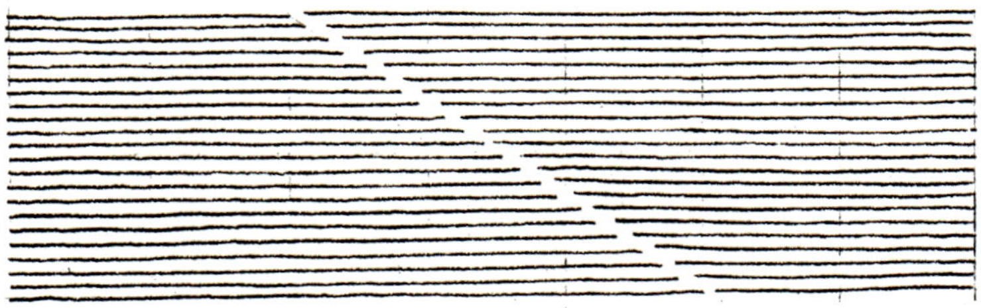

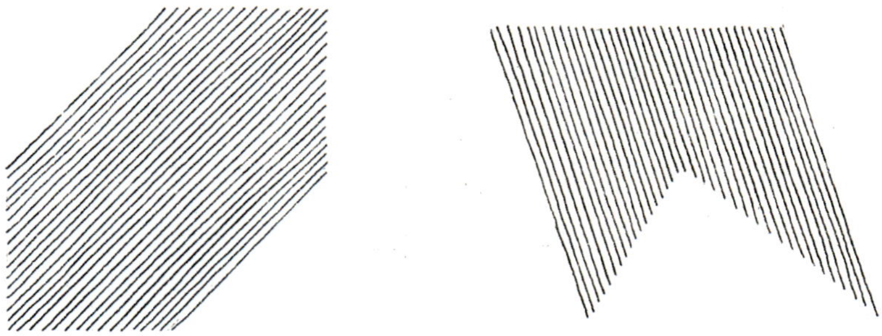

Drawing Curved Lines: Exercise 1

Step 1: Similar to the straight-line exercise, we'll start by drawing curved lines that are horizontal and parallel to each other. Practice drawing curves that arc downward as well as upward.

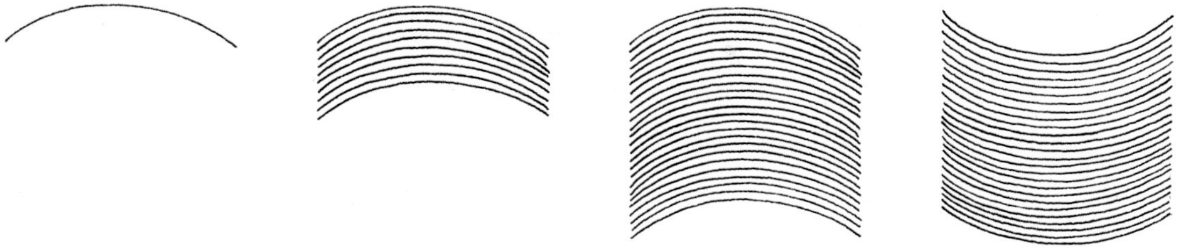

Step 2: Once you've practiced the horizontal curves, move on to drawing them in different directions, such as vertical, diagonal, or any other angle. You can also try drawing wave patterns to create lines that curve twice.

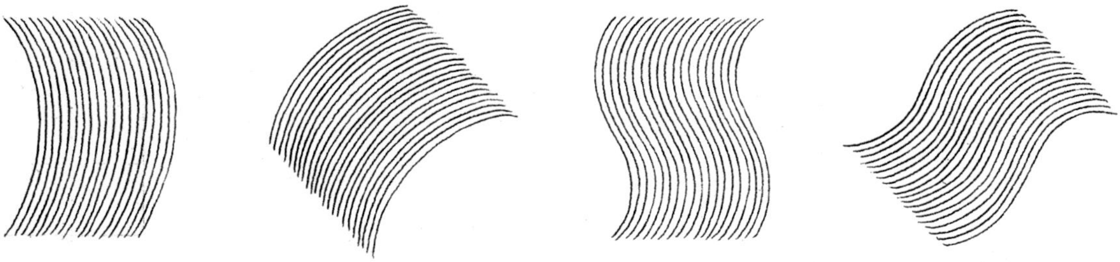

Drawing Curved Lines: Exercise 2

Step 1: Let's practice a technique where you lift the side of your hand off the paper to draw lines of varying lengths. Start with short, simple curves or waves, then gradually increase the length with each subsequent line. To draw longer strokes, relax and let your hand slightly touch the paper while moving to make the lines smoother.

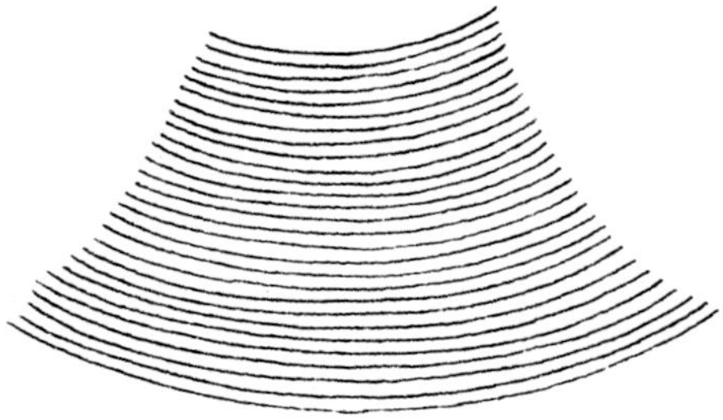

Step 2: Practice this exercise by drawing lines in different directions, such as vertical, diagonal, and a wave pattern.

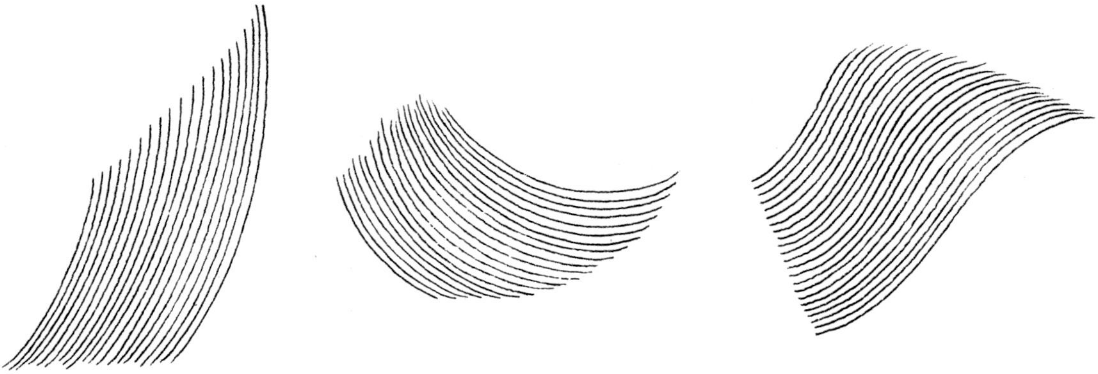

SHAPES

Since we were kids, we've learned about basic geometric shapes like circles, squares, rectangles, triangles, etc. These are the foundational shapes we'll be practicing in this section. However, instead of using rulers or any supportive tools, we'll draw everything freehand, relying on our own feelings. Practicing these shapes is all about combining the simple lines we worked on earlier. Let's get started!

Shapes with Straight Lines

Step 1: Use the straight lines you practiced earlier to start drawing a square with sides about 1 inch (2.5 cm) long. You don't have to draw it in one continuous line; you can lift your pen to draw each side separately.

Step 2: Draw another smaller square inside the first one. The sides of this second square should be parallel and about 1 mm away from the sides of the first square (just like the single-line exercises we did).

Step 3: Continue drawing smaller squares using the same method. Keep going until the smallest square is at the center of the shape.

1

2

3

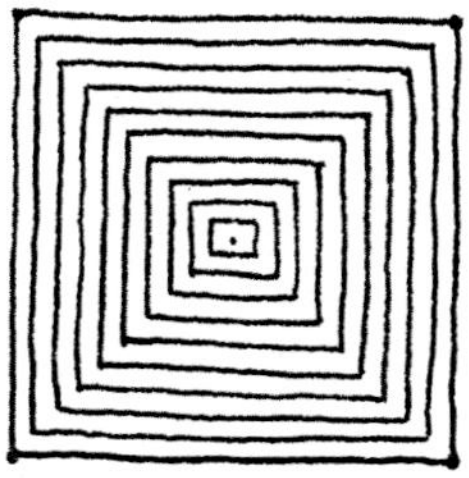

Step 4: After you've drawn the gradually smaller squares, let's reverse it. Now, increase the size of the squares. Starting from your original square, draw new squares outside of it, keeping the distance between each square about 1 mm. Continue drawing until the outer square reaches about 2 inches (5 cm) on each side.

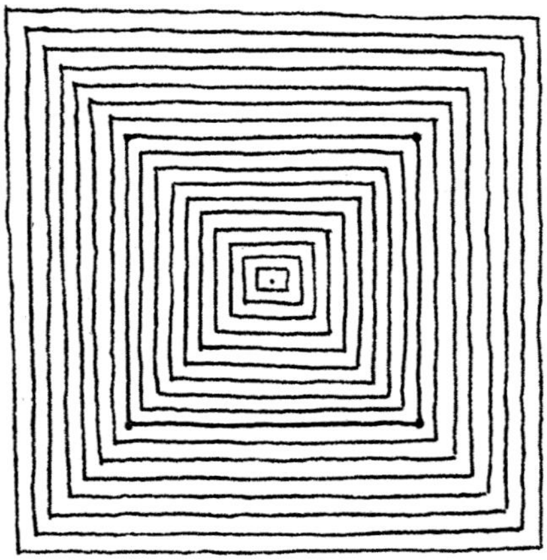

Step 5: Apply the same technique to draw other basic shapes, like rectangles, parallelograms, triangles, trapezoids, and any random shapes you can think of (but keep them simple).

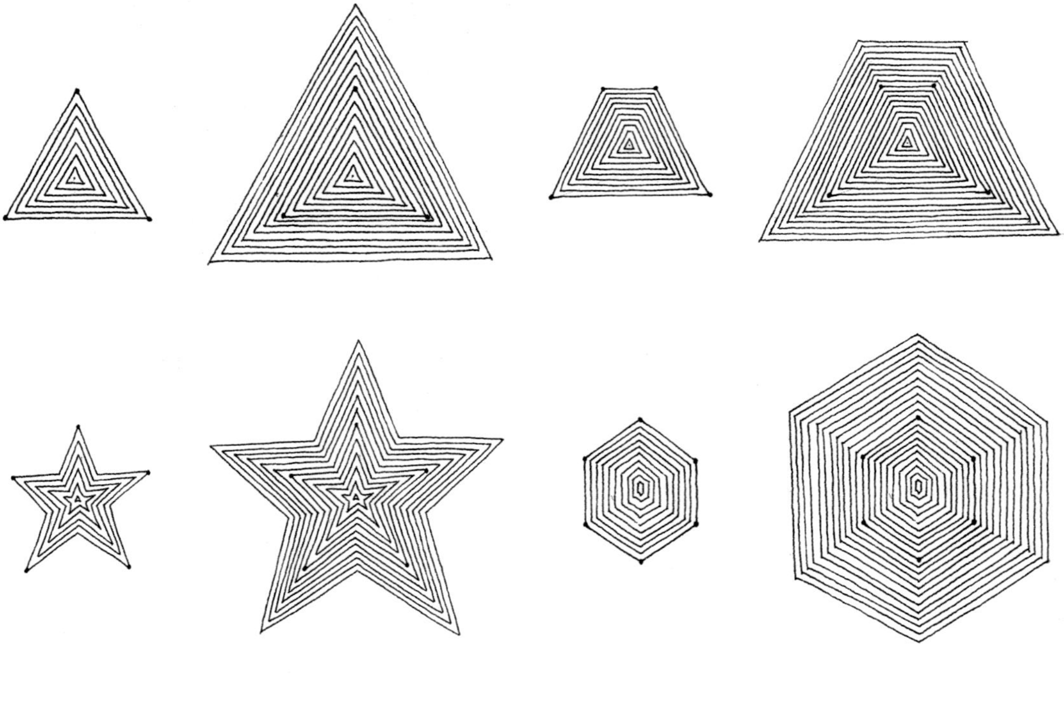

Shapes with Curved Lines: Exercise 1

Step 1: A circle is one of the best shapes to practice curves because of its balance. Draw a circle with a diameter of about 1 inch (2.5 cm) using just your feel, without a compass or ruler. You can sketch with a pencil first if you want the circle to be more accurate.

Step 2: Draw a smaller circle concentric with the first one, leaving about a 1-mm gap between the two circles.

Step 3: Continue drawing smaller circles, gradually decreasing in size, until the circles become very small.

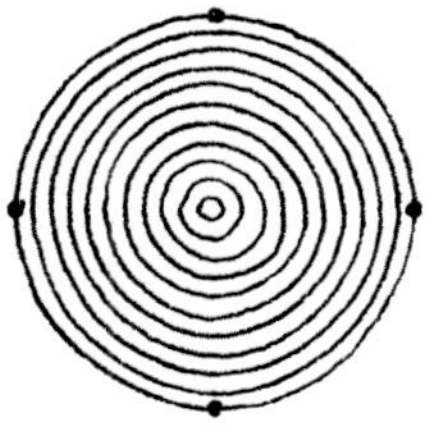

Step 4: As the circles get smaller, controlling your lines might become more challenging. Relax your hand, and draw gently to keep the lines light and smooth. Don't worry if the circles aren't perfect; keep practicing to improve your hand movement when drawing curved lines. You can also practice increasing the size of the circle.

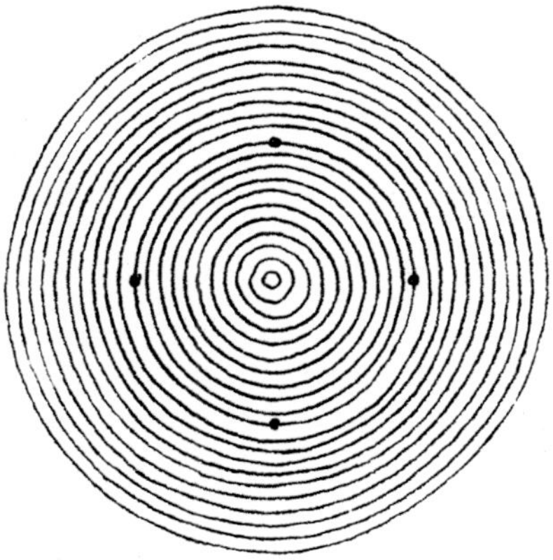

Shapes with Curved Lines: Exercise 2

Step 1: In addition to drawing circles, you can practice curved lines with randomly shaped curves to improve the flexibility of your hand. Try drawing random shapes, and using the same method as with circles, draw smaller and larger versions of those shapes.

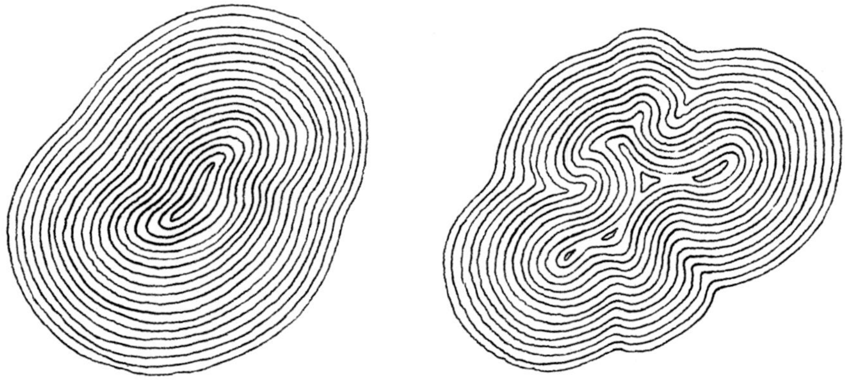

Shapes with Curved Lines: Exercise 3

Step 1: In addition to practicing circles and ellipses, you can apply curved lines to basic geometric shapes with straight lines. The method here is to "distort" the shape by replacing straight lines with curved ones. Try drawing a square with sides about 1 inch (2.5 cm) long, but replace the square's sides with curved or wavy lines.

Step 2: Draw similar shapes inside and outside the original square, making sure the lines are parallel and about 1 mm apart.

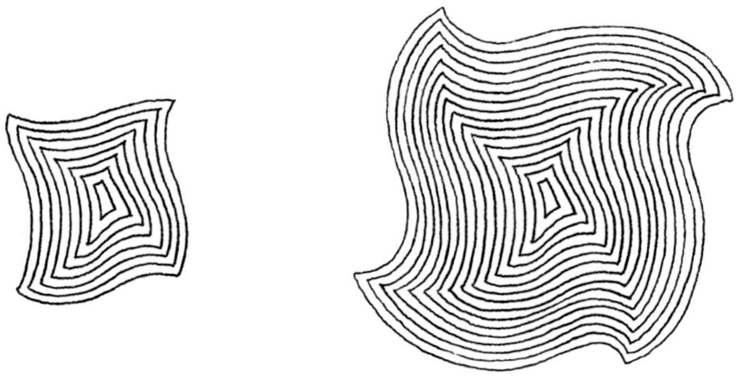

Step 3: Explore other geometric shapes, like triangles, parallelograms, or any random shapes you can think of.

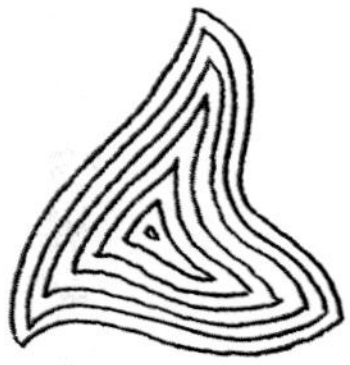

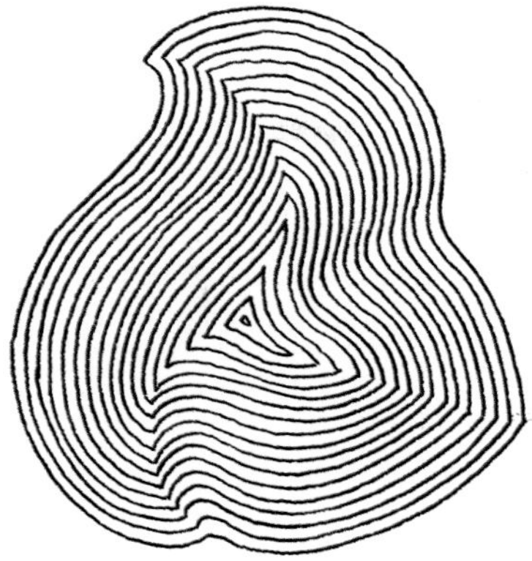

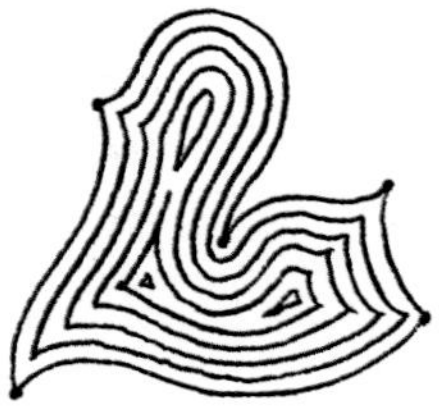

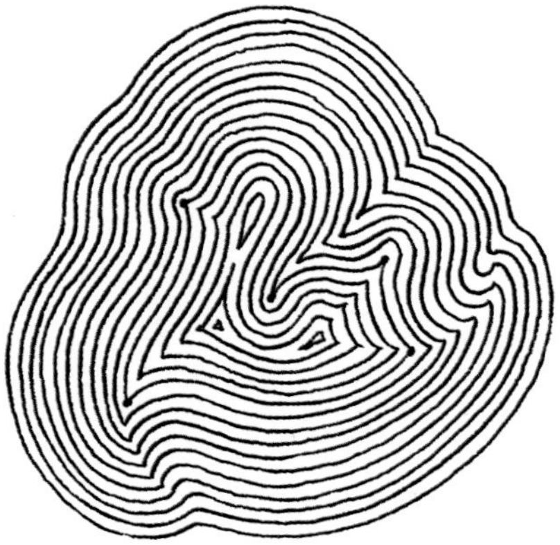

Congratulations on completing the second part of the basic drawing technique! We have just one more section to go before finishing this chapter: forms. Let's turn the page and explore it together!

Forms

Simple lines form shapes when combined together, and shapes create forms. In drawing, a form is any 2D drawing that creates the illusion of three-dimensional space. Practicing forms helps you gain a deeper understanding of how to depict volume and structure, laying the groundwork for more complex subjects in the future.

One of the fundamental (and exciting) concepts for representing depth and three-dimensional space is the theory of linear perspective. We'll discuss this in more detail in the next section, along with constructive sketching and outline drawing. For now, let's start with some simple exercises to draw basic forms, including cubes, spheres, and cylinders.

Cube

Step 1: Draw a square with sides about 1 inch (2.5 cm) long.

Step 2: Focus on the top-right and bottom-right corners of the square. Draw two diagonal lines, each about 1 inch (2.5 cm) long, slanting upward at a 45-degree angle.

Step 3: Draw a vertical line connecting the endpoints of the two diagonal lines.

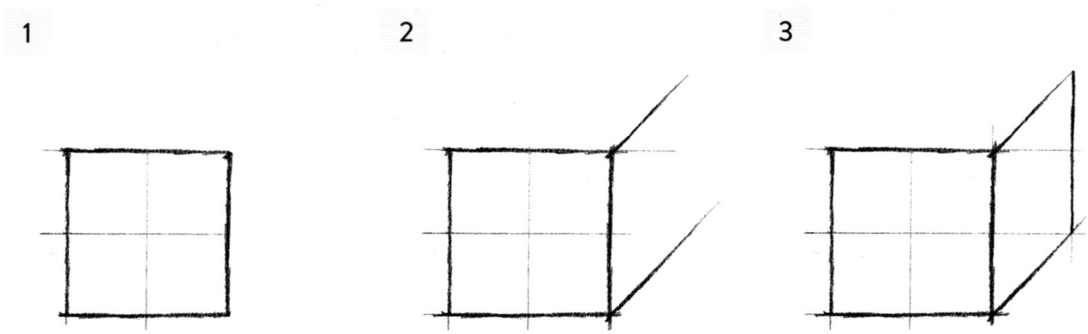

Step 4: From the top-left corner of the original square, draw another diagonal line parallel to the other diagonal lines. Connect the end of this line to the previous vertical line. Voilà! You've drawn a basic cube form. Easy, right?

Step 5: To express the invisible parts of the cube, you can use the same drawing technique but with dashed lines. This approach will help you better represent the 3D space of the form, enhancing the sense of structure and space in your subject.

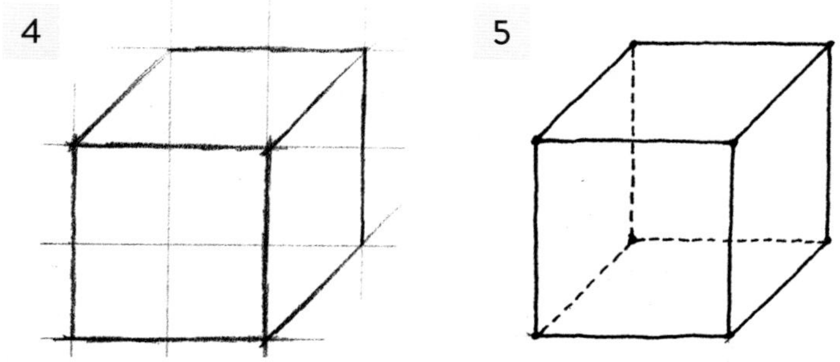

Sphere

Step 1: Draw a circle with a diameter of about 1.5 inches (3.5 cm) to start, and the exercise is completed!

Step 2: Just kidding! But that's the tricky part of drawing a sphere. Without shading or additional details, simple lines can't convey the three-dimensionality of a sphere. There is a solution: Use a pencil to mark the central point of the circle, and draw a vertical line and a horizontal line through that central point (with pencil as well).

Step 3: Keep using pencils to draw two oval shapes in vertical and horizonal directions with heights equal to the diameter of the circle and widths about ¼–½ inch (0.6–1 cm). These oval shapes' central points are aligned to the circle.

Step 4: Start using a fineliner to draw half of the oval shapes based on the vertical and horizontal axis. By doing this, you've created curved lines to express the curved structure of this form.

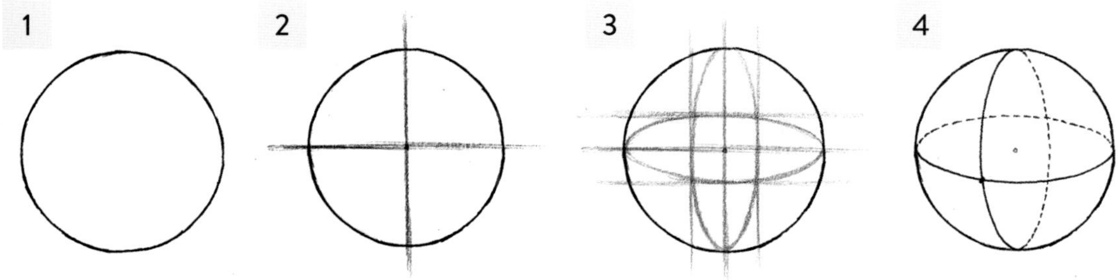

Cylinder

Step 1: Draw a vertical rectangle with a height of 2 inches (5 cm) and a width of 1 inch (2.5 cm).

Step 2: Focus on the horizontal line at the top and bottom of the rectangle. Draw two oval shapes with widths equal to the rectangle's width and heights of about ½ inch (1 cm).

Step 3: Use a fineliner to outline the cylinder based on your sketch. From a slightly top-down view, the top of the cylinder will appear as a complete oval, while the bottom will be a combination of solid and dashed lines to show the visible and invisible parts. The width of the cylinder is represented by two simple vertical lines.

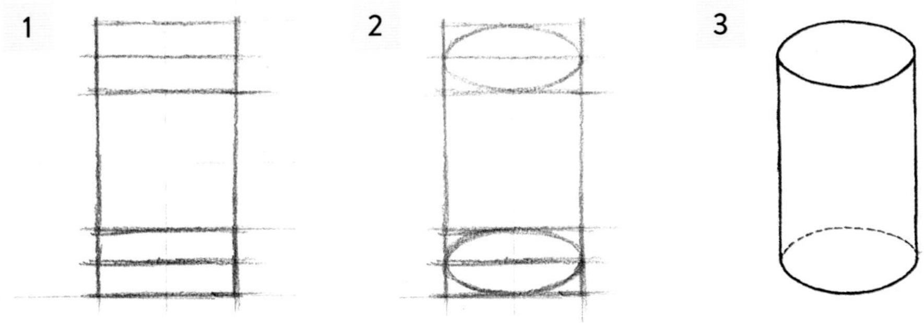

Cone

Step 1: In addition to the cylinder, you can also practice with a similar form: the cone. The key difference is that the cone has a pointed tip. To draw this, follow the same sketching steps as for the cylinder. Then, find the center of the top oval, and connect this point down to meet the two outer points of the oval at the base.

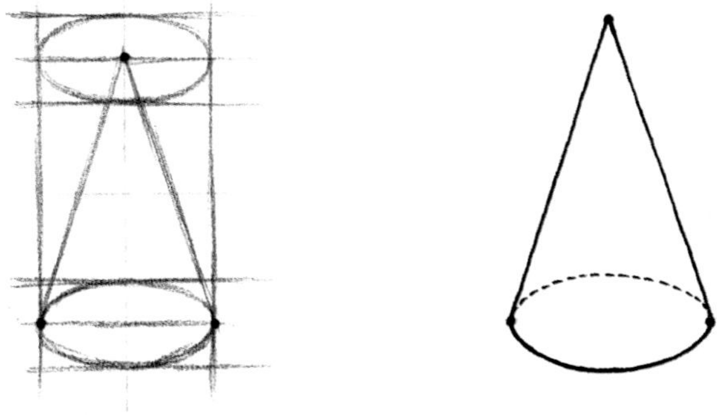

An Easy Guide to Linear Perspective

How can we use lines, shapes, and forms from the previous section to draw a complete work? The first step: sketching. Sketching is how we depict the unique and major shape of a subject through simple lines, not including shading techniques. To practice this technique effectively and achieve more accurate results, let's briefly talk about linear perspective and constructive sketching.

What Is Linear Perspective?

First, take a moment to observe the space around you, or go for a walk outside and look at the natural scenery or streets. You might notice that objects farther away appear smaller than those closer to you. Even though the trees along the roadside are similar in height, from our perspective, they appear before our eyes in various sizes. This applies to everything you see, like the road in front of you, buildings, cars, or a train approaching the station.

To simplify the concept of linear perspective, think of it as a way to create the illusion of depth to express three-dimensional space by using two-dimensional drawings on paper. This means depicting objects in different sizes depending on their distance from us and arranging them logically to create a lively world.

Linear perspective can be simple or complex, depending on various factors like your learning goals or how precise you want your spatial representation to be. Learning linear perspective can be a long journey, and the best approach is to experience it step by step. In these initial stages, let's practice the most basic and simple elements together so you can equip yourself with the essential skills needed to support your pen-and-ink drawing.

Our goal in the following exercises is to understand the fundamental concept and theory of linear perspective. Therefore, feel free to use a ruler for more precise lines. Additionally, you can use a pencil (HB or 2B) for sketching and a fineliner (01 or 03) for outlining the drawing.

Linear One-Point Perspective

Step 1: Do you enjoy the beauty of the ocean? Look far out to where the vast sea meets the sky in a horizontal line—that's the horizon. This is the most important starting point in learning perspective, and everything else will depend on how you define this horizon line. Now, keep that expansive ocean scene in mind, and use a pencil or a fineliner to draw a long, straight horizontal line right in the middle of your paper or sketchbook to represent the horizon.

Step 2: Next, draw a small dot on the horizon line, near the right edge of your paper (about 1–2 inches [2.5–5 cm] from the edge). We'll call this dot the Vanishing Point.

Step 3: Start drawing three square shapes near the left edge of your paper, following this instruction: One square should be centered on the horizon line (so the horizon cuts through the middle of it), one square should be above the horizon line (in the sky), and one square should be below the horizon line (in the ocean).

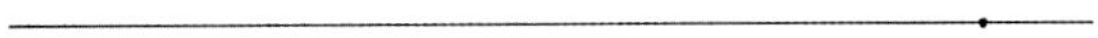

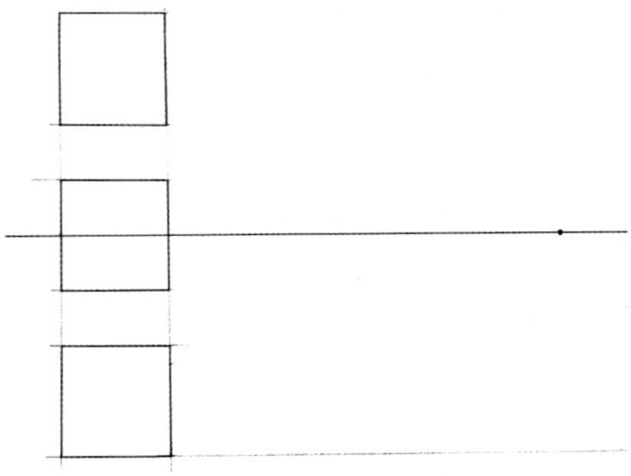

Step 4: Focus on the corners of each square. Use straight lines to connect these corners to the dot on the horizon line that we drew in Step 1.

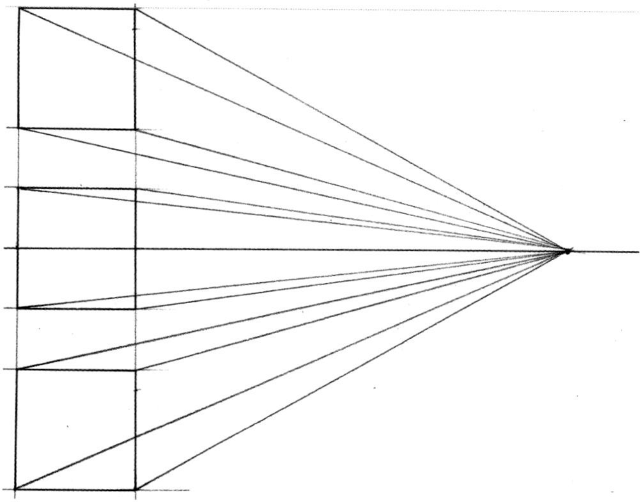

Step 5: Draw vertical and horizontal lines that intersect the connecting lines at different points *(as shown in the illustration)* to create cubes seen from various perspectives.

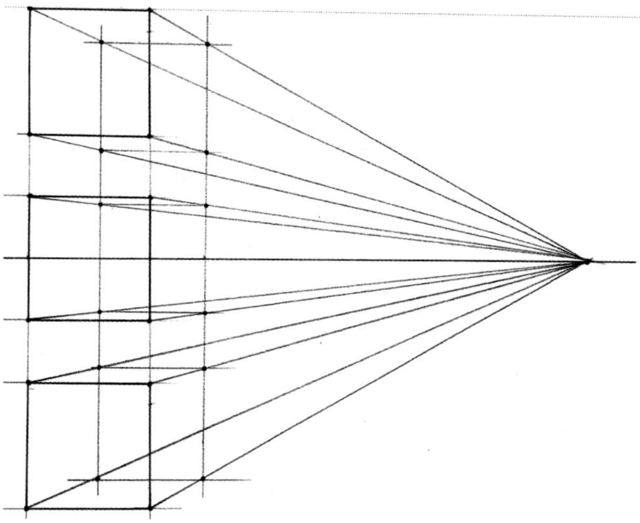

Step 6: Use a fineliner to outline the cubes. For the invisible parts, you can apply the dashed-line technique, like we did when drawing basic forms. When completed, you can erase the sketching. And there you have it! That's how we create a one-point linear perspective with cube-forms drawing.

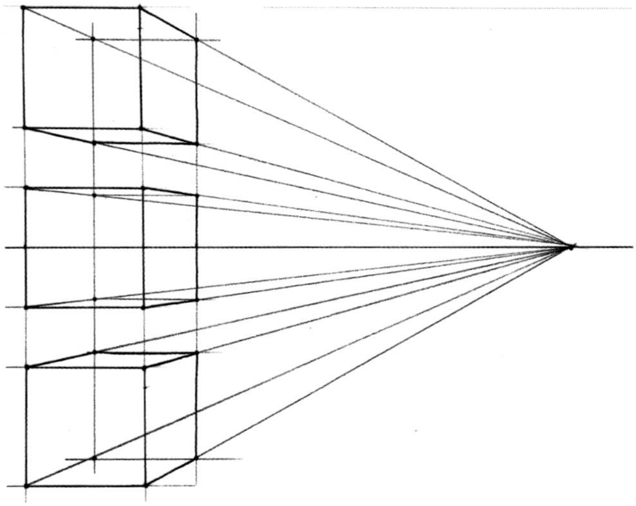

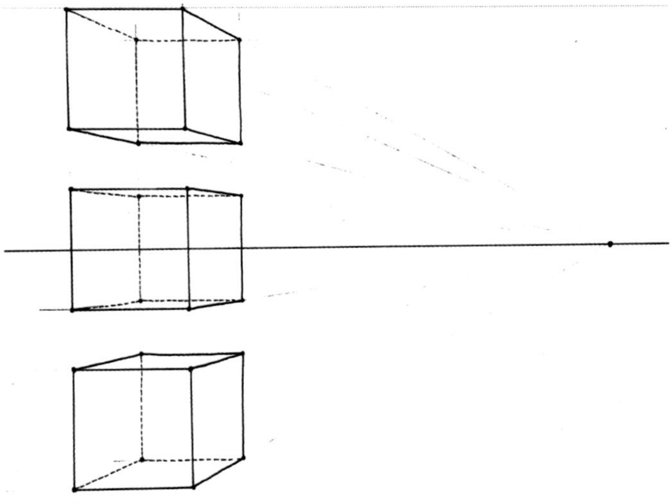

Linear Two-Point Perspective

Step 1: Turn to a new page. Similar to the previous exercise, draw a horizontal line to represent the horizon. Then, draw two small dots on the horizon line, one far to the right and one far to the left, both about 1–2 inches (2.5–5 cm) from the edge of the paper. We'll call these points Vanishing Point 1 (on the left) and Vanishing Point 2 (on the right).

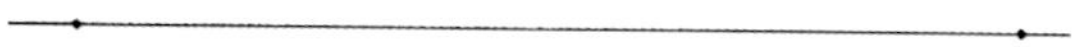

Step 2: Next, draw three vertical lines, each about 1 inch (2.5 cm), on the right side of the drawing, in the following positions: one line right in the middle of the horizon line, one line in the sky above the horizon, and one line in the ocean below the horizon. All three lines should be aligned vertically.

Step 3: Connect the top and bottom points of these vertical lines to both Vanishing Points on the horizon line that you drew in Step 1.

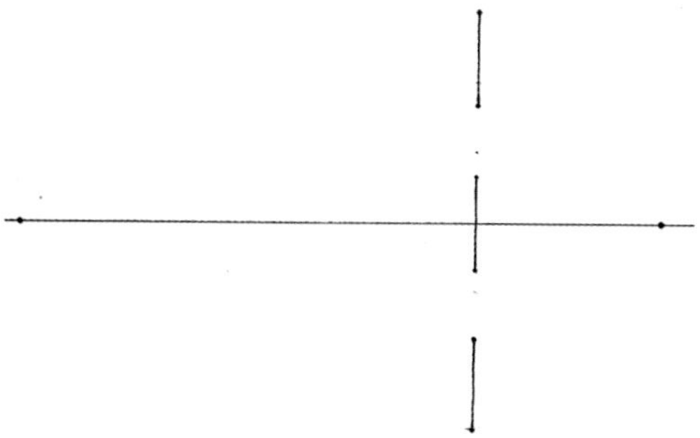

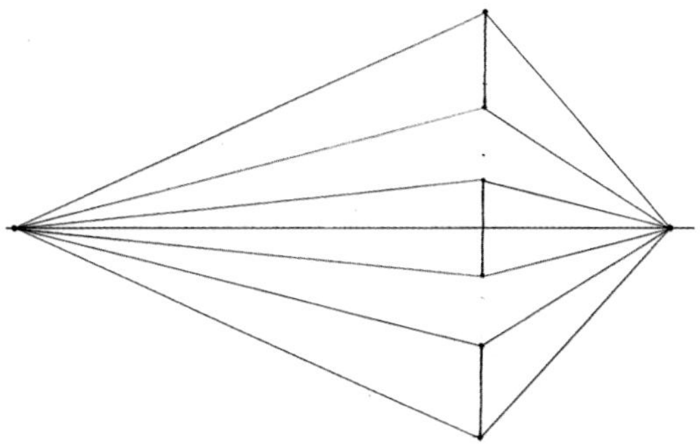

Step 4: Based on the vertical line in the center, draw two more vertical lines, one to the left and one to the right. The distance from the center line to the right line will be shorter than the left line, based on the perspective and the object's position (more on the right side of the drawing). These lines will also intersect with the connecting lines to the Vanishing Points at different points.

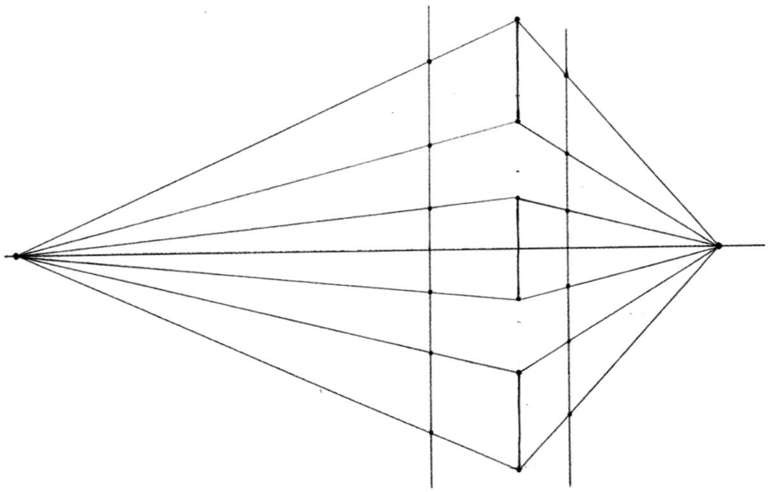

Step 5: From the marked intersections, draw lines connecting these points to both Vanishing Points. Now, take a step back and observe—do you see cubes floating in a three-dimensional space?

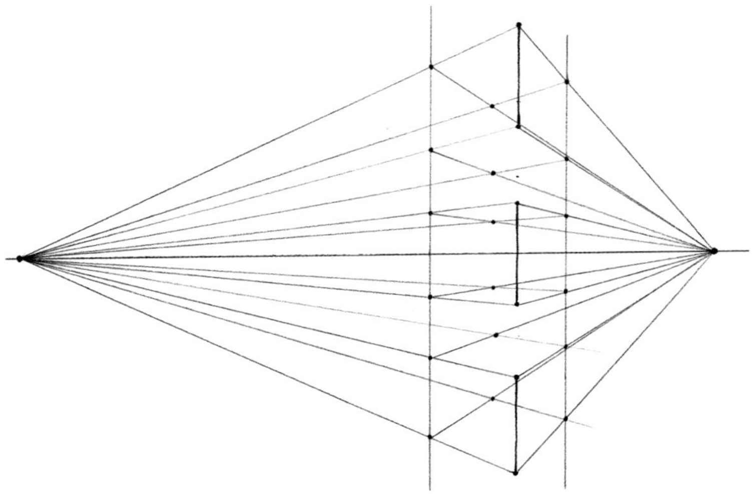

Step 6: Use a fineliner to combine solid and dashed lines to outline these cubes. You can also erase the sketch lines to make the drawing clearer. We've now completed the Linear Two-Point Perspective exercise!

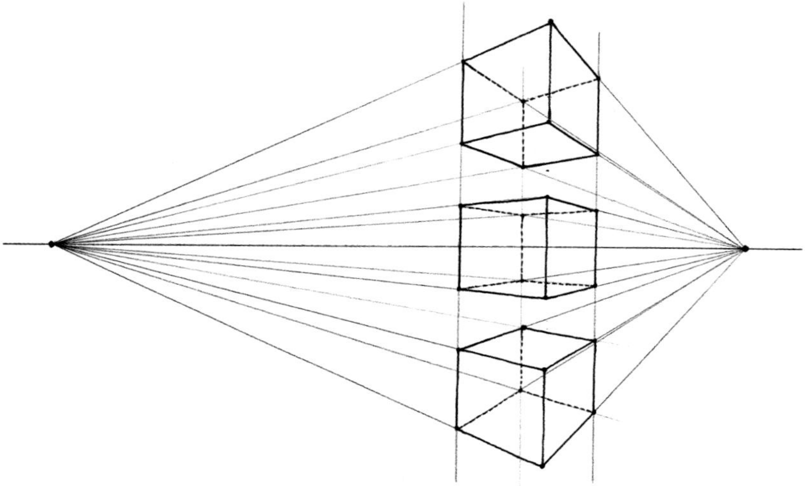

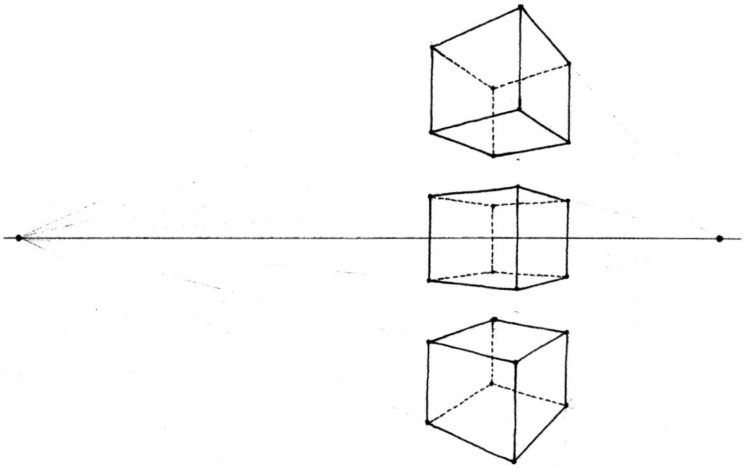

Constructive Sketching Made Simple

When we observe any subject for drawing, it's easy to get lost in small details. However, focusing too much on tiny areas can make us forget about the overall shape and composition, leading to imbalance in the complete artwork. To create a desired sketch and achieve a good overall composition, one of the highly effective sketching methods used in most art schools is constructive sketching.

Basically, constructive sketching is the method of sketching a subject from simple shape to detailed structure. To achieve this, we can get started by simplifying the subject forms, expressing the major shapes, and then working on the details in the last step. Let's learn more about this method by drawing a simple still life as illustrated below.

Use a Rectangle to Determine the Composition

Step 1: As usual, select a very simple subject. In this exercise, we will draw a still life with objects that have similar shapes to basic forms, including a small vase, an apple, and a notebook. Observation is crucial before you start drawing, as it helps you grasp the space, form, depth, and lighting in the composition.

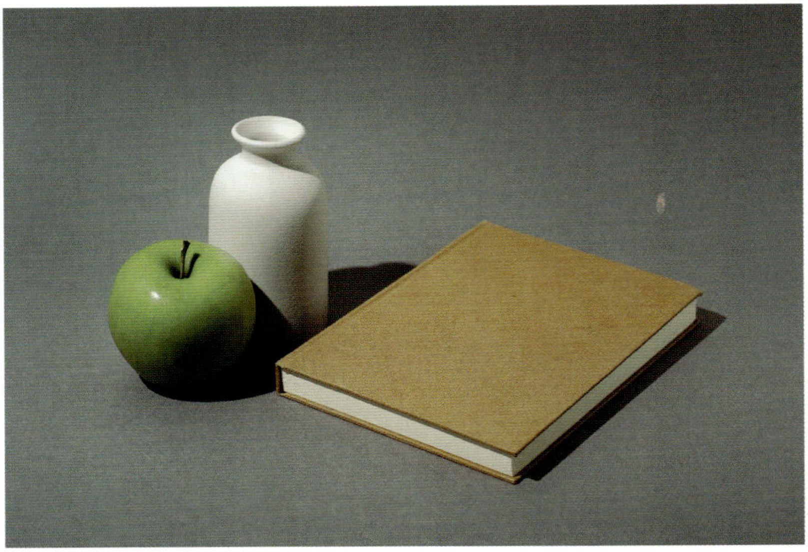

Step 2: Use an H or HB pencil to identify the highest, lowest, far-right, and far-left points of the overall composition that include all the subjects in the scene. Draw a rectangle with edges passing through these points to create a framework for the overall composition.

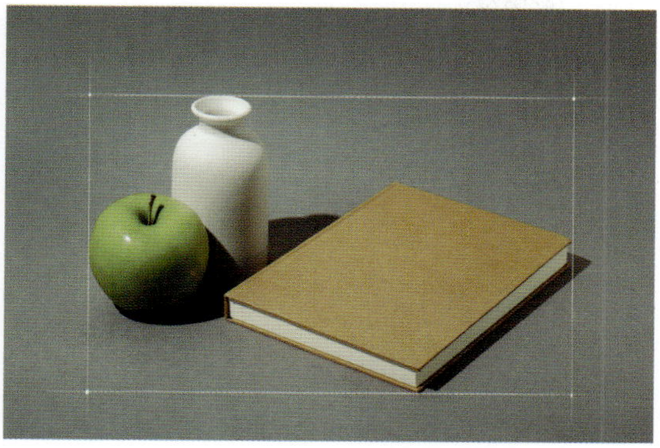

Step 3: Observe and measure the relative proportions and positions of the subjects, then draw rectangles around each subject. At this point, you've just defined the position and composition of the drawing.

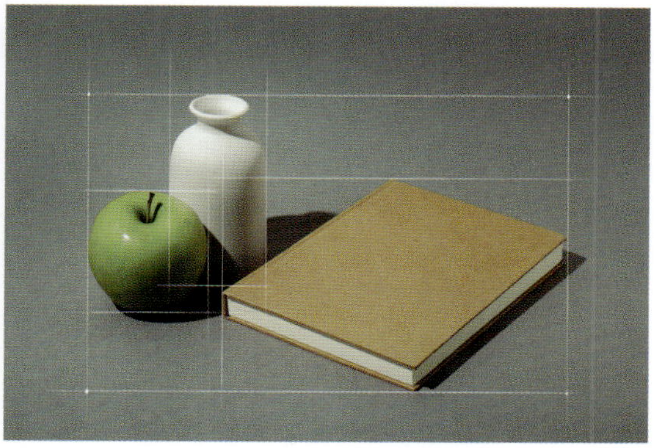

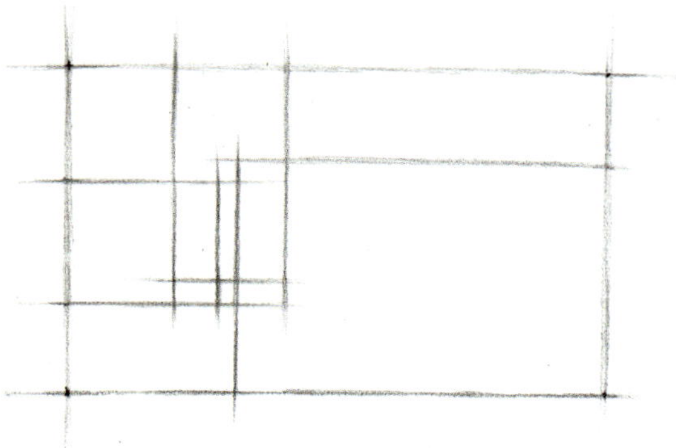

Simplify the Forms

Step 4: Every subject has its own unique shape. That's why it can be challenging to capture that shape accurately right away. To help with this, we'll use the method of simplified forms. Take a good look at the overall shape of each subject, and imagine which basic form it resembles by comparing similar features. In this illustration, you can see that the vase has a rounded outline, so it closely resembles a cylinder form. Similarly, keep imagining and comparing: The apple has a spherical shape, and the notebook looks like part of a cube.

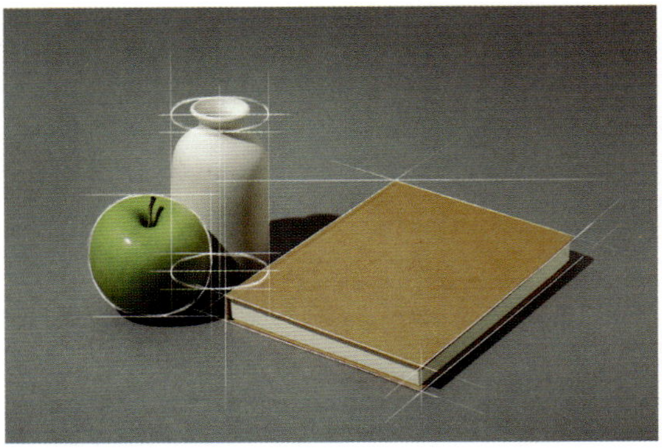

Step 5: Place these simplified forms in the corresponding positions of the subjects.

Step 6: Once you have these basic shapes, analyzing and representing the objects' forms become much easier. Use simple sketch lines like straight lines *(or just slightly curved ones)* to roughly define the shape of the subject. At this stage, you don't need to worry about small details—just focus on the overall composition and the arrangement of the subjects within it.

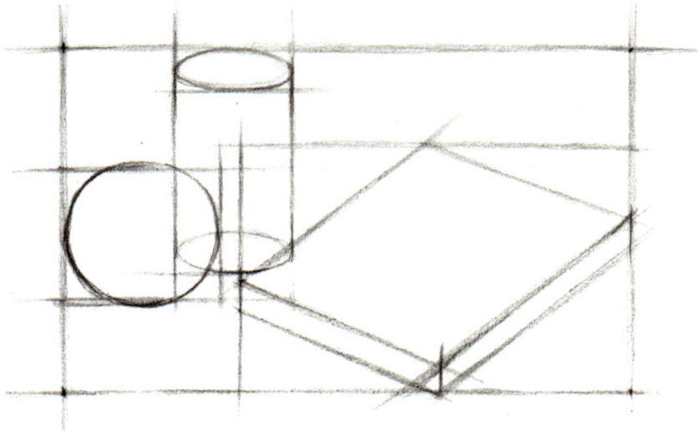

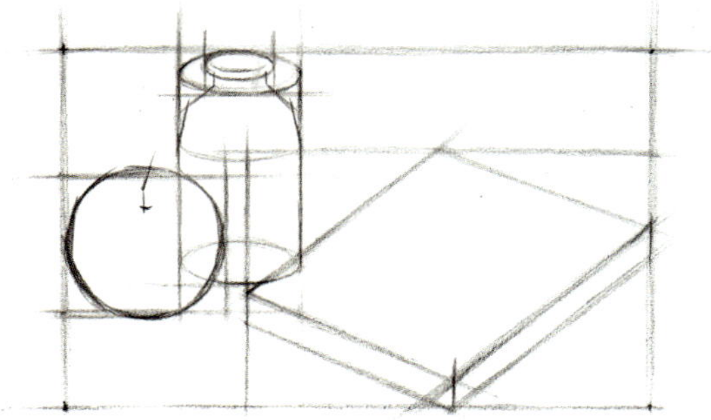

Outline the Subject

Step 7: To capture the unique shape and fine details of the subjects, start with a pencil. You can use a slightly darker pencil than the one used in the sketching step to make the lines clearer. Focus on the simple straight sketch lines you've drawn. When connected, these lines will form angular paths. For subjects with curved shapes, you can round off these angular paths to represent the curve. In this illustration, the subjects with curved lines are the vase and the apple. In addition, you can also sketch the areas of cast shadow (the objects' shadow) to capture the context for the drawing.

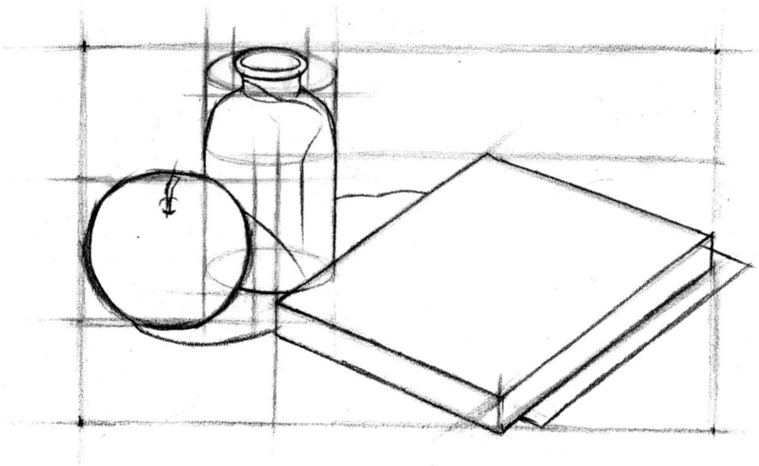

Step 8: For subjects with straight lines, like the notebook, you can keep the initial sketch lines and add a few more to show details like the thickness of the book cover. Keep this sketch, as we'll use it again for shading practice in the upcoming chapters.

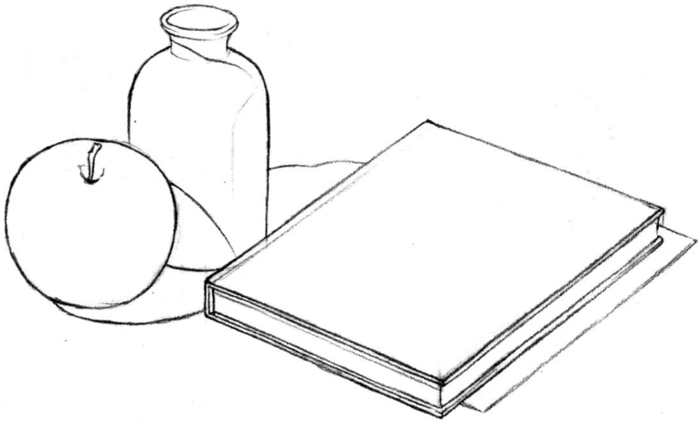

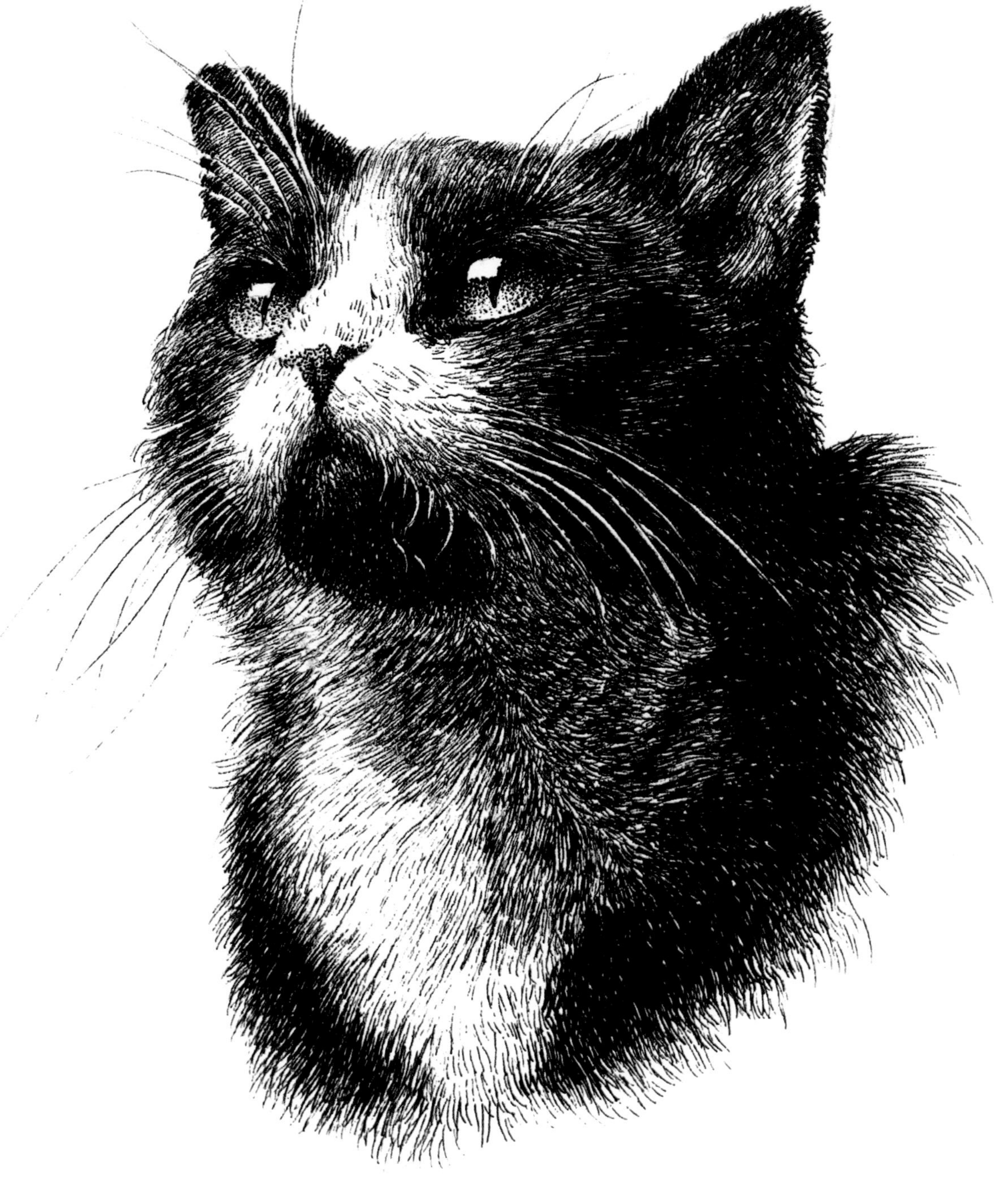

Chapter 4
Shading Theory Made Easy

In this chapter, we delve into shading theory, a fundamental concept in visual art. Shading is the technique through which we convey light and dark areas, using various methods to depict drawings with a sense of three-dimensionality. We'll explore two key concepts in shading: value and shading key components. Let's gain a deeper understanding with the following sections.

Although this book focuses on pen-and-ink techniques, we'll be using a pencil in this chapter to make the practice easier and more effective. Using a pencil will give you more flexibility with shading and allow you to focus more on the shading theory and understand the concept in depth.

What Is Value?

In shading and visual art, value refers to the range of brightness levels observed on a subject under the influence of light sources. Areas that are brighter exhibit higher values, while darker areas have lower values. Practicing value enables us to refine our shading techniques and enhance our skills in representing three-dimensional forms. One of the fundamental and effective exercises for understanding value is the value scale, which will be demonstrated in the following exercise.

Basic Solid Value Scale

Step 1: Start by drawing a series of ten connected squares, each about 1 inch (2.5 cm) in size, arranged horizontally.

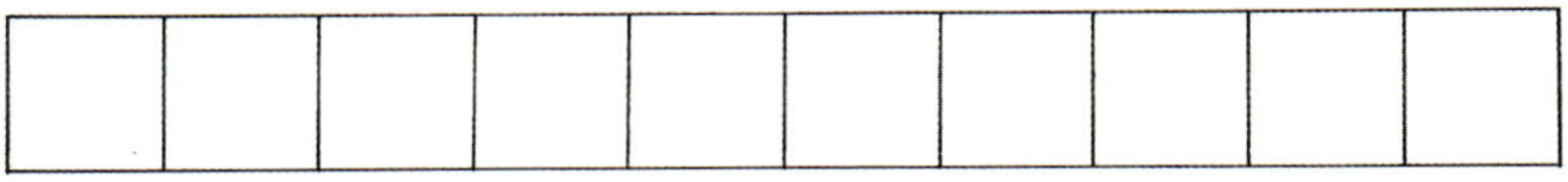

Step 2: Imagine that the first square will be the darkest, and the last square will be the lightest (almost white). Our goal is to gradually lighten the squares from left to right. Begin with the first square, and shade it as dark as possible. You can use an 8B pencil or charcoal to fill it in completely.

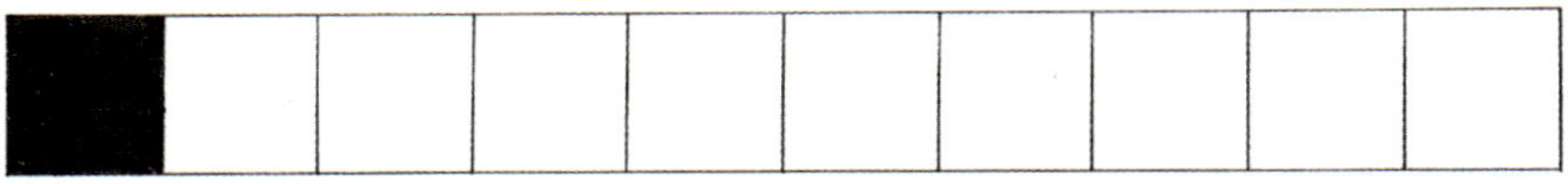

Step 3: Shade the second square, but make it slightly lighter than the first one, like a dark gray. As you draw, keep the entire value scale in mind so that by the time you reach the last square, you'll have created a smooth transition to white.

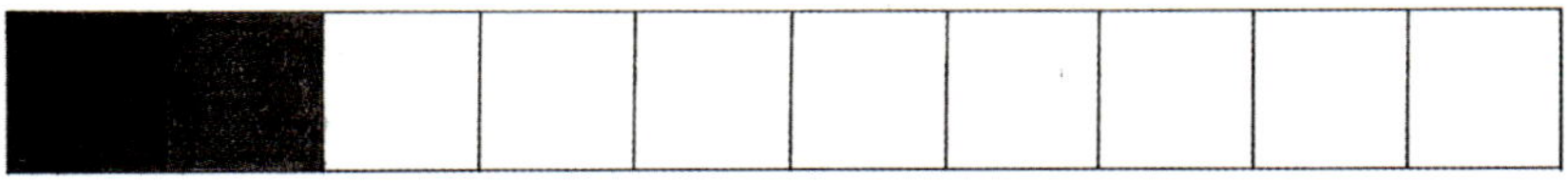

Step 4: Continue with the same approach, shading the third square a bit lighter than the second. You might want to switch to a 4B or 5B pencil for easier control over the value. Proceed with the next squares, gradually decreasing the pencil grade to 3B or 2B. By the time you reach the fifth or sixth square, you'll notice a neutral gray tone, representing a balanced mix of black and white.

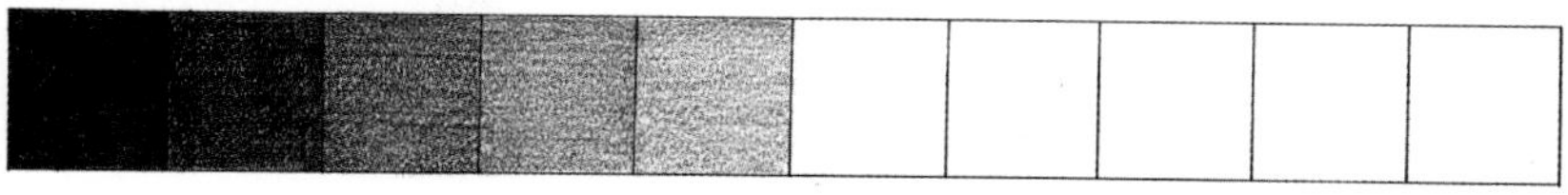

Step 5: From the neutral square, use progressively lighter pencils, from 2B to HB, to create the lighter values. Continue shading squares seven to nine so that the ninth square appears as a very light gray.

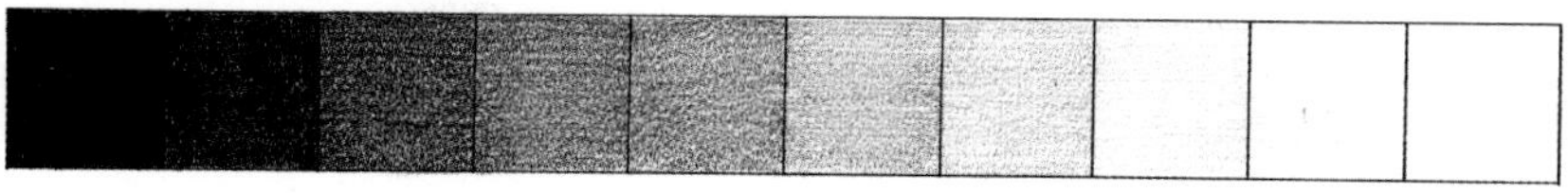

Step 6: If you feel the transition of values is smooth, you've completed the exercise! However, sometimes the value scale may not turn out as expected. In that case, you can make adjustments to some squares to create a more balanced value transition. In this illustration, I made the values in the middle squares a bit darker.

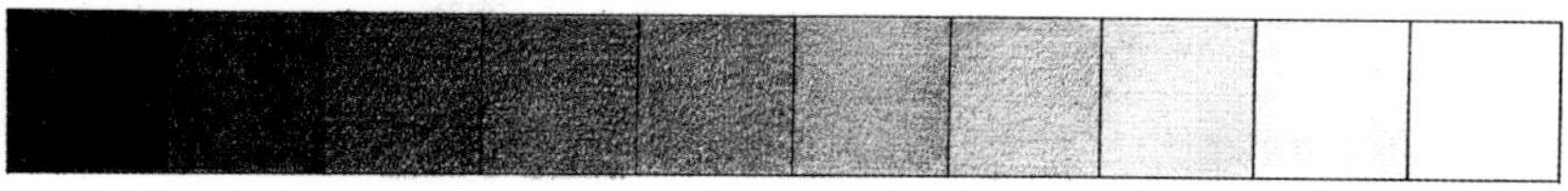

We have just completed a basic value scale with squares of varying lightness and darkness. To achieve a smooth transition and blend the values together, let's move on to the second exercise.

Transitional Value Scale

After practicing the solid value with the basic value scales, let's practice smooth transitions between the values. Practicing value transitions improves flexibility in shading techniques and helps you express realistic work.

Step 1: You don't need to draw a full-length value shape like in the previous exercise. Start with a horizontal rectangle about 3 inches (8 cm) long and 1 inch (2.5 cm) tall.

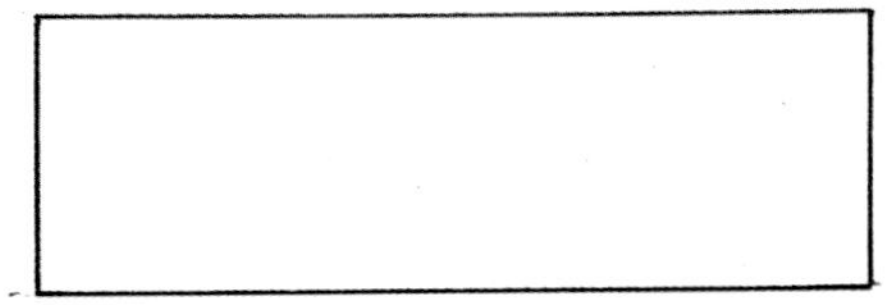

Step 2: One of the most effective shading methods is the layering technique. Use an HB pencil to create a light gray layer, covering almost the entire shape while leaving a small section on the right side unshaded. Adjust the hand pressure when shading to ensure a smooth transition in value.

Step 3: Continue using the HB pencil for the next shading layer. Just like in the previous step, leave part of the first shaded area untouched, and control the pressure of your hand to create a smooth transition in value.

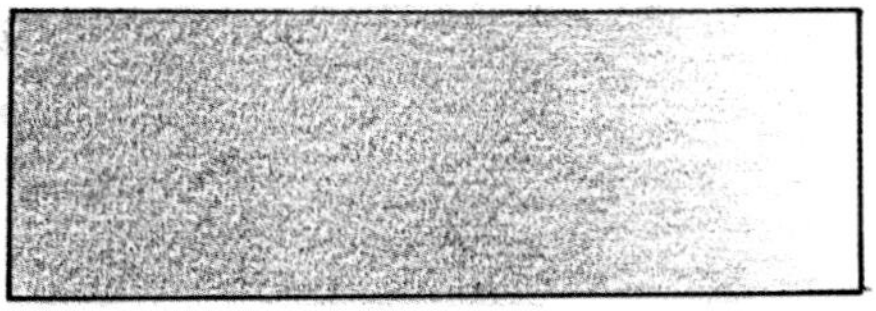

Step 4: Switch to a 2B or 3B pencil, and continue shading the next layer. At this point, you should start to see a clearer transition in value, from neutral gray to white, moving from left to right.

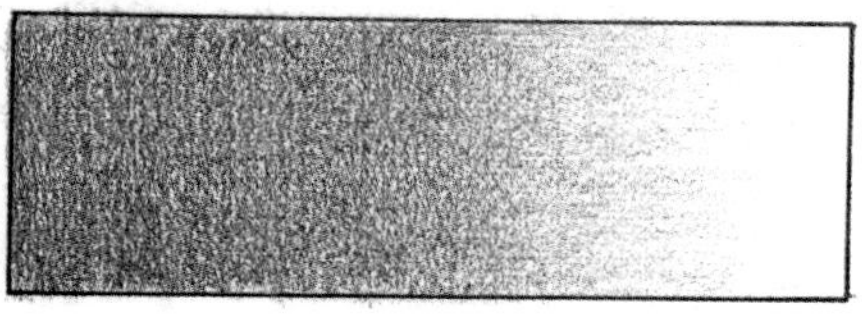

Step 5: Apply the same method for the following layers. For areas that need to be darker, you can switch to a 5B or 6B pencil.

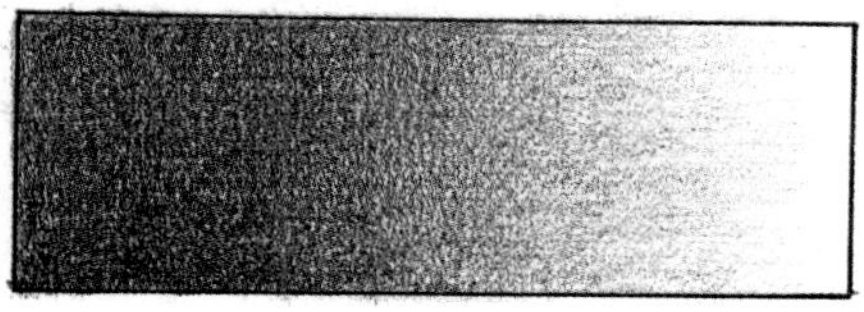

Step 6: On the far left of the value scale, shade as dark as possible using an 8B pencil. Once you've finished, feel free to adjust and balance the values to ensure a smooth transition from left to right. And that's it—you're done!

THE KEY COMPONENTS TO KNOW

Shading is essentially the art of arranging values to establish a three-dimensional structure for a subject. When a subject is illuminated by light, the levels of brightness and darkness (value) vary across its surface. Areas directly exposed to light have higher values, whereas those in shadow possess lower values. To achieve realistic and precise shading, we identify crucial value positions known as *key shading components*. To begin our exploration, let's closely examine a basic form (in this case a sphere) to gain a deeper understanding of this concept.

Overall Value

Shading a basic sphere is one of the best ways to learn about the key shading components due to its smooth value transitions and balanced form.

Step 1: Draw a circle with a diameter of about 1.5–2 inches (4–5 cm) to represent the sphere. A subject's depth and light-dark contrast depend on how the light interacts with it. For this initial practice, we'll use a basic and traditional light setup. The light will come from above and slightly to one side (the left) so that it covers about two-thirds of the sphere.

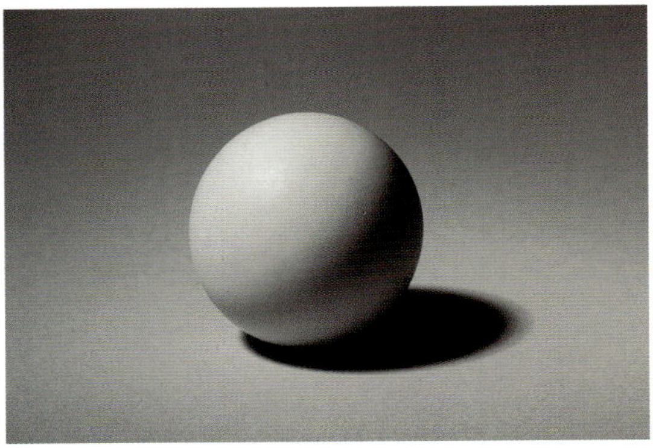

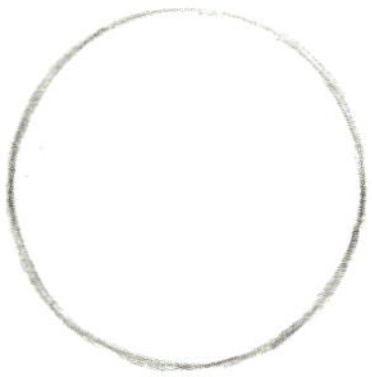

Step 2: With this light setup, observe how the light and dark areas are divided on the sphere. Define the position of this division line, and draw it on the circle. This is usually a diagonal curve where the light and dark areas meet. Let's refer to this division line as line (d) for easier explanation.

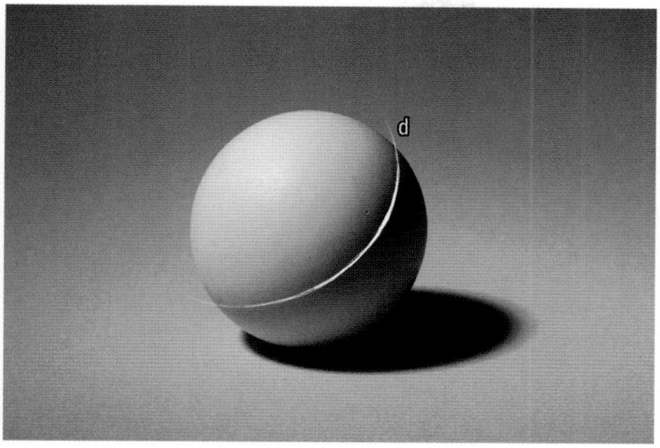

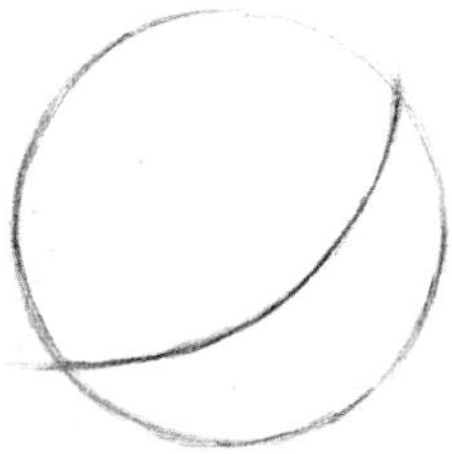

Key Shading Components

Step 3: Let's start analyzing the key shading components in this sphere. Begin with the highlight. The highlight is where light directly impacts and is perpendicular to the subject, creating a small, very bright area. With the current light setup, you can see the Highlight (H) near the upper-left corner of the sphere. Use your pencil to draw a small oval to mark the highlight position.

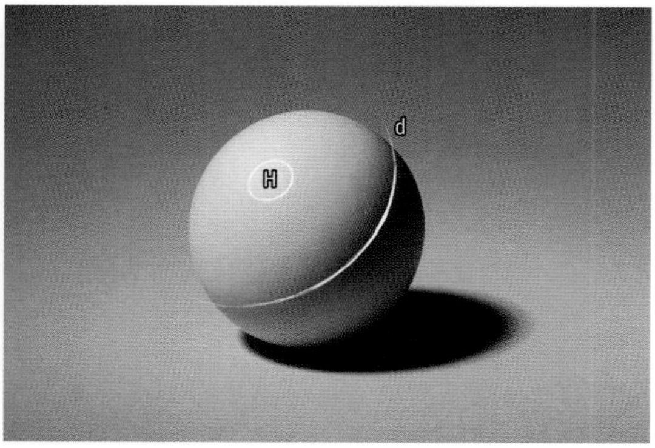

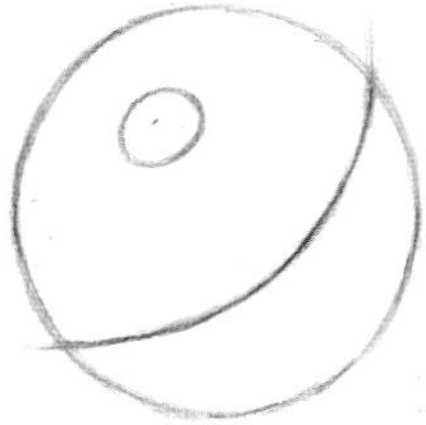

Step 4: Based on the division line (d), observe the position about one-third into the shadow area from the line (d). This is where we will show the lowest value on the sphere, known as the Core Shadow (C). Draw a curved or wavy line to define this key shading component.

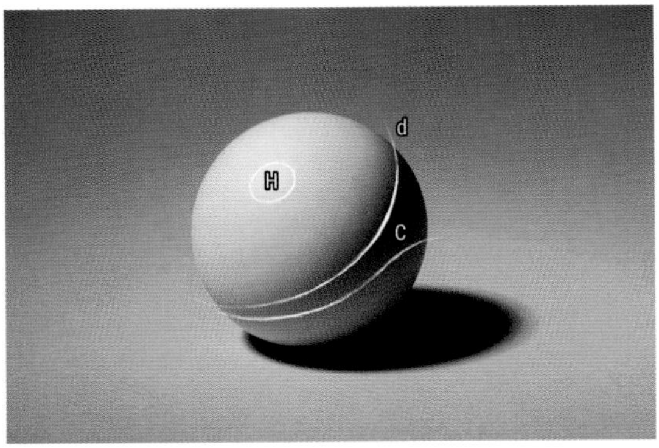

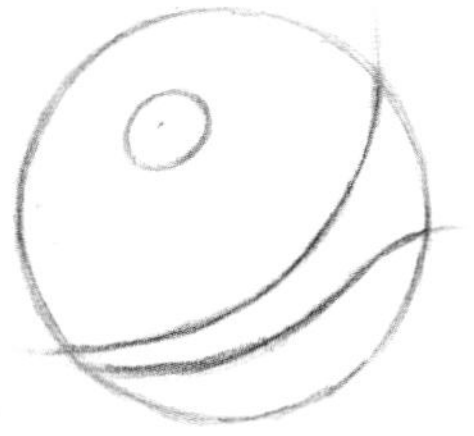

Step 5: On the subject, the area where light directly hits but is not necessarily perpendicular is called Direct Light (D). This area typically surrounds the highlight and covers a larger area. Draw a larger oval to mark the area of direct light.

The division line (d) marks the transition between light and shadow on the subject, and it is also where the Mid-Tone (M) is located. In other words, the mid-tone is the transition area between direct light (D) and core shadow (C).

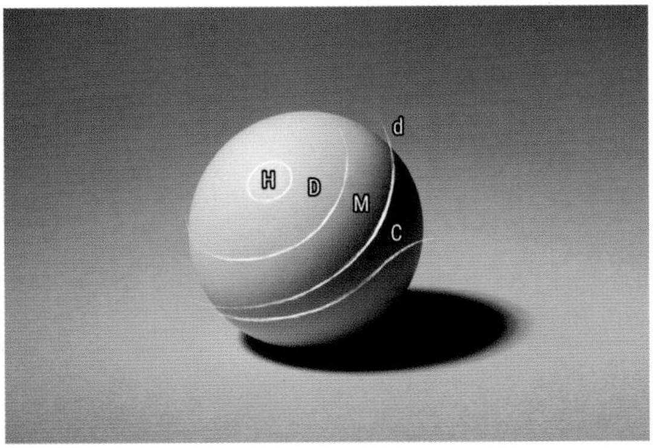

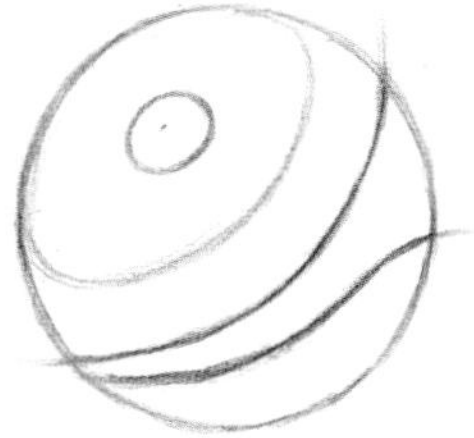

Step 6: We have covered some basic shading components. To enhance the depth and 3D quality of the subject, let's discuss Reflected Light (R). When the sphere is placed on a light-colored surface, you can see some light reflecting from underneath, back onto the sphere. Therefore, the area on the lower right side of the sphere will be slightly brighter, and we call this area reflected light (R). This means if the subject is placed in a very dark space with minimal reflected light from its surroundings, it will be difficult to determine the position of the core shadow. However, using reflected light in your drawing achieves a more dynamic and impressive depiction of depth and structure. Mark the reflected light on your sphere, as shown in the image below.

Step 7: Finally, to complete the drawing and convey a sense of space, we cannot overlook the Cast Shadow (Ca). The cast shadow is the shadow cast by the subject onto its surroundings. As you can see, the shadow of the sphere in this illustration is an oval shape on the surface. Depending on the strength of the light (soft or hard), the cast shadow can be either sharp or blurred. Draw the cast shadow now.

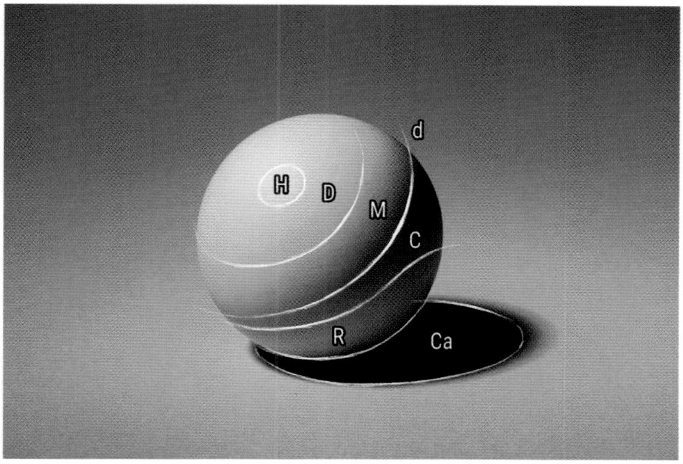

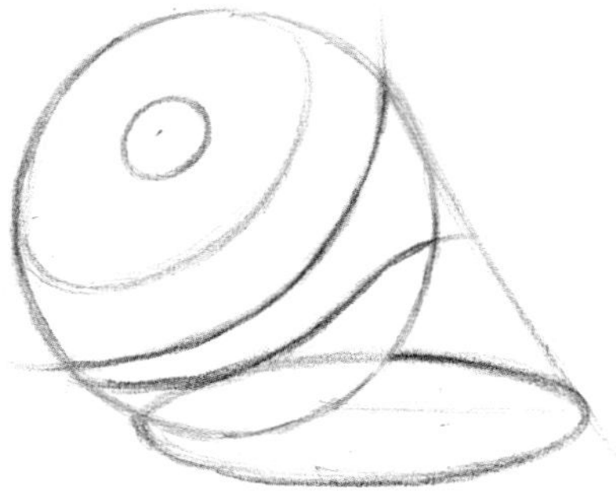

Shading the Sphere with Pencils

Step 8: After establishing the overall light area, we'll determine the overall value by shading a layer of light gray on the whole sphere except the highlight. In this demonstration, I'm using an HB pencil.

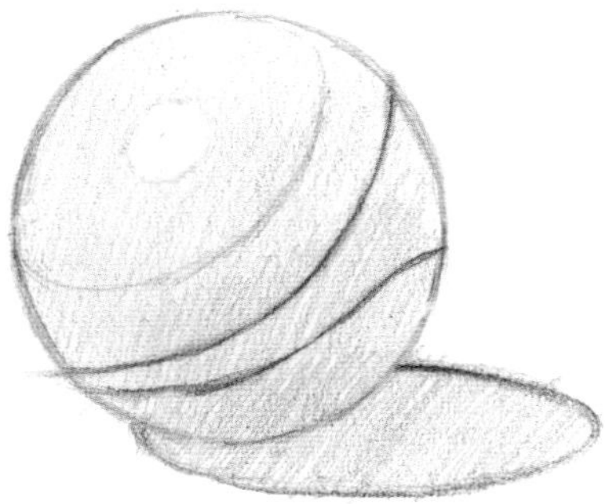

Step 9: Switch to a 2B pencil to shade the entire dark area of the sphere. The dark area is defined by the dividing line (d). Make sure to shade the entire core shadow, reflected light, and cast shadow.

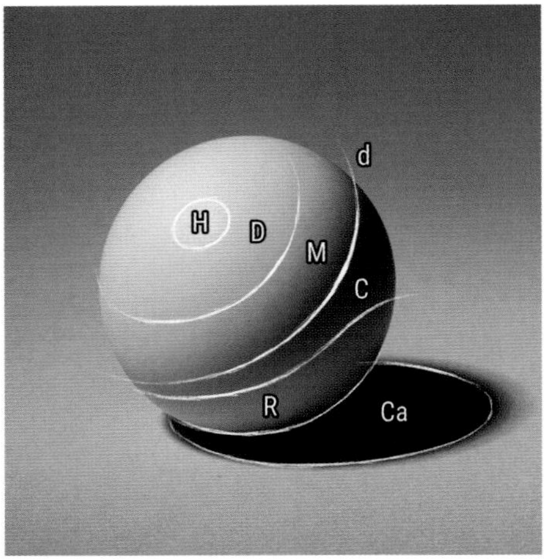

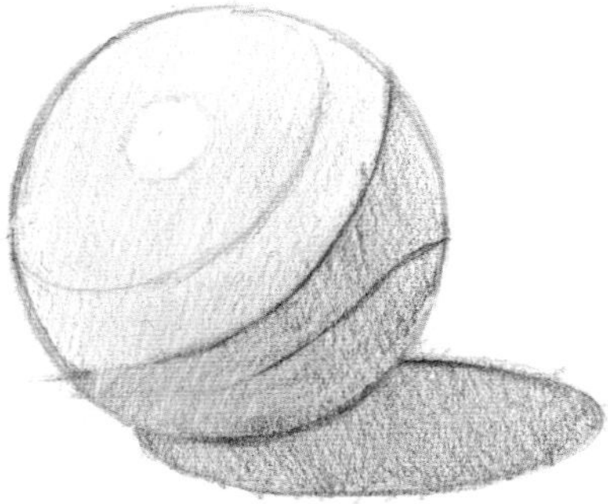

Step 10: Continue using the 2B pencil or switch to a 3B to darken the core shadow and cast shadow (reducing the value, or making it lower). At this point, you should be able to see the reflected light more clearly.

Step 11: Use a lighter pencil, such as an HB, to slightly darken the reflected light and mid-tone areas. You just need to make these areas a bit darker, but keep them lighter than the core shadow and cast shadow.

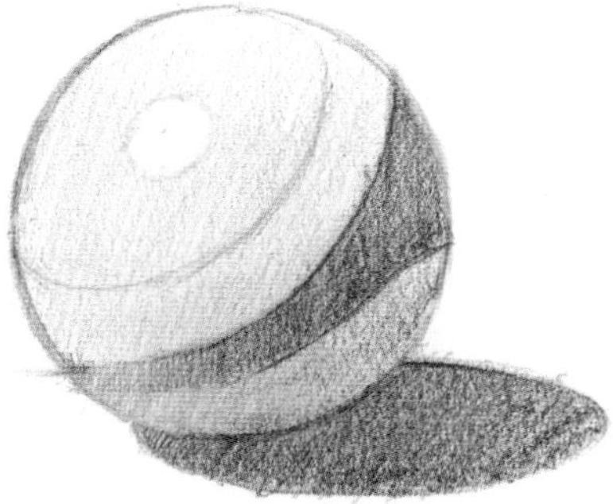

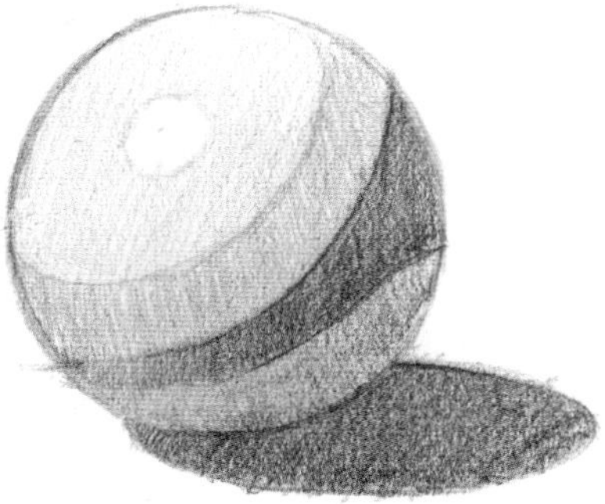

Step 12: Apply the value transition and blending techniques to create natural shading on the sphere. You can also use a tissue or your finger to gently blend the pencil marks on the paper for a smoother transition.

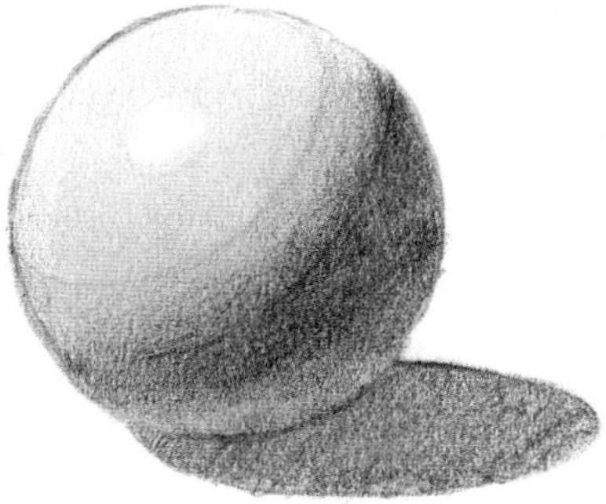

Step 13: Use a darker pencil, like a 5B or 6B, to emphasize the darker areas of the sphere, such as the core shadow and cast shadow. While shading, adjust the pressure of your hand to blend the values harmoniously. For the cast shadow, the area closest to the sphere should be darker than the areas farther away.

Step 14: Observe and compare your work with the reference photo to make any necessary adjustments until you're satisfied. You can exaggerate the darker areas to create higher contrast, which will help emphasize the form of the subject. We have successfully completed the shading of a sphere!

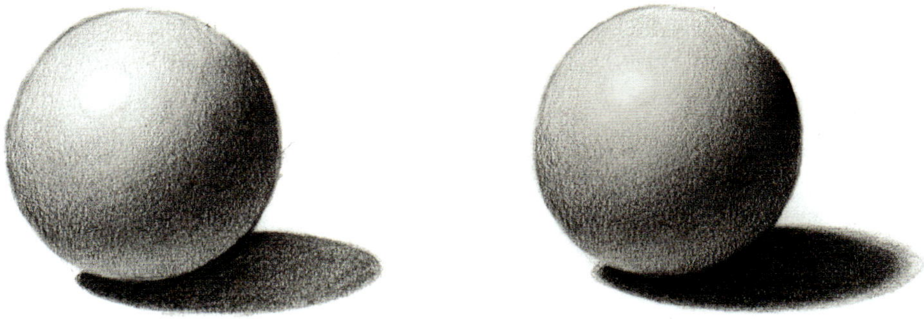

Let's quickly review the key shading components we've explored:

- **Highlight:** The brightest value, found where light squarely hits the subject.
- **Direct Light:** The area directly illuminated by the light source.
- **Mid-Tone:** Positioned between light and dark areas, often at the division line.
- **Core Shadow:** The darkest area on the subject, where minimal light reaches.
- **Reflected Light:** Reflection from the surrounding environment onto the subject, contributing to its illumination.
- **Cast Shadow:** The shadow cast by the subject onto its surrounding environment.

Practice Shading Theory with Basic Forms

To help you better understand the theory of shading and practice your basic shading skills with simple shapes, let's work together on an exercise drawing basic forms, including a cube and a cylinder.

Step 1: Use the constructive sketching method (page 48) to draw the cube and cylinder. At the same time, identify the position of the cast shadow to show the space around the subjects.

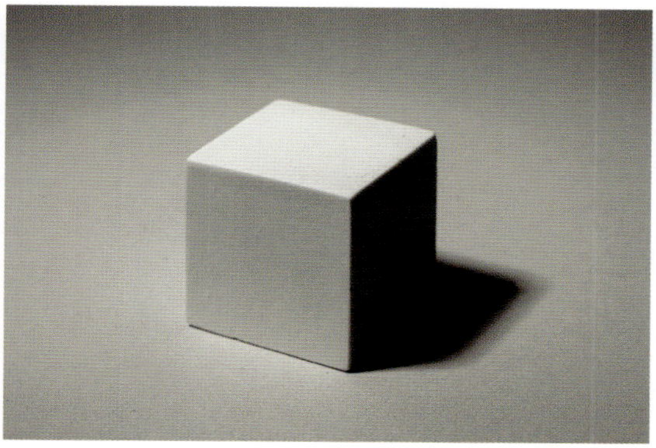

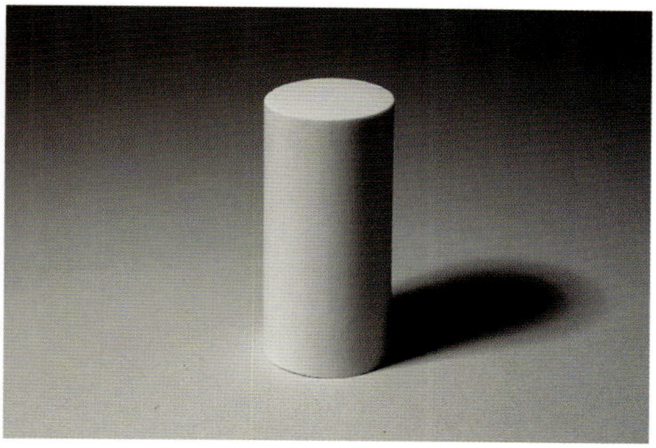

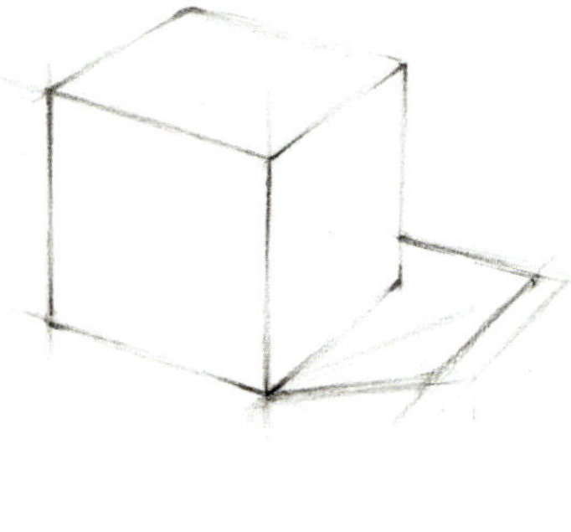

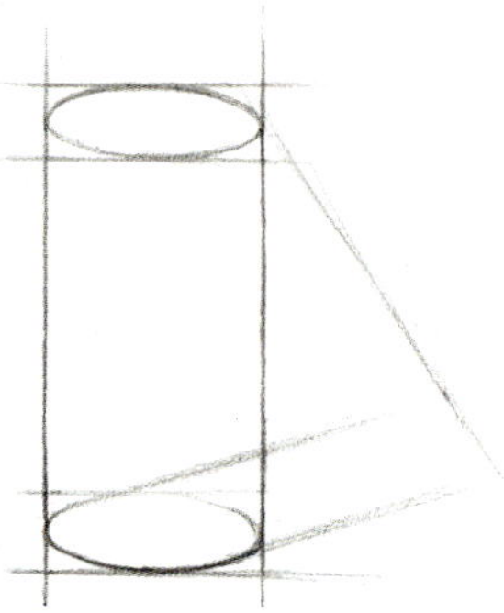

Step 2: Determine the key shading components by observing your reference. For the cube, some of the key shading components are already defined by the corners and edges of the shape. For the cylinder, draw vertical lines to divide the key shading areas.

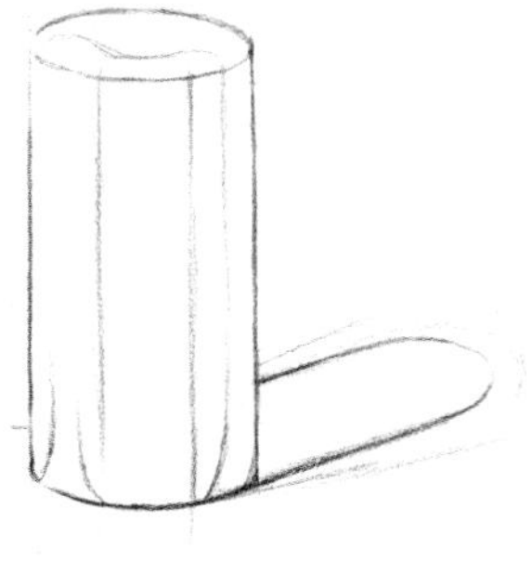

Step 3: Define the overall value by dividing the form into two main light and dark areas.

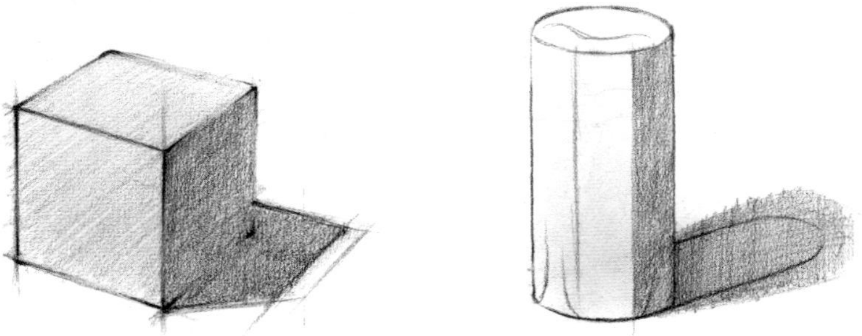

Step 4: Locate the core shadow and cast shadow, and darken these areas. At this stage, you don't need to focus on the exact value.

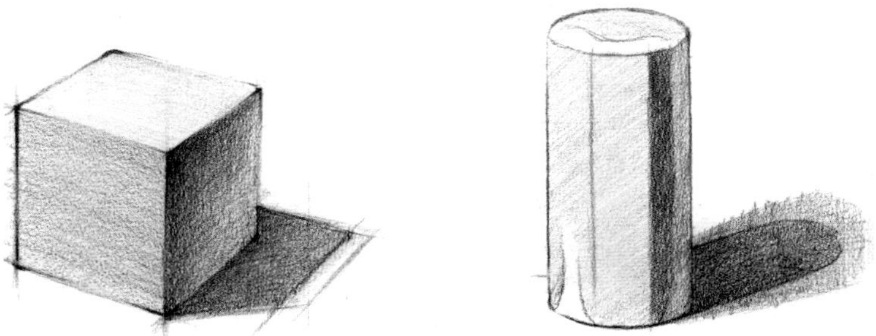

Step 5: Blend these values together by adjusting the hand pressure when shading with pencils. For the cube, which has sharp angles and edges, you only need to blend the core shadow and reflected light. For the cylinder, make sure the values transition smoothly to show the curved surface.

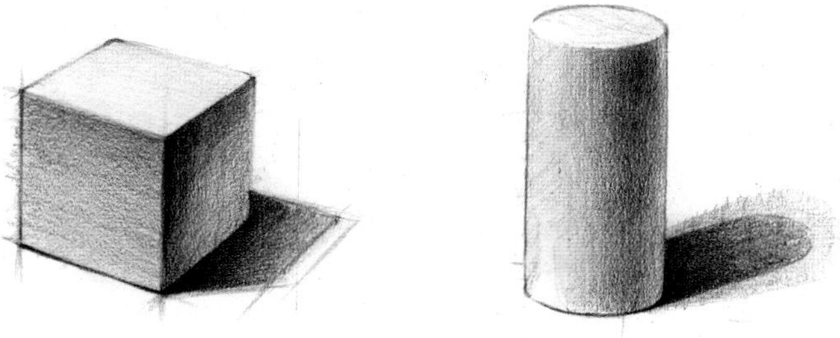

Step 6: Emphasize the dark values, such as the core shadow and cast shadow, once again. At the same time, continue blending the values until the drawing's light matches that of the reference.

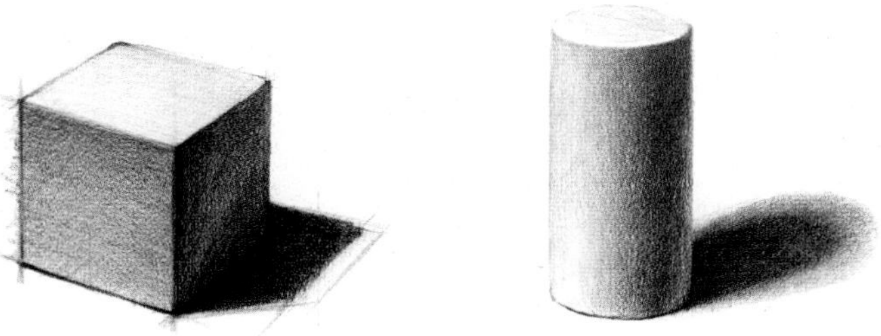

Step 7: To emphasize the form and create depth, you can add a background (optional). Observe, compare, balance the values, and make adjustments until you're happy with the result.

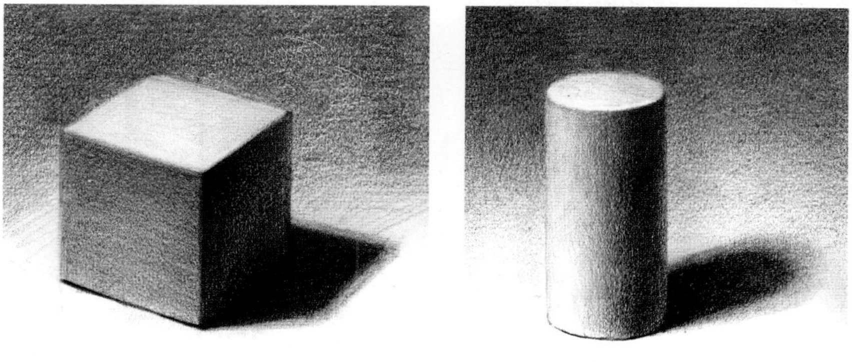

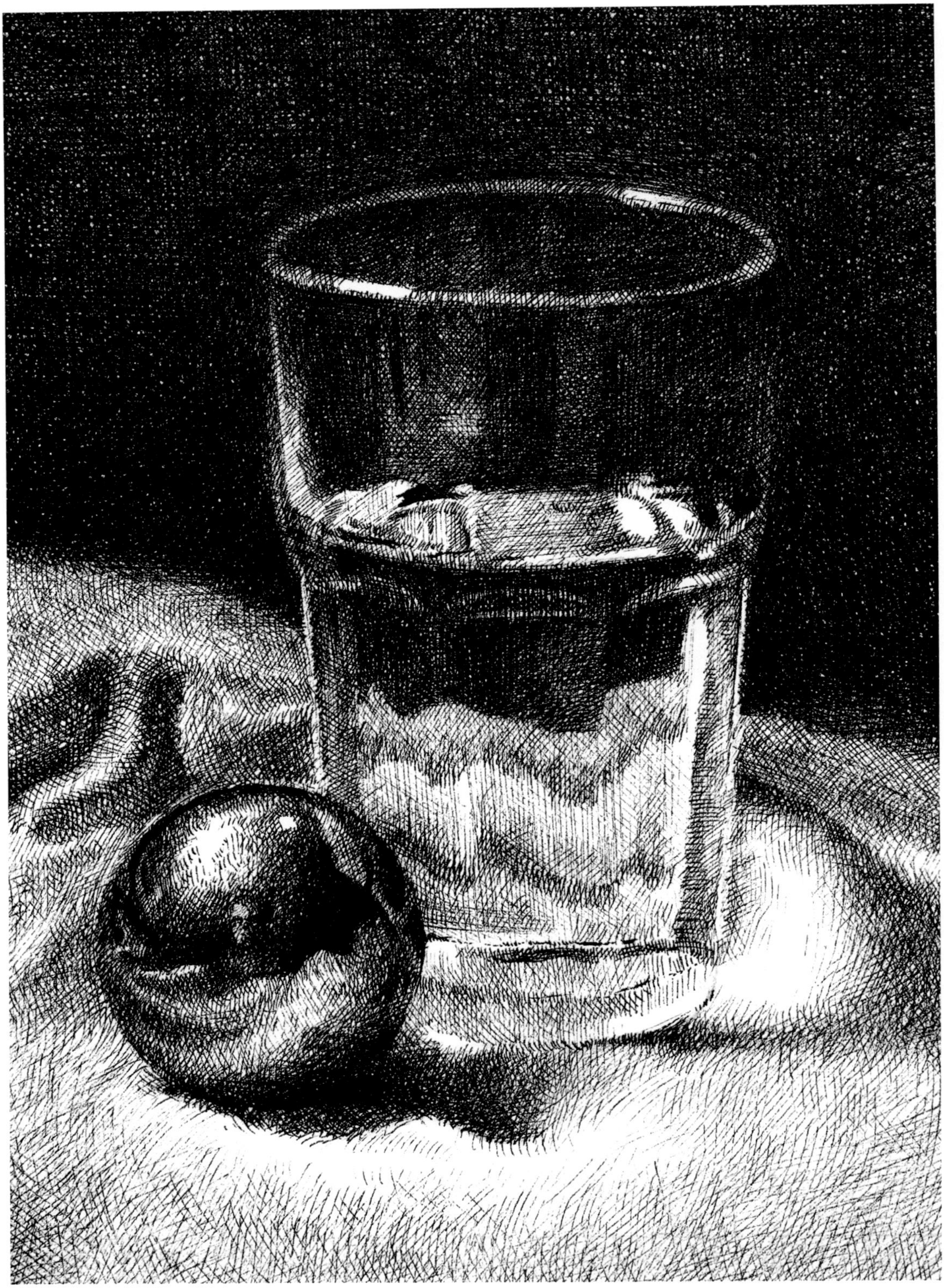

Chapter 5
Creating Depth with Shading Techniques

Based on what we've learned and discussed earlier about shading, in this chapter, we'll explore different pen-and-ink shading techniques such as hatching, cross-hatching, stippling, cross-contour, line thickness, and a few additional methods.

Understanding value and key shading components is the most essential foundation for expressing shading with different mediums, including pen and ink. Through practical exercises and detailed step-by-step demonstrations, this chapter will help you master the most important basic techniques. Let's get started!

HATCHING AND CROSSHATCHING

In drawing, hatching and crosshatching are considered the most common techniques for shading. Their advantage lies in their versatility for representing value, as discussed in the previous chapter. Mastering these techniques enables you to effectively convey depth and three-dimensional structure in your drawings. Let's begin with a closer look at the hatching technique.

HATCHING

Essentially, hatching involves using parallel lines to convey value. By drawing multiple parallel strokes, the area covered will appear as a light gray tone. As we add more layers of hatching, the value becomes darker. To get used to this technique, let's do a few exercises.

Start with Simple Straight Lines

Step 1: Similar to the warm-up exercise at the beginning of the book (page 18), draw parallel horizontal lines at a moderate hand-movement pace. The difference here is to gradually taper the end of each line by lifting the pen off the paper while still moving your hand. You'll notice that the line's end becomes very fine, natural, and fluid.

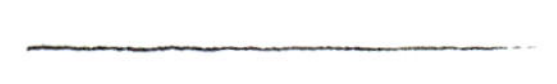

Step 2: Continue drawing parallel lines with even spacing of about 1 mm between them. Always try to lift the pen off the paper while your hand is still in motion.

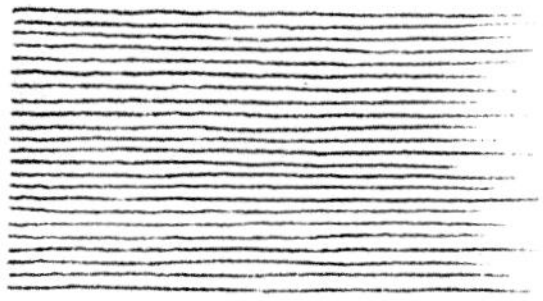

Step 3: Practice this method with different line directions, including horizontal, vertical, and diagonal lines.

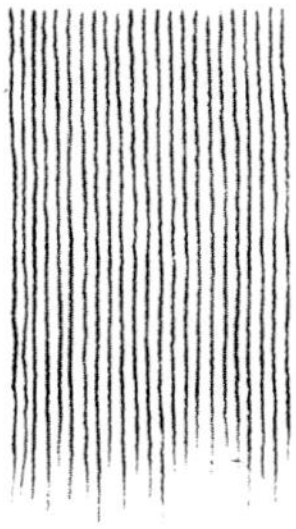

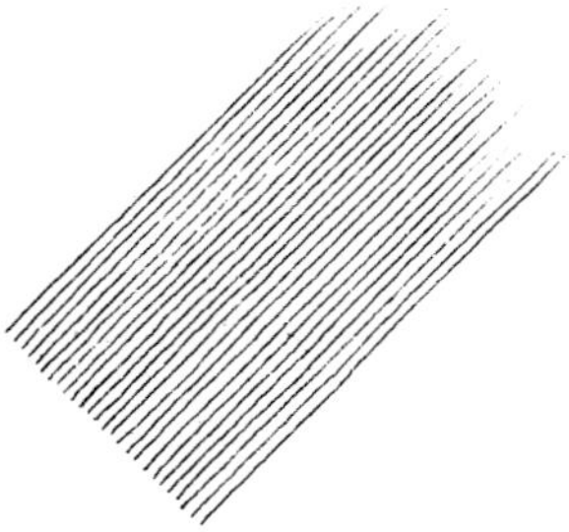

Increase Hand Pace Gradually

Step 1: Follow the previous exercise, but gradually increase the pace of your hand movement with each line you draw. As you draw faster, the accuracy of the lines may decrease, and you might create lines that don't match your expectations. Don't worry about that; in this exercise, maintaining a smooth and consistent hand pace is more important than the precision of the lines.

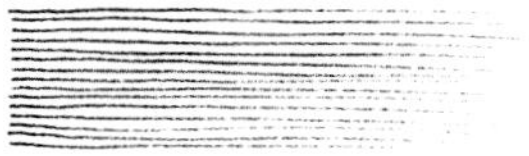

Step 2: Continue to increase your drawing speed until your hand moves quickly, creating lines that lightly glide across the paper.

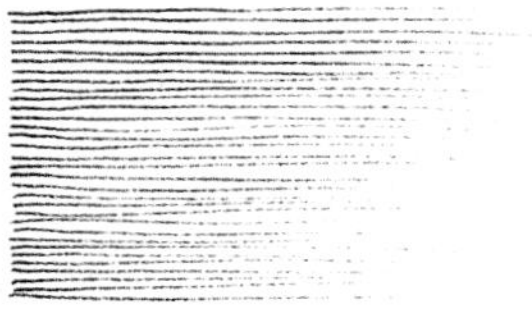

Step 3: Practice with various line directions and hand movements to get used to working at a faster speed.

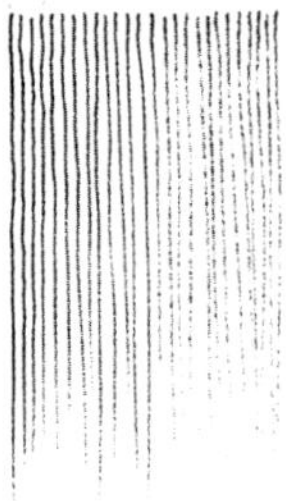

Vary the Distance Between Lines

Step 1: Let's do a more challenging exercise by drawing hatch lines closer together. Start with lines spaced about 1 mm apart, and then gradually decrease the distance between them as you go. Keep drawing until the lines are almost touching (but not quite). If some lines end up touching or crossing, don't worry—just keep practicing and refining your technique.

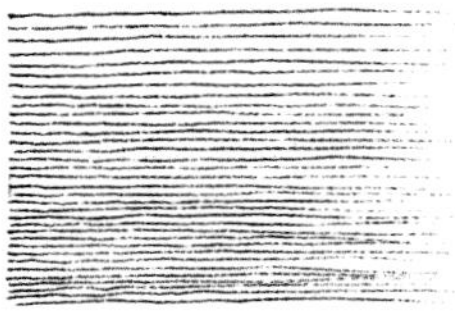

Step 2: Practice this method with different line directions, including horizontal, vertical, and diagonal lines.

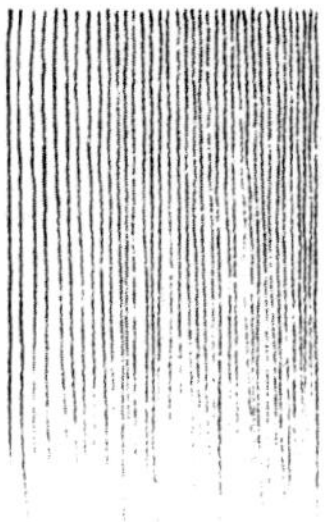

Express Value with Hatching

Step 1: Let's start applying the hatching technique to create different shades of gray. Begin with a layer of hatching using a fast hand movement and closely spaced lines to create a light gray shade.

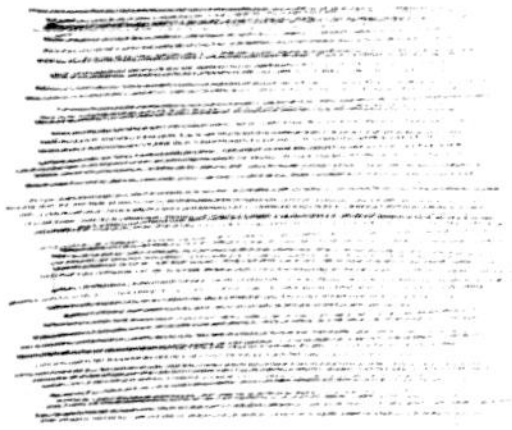

Step 2: Draw another layer of hatching in the same direction, overlapping the first layer. It's okay if the lines touch and overlap with each other. After completing the second layer, you'll notice that the gray becomes darker than the first layer.

Step 3: Continue this process with additional layers, such as the third, fourth, and so on. Make sure each layer has the same direction and hand movement. The more layers you add, the darker the shaded area will become.

Step 4: Keep drawing until you achieve a very dark gray or nearly black shade, and you'll have completed the exercise!

CROSSHATCHING

Crosshatching is a drawing technique that uses strokes in multiple directions. These strokes intersect harmoniously, helping you create depth and shading in your artwork. This technique is widely used in drawing in general and pen-and-ink drawing in particular. Crosshatching allows you to achieve a wide range of values, effectively conveying detail and texture.

Create Solid Value with Crosshatching

Step 1: Start with a light layer of hatching in a square shape with horizontal lines to create a light gray tone, just like in the previous exercise.

Step 2: Now, let's change the direction of your strokes. For crosshatching, we'll follow the same approach as hatching, but this time, angle your strokes about 15 to 45 degrees (30 degrees is ideal) from the direction of the first hatching layer. Create this second layer to achieve a darker gray tone.

Step 3: Continue by changing the direction of your strokes in the third hatching layer. If you chose a 30-degree angle for the second layer, then the third layer should be at a 60-degree angle to the horizontal strokes.

Step 4: Keep applying this method in the following hatching layers until you complete a full 360-degree rotation. With each layer, you'll notice the shaded area gets progressively darker. This is how crosshatching works. So, what should you do once you've completed a 360-degree rotation?

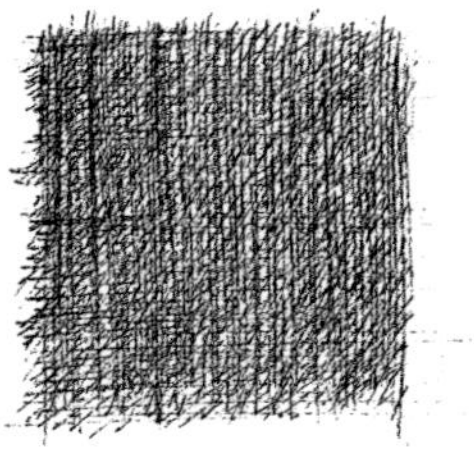

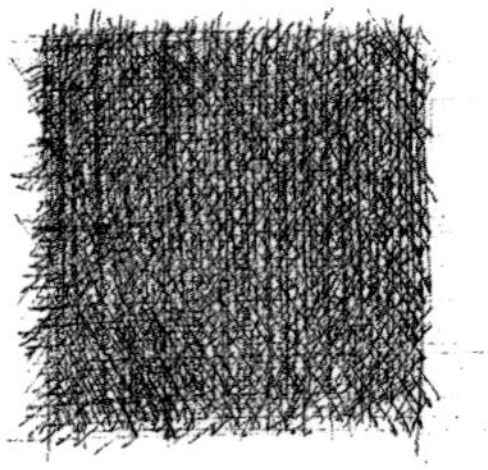

Step 5: At this point, with a high density of crosshatching, you can continue adding more layers in any direction you choose. It's okay if new strokes overlap previous layers. The key is to continuously change the layering and ensure that the intersecting strokes feel balanced. Keep crosshatching until you achieve a very dark gray or nearly black shade.

Draw a Value Scale

Step 1: Now, let's apply the technique we just learned to create a value scale as we studied in the "Shading Theory Made Easy" chapter. Start by drawing ten squares, each about 1 inch (2.5 cm) in size, lined up horizontally.

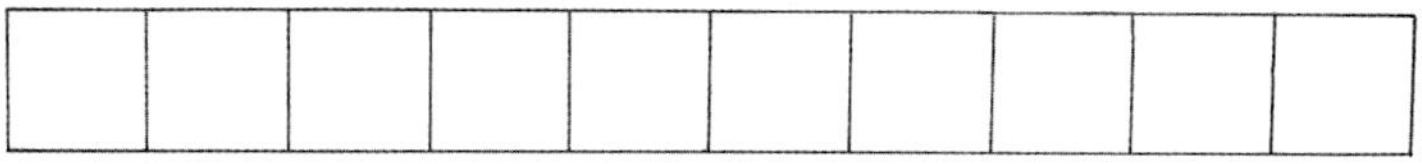

Step 2: Use the hatching technique to create a light gray shade that covers all squares from one to nine, leaving the tenth square blank to represent the highlight.

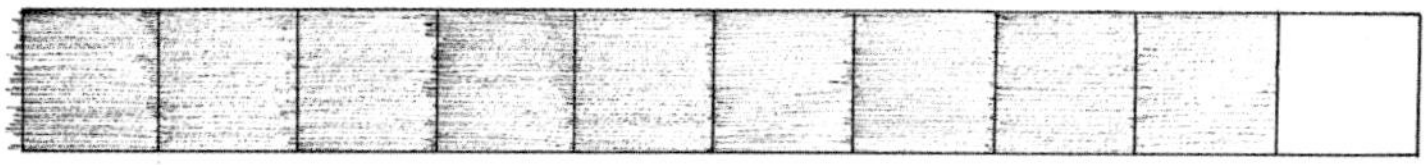

Step 3: Change the direction of your strokes to create a crosshatching layer over squares one to eight, leaving square nine as a light gray layer.

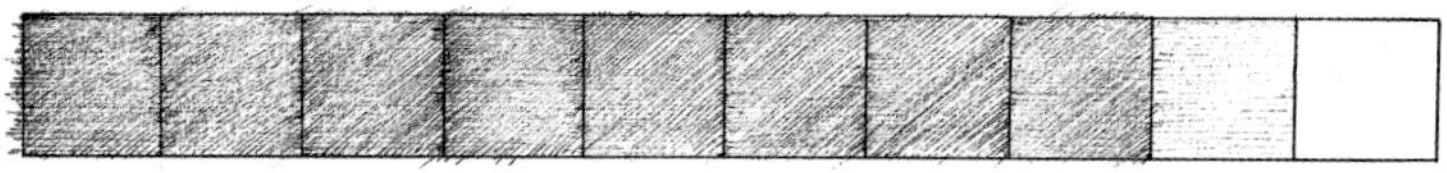

Step 4: Continue with the same technique, layering crosshatching and leaving out squares in a countdown from eight, seven, six, and so on, until you finish with square one. By doing this, you'll create a gradient of values. You can modify this value scale more by adding more crosshatching layers if you want to make the value lower.

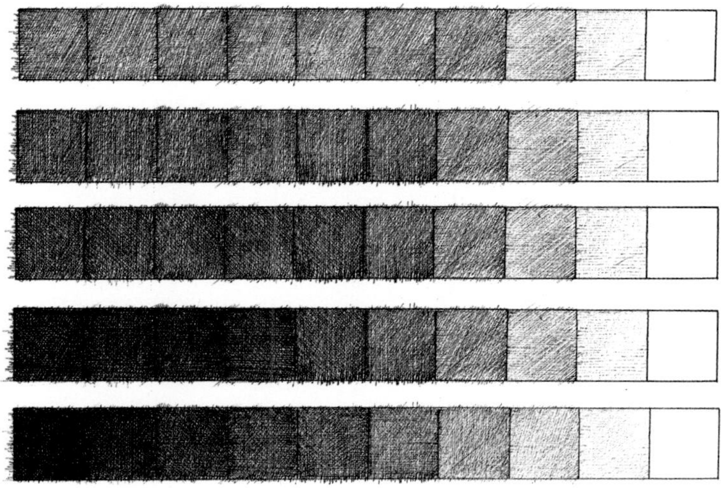

Blend Values Using Crosshatching

Step 1: Let's dive into an exciting exercise: blending different values to create a smooth gradient from light to dark. To keep things manageable, start by drawing a square about 1.5–2 inches (4–5 cm) on each side to define your drawing area.

Step 2: Begin with light hatching in any direction you prefer to create a very light gray shade that covers almost the entire square. In this demonstration, I'll start with diagonal hatching lines at a 45-degree angle. Leave a small area on the right edge of the square blank to represent the highest value (the lightest shade). It's okay if your lines extend slightly outside the square.

Step 3: Apply crosshatching for the second layer to create a darker shade. The goal here is to blend values to achieve a smooth transition from light to dark. With this second layer, leave a bit of the first hatching layer visible on the right side. After that, you should begin to see the value transition in this position.

Step 4: Continue adding layers of crosshatching. For each new layer, adjust the direction of your hatching lines, and leave a small part of the previous crosshatching layer visible on the right side. Keep going until you achieve a smooth gradient from dark (left side) to light (right side).

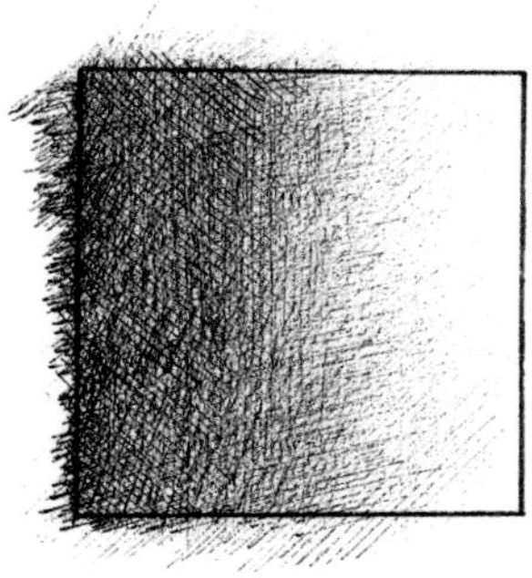

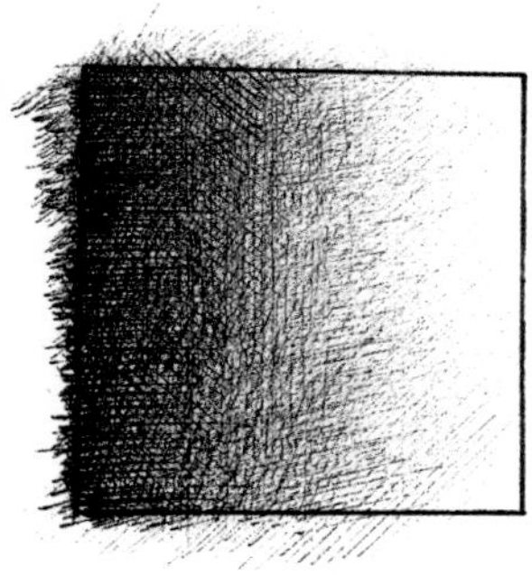

Step 5: You can refine your gradient further by adding additional crosshatching layers as needed. On the left side of the square, you can modify and add more layers of crosshatching to make it almost black. Move your hand gently, drawing and adjusting as you observe and compare until you're satisfied with the result. And that's it—you've completed the value blending exercise!

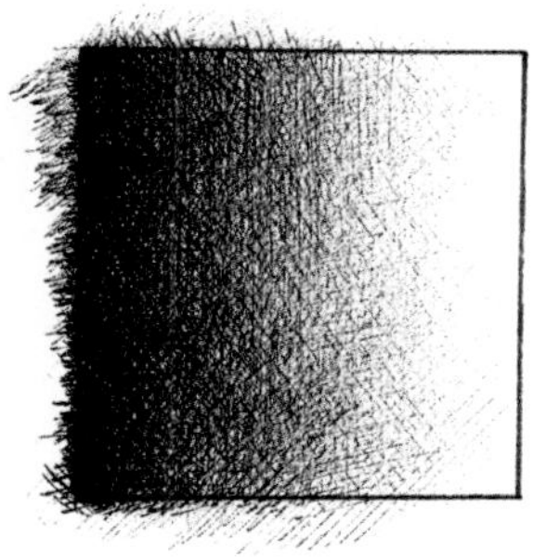

Let's Put It All Together

We've explored hatching and crosshatching techniques to represent different values and blend them smoothly. Now, let's use these techniques as tools, combined with the shading theory we've learned, to work on a practical exercise together.

Constructive Sketching and Outlining

In this exercise, we will be drawing a simplified bird sculpture. Subjects with simplified forms are very useful for practice because the minimized details allow you to focus more on shading, structure, and form.

Step 1: Start by observing the reference photos, analyzing them, and drawing a simple rectangular shape around the entire subject.

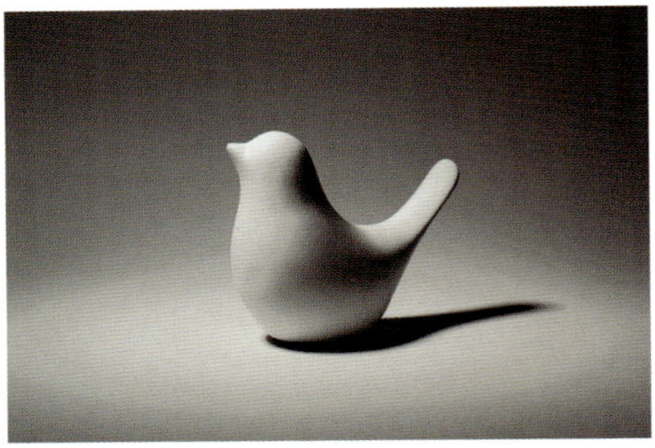

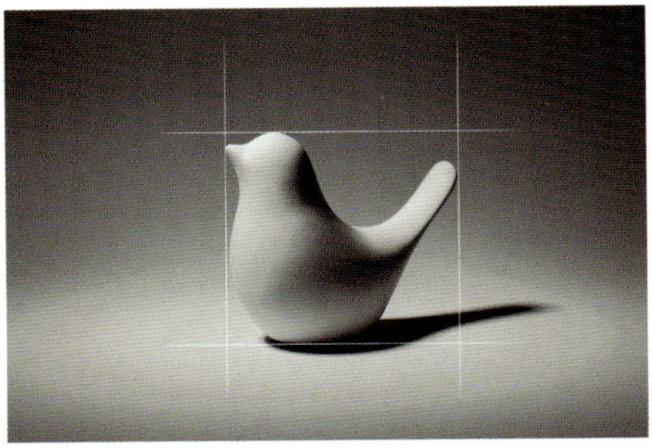

Step 2: Identify key points on the subject, such as the top of the head, the sides, the tail, and the bottom of the bird. Then begin drawing a constructive sketch using simple straight lines to capture the overall simplified shape of the sculpture. At the same time, you can determine the position of the cast shadow.

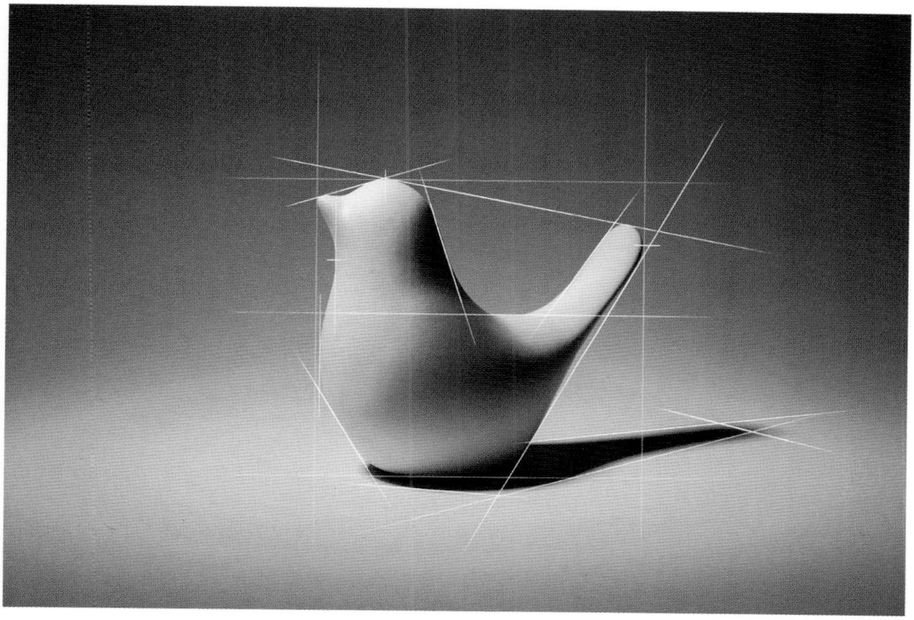

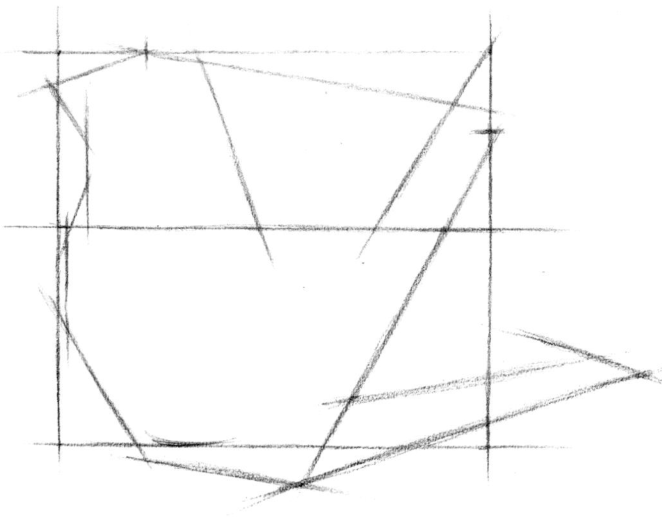

Step 3: Based on the constructive sketch, use curved lines to outline the shape of the bird. Continuously refer to the reference photo to create an outline you're happy with. Once the outline is complete, you can erase any unnecessary sketch lines to make the bird's shape clearer.

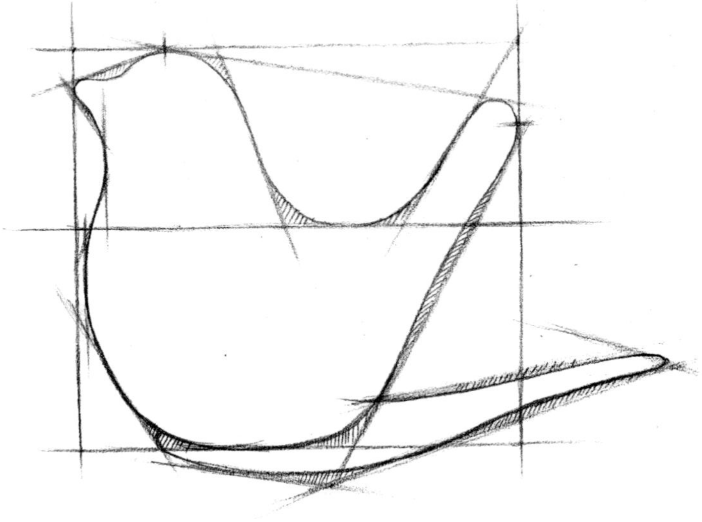

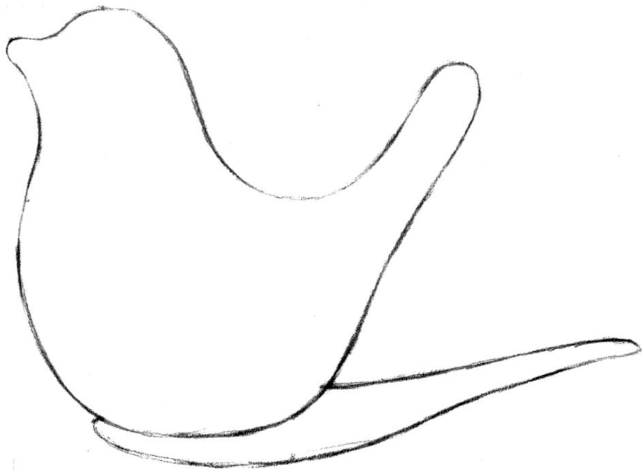

Key Shading Components

Step 4: Observe the reference photo; you'll notice that the light is divided relatively clearly. Start by drawing the overall light–dark division lines to grasp the overall value of the drawing.

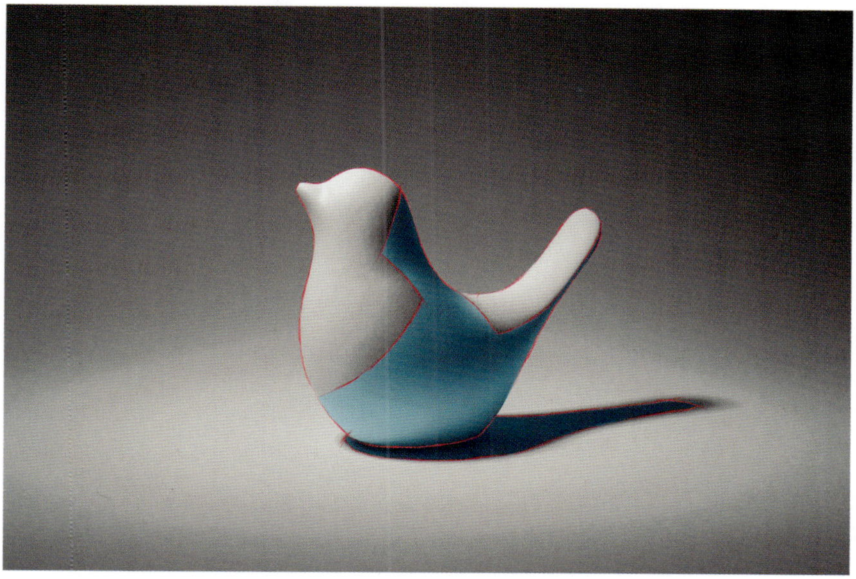

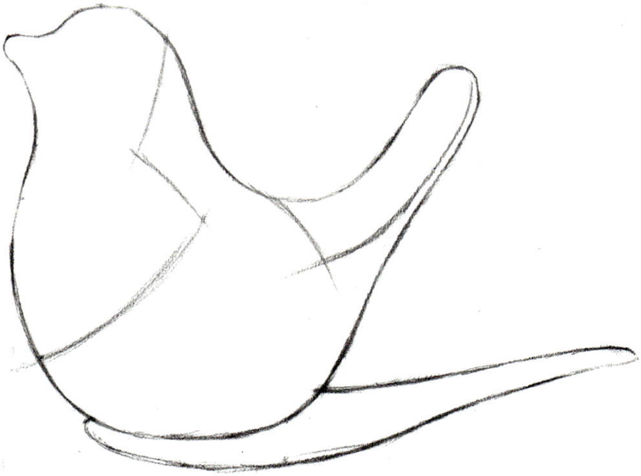

Step 5: Based on the overall value, identify the key shading components, including the highlight (located on the top of the bird's head), direct light, mid-tone, core shadow (found at the back of the head, the center of the body, and the tail edge), reflected light, and cast shadow. Flip back to page 59 if you need a refresher on these terms.

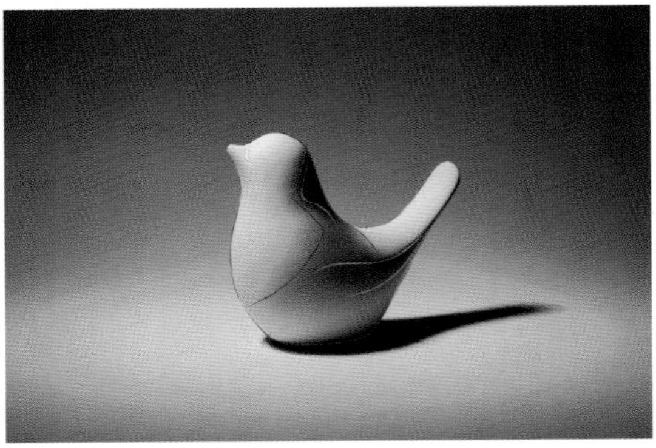

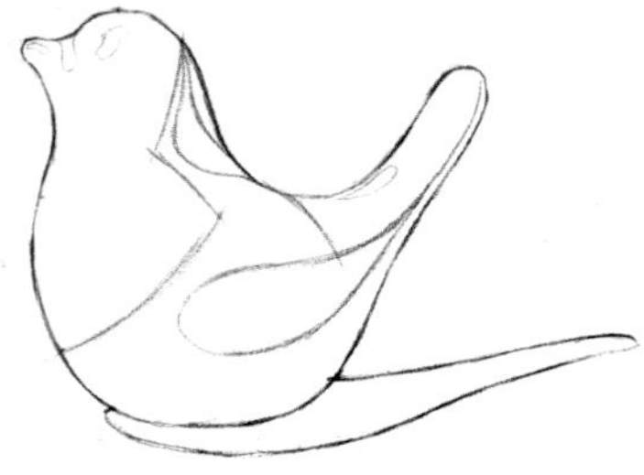

Hatching and Crosshatching

Step 6: After finishing the sketch and defining the key shading components, let's begin to express the overall value with hatching and crosshatching. Using a fine-tipped 005 fineliner is recommended to keep this layer from becoming too dark. In this step, we'll work with quick hand movements to create a light hatching layer that covers the dark areas of the subject, based on the overall value in the pencil sketch. You can also work on the background areas surrounding the bird to emphasize the light areas. Since the bright areas of the drawing can be difficult to define on a white sheet of paper, you can add shading on the background around the high-value areas to clarify the shape of the bird.

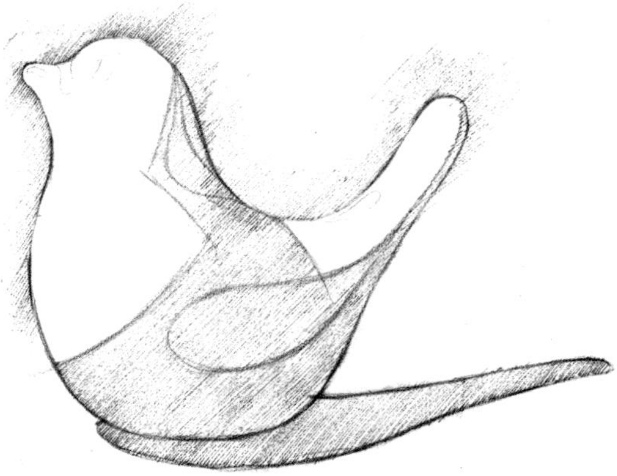

Step 7: Use the crosshatching technique to create a thin layer over the entire subject (including the dark areas), leaving only the highlight untouched. The lines in this crosshatching layer should be at a 30-degree angle to the hatching lines from Step 6.

Step 8: Identify the positions of the core shadow and cast shadow, and apply a crosshatching layer to these areas to make the key shading components stand out more clearly.

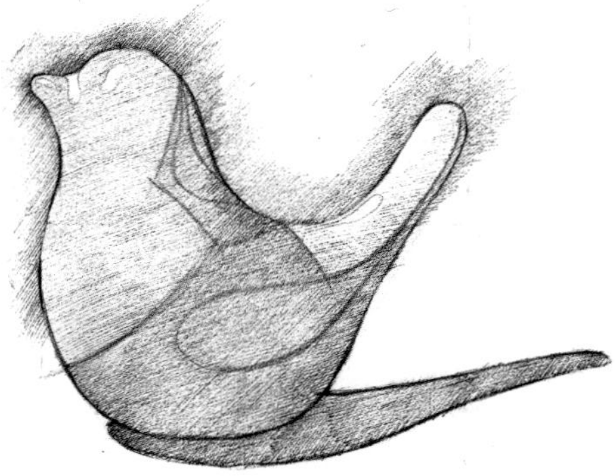

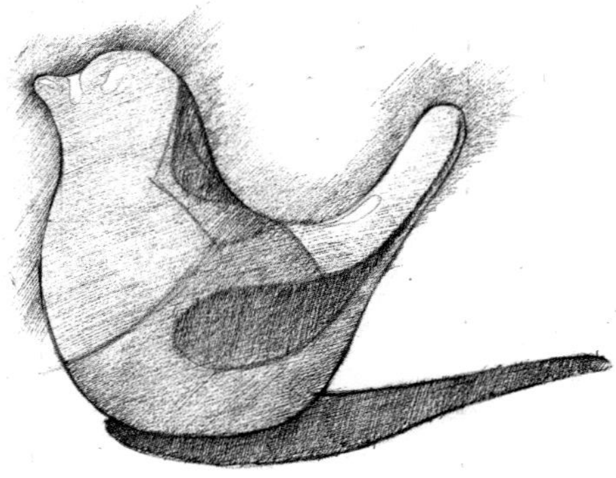

Step 9: Based on the identified key shading components, blend the values together to create a smooth transition. You can apply the crosshatching blending technique learned in the previous section. At this point, you may also erase any unnecessary sketch lines to better observe the values.

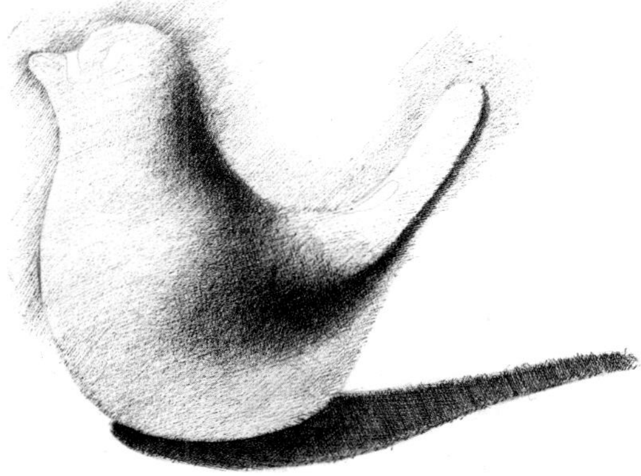

Step 10: Emphasize the core shadow and cast shadow to darken these areas so that the values closely match the reference photo. You can keep using the 005 fineliner or switch to 01 pen in this step.

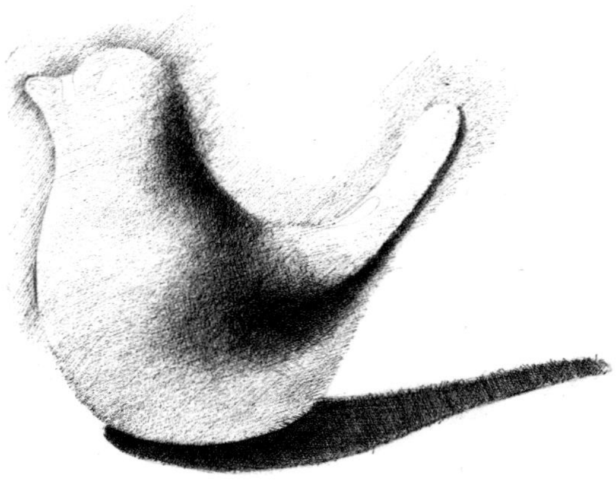

Step 11: Switching back to 005, using the values of the core shadow and cast shadow as a guide, shade the reflected light (located beneath the bird's body) and the mid-tone areas.

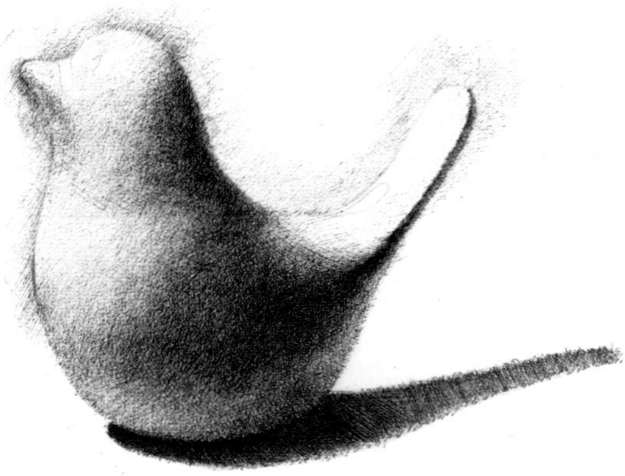

Step 12: While drawing a background is optional in these exercises, sometimes, taking the time to add one can help you observe and balance the values better. It also enhances contrast, making the drawing livelier and more realistic. For this exercise, the background will be a neutral gray layer created using the crosshatching technique.

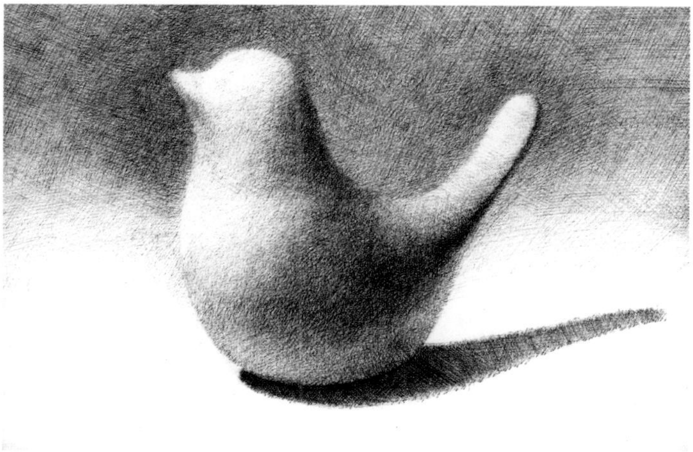

Step 13: Observe your drawing, comparing it to the reference. Now you can adjust and balance the values until you're satisfied with the result. Congratulations! You've just finished your very first complete pen-and-ink drawing with the crosshatching technique.

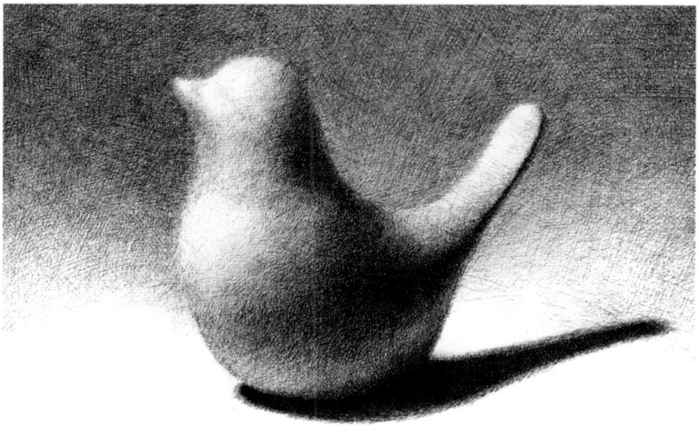

Stippling: The Art of Dots

Stippling is a technique that demands meticulous and careful execution. While it may require more time to achieve the desired results, the effect it creates is impressive and can represent a variety of textural expressions. This is a technique that uses small dots to express value. By layering multiple dots in a specific area, we can darken or reduce the value. The more dots we add, the lower the value becomes. Let's get started by doing some practical exercises!

Learning the Technique

In stippling, value is expressed through the "density" of small dots. The more dots you place in a specific area, the darker the value will be.

Before diving into the practice, let's discuss how to hold your pen for stippling. Hold the pen with your index, middle, and thumb fingers, just as you would normally. Then, keep the pen almost perpendicular to the paper. This way, you can create small, round, uniform dots that match the nib size. Lightly touch the nib to the paper and lift it quickly. Relax your hand, and continue to place dots at different positions, aiming for an even rhythm in your movement.

Creating value with stippling takes more time and requires more patience compared to other pen-and-ink techniques. So, relax and enjoy watching the light gradually take shape in your drawing—it's a fascinating process!

Solid Value Expression with Dots

Step 1: Start by sketching a square with sides about 2 inches (5 cm) long. Next, draw 45-degree diagonal lines to divide the square into smaller squares, each about ¼ inch (0.6 mm) in size, following the illustration as a guide.

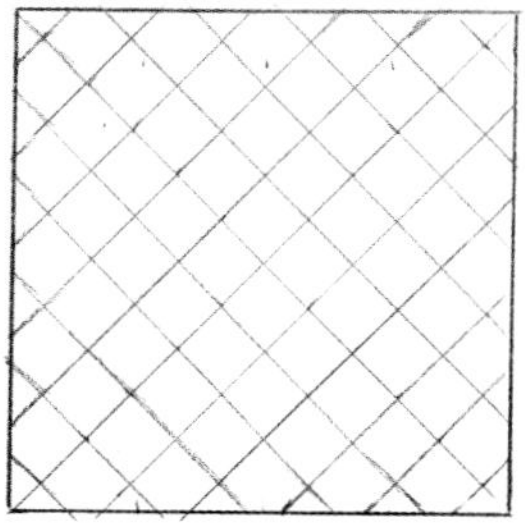

Step 2: Leave the four squares in the center empty. Use the stippling technique to create a layer of tiny dots around the four squares. Be gentle with your dots, keeping them sparse to represent a light gray tone that signifies direct light.

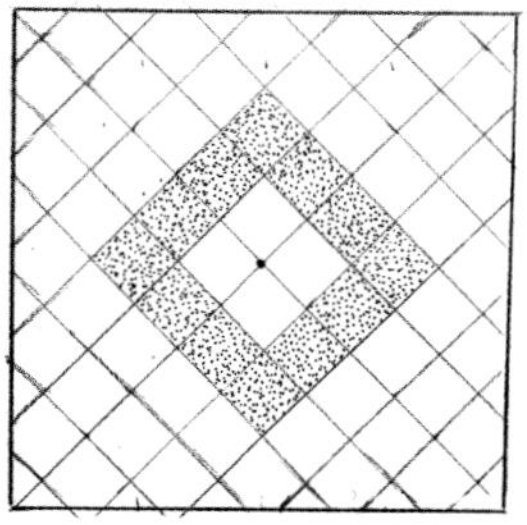

Step 3: Pay attention to the four corners of the larger square. Add a lot more dots to these areas, making them densely packed so that the value becomes very dark, almost black.

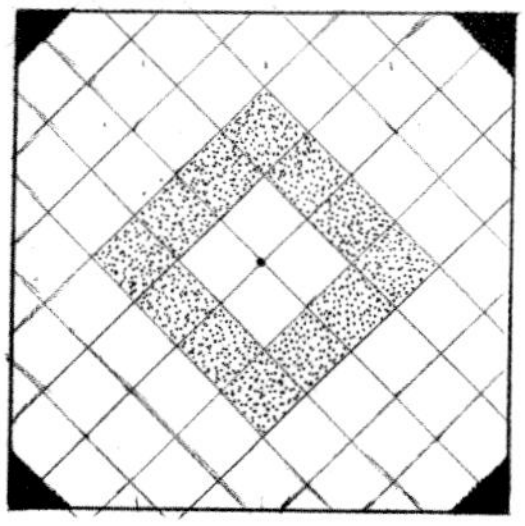

Step 4: With the light value in the center and the very dark value in the corners, create a neutral value in between. The density of your dots here should be balanced, not too many but not too few either.

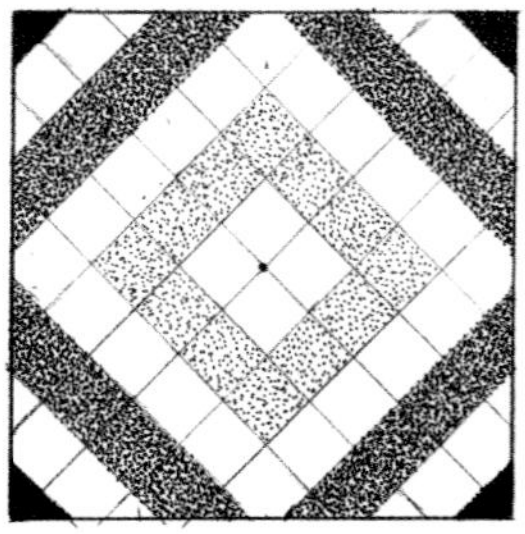

Step 5: Using the same method, adjust the density of your dots to create in-between values for the remaining areas. Once you're finished, you should see a smooth transition of value from light in the center to dark in the corners.

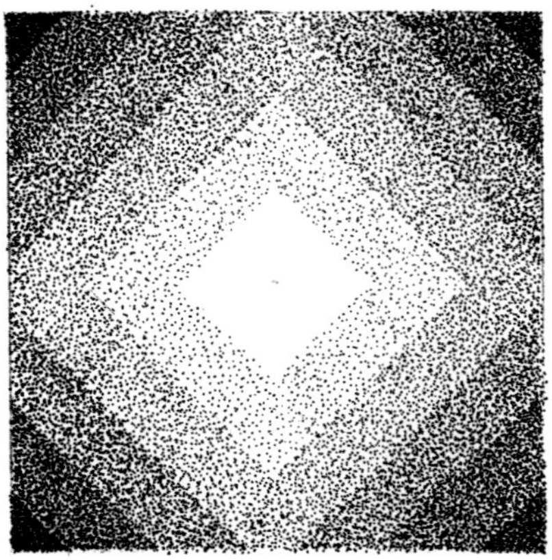

Blending Value Expression with Dots

Step 6: Building on the solid values we just created, now let's blend the values together to achieve a smooth light transition. First, sketch circles inside each of the squares.

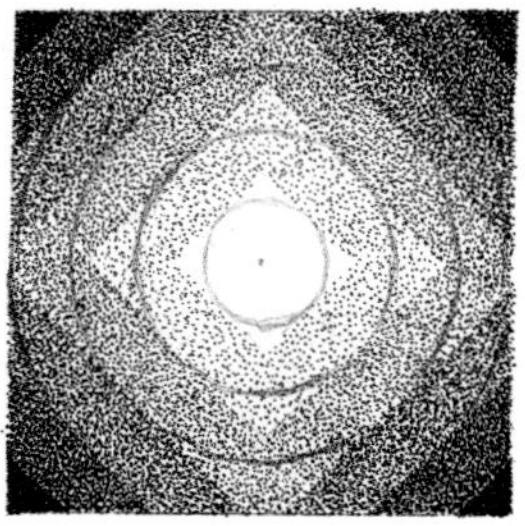

Step 7: Using the same technique as in the previous exercise, apply solid values to the circular shapes you just drew.

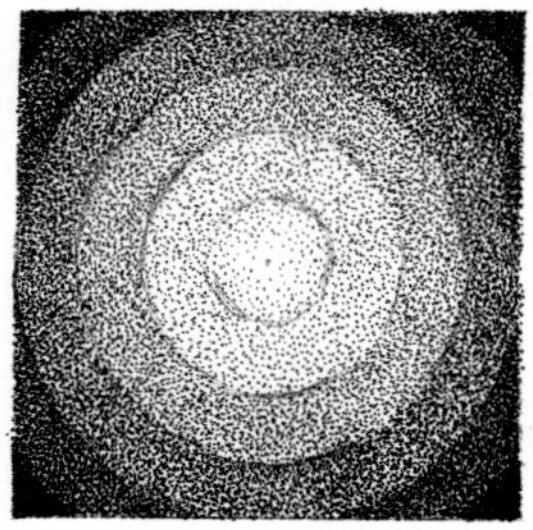

Step 8: Focus on the center of the circle. Blend the value at the center (highlight) with the surrounding area (direct light). To create this transition, gradually reduce the density of your dots as you move toward the center, allowing for a smooth light shift.

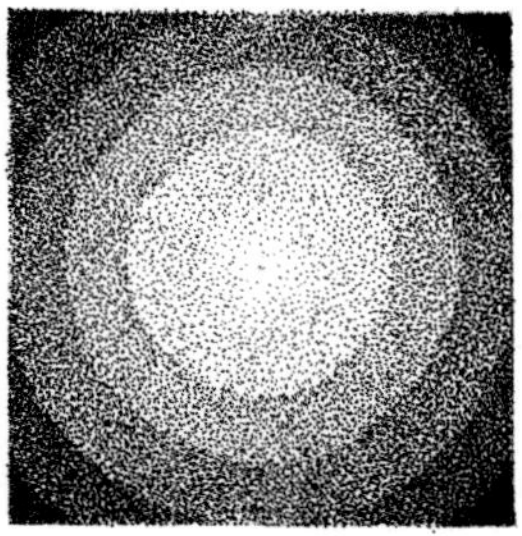

Step 9: Continue applying the same method to the other circles. Adjust the number of dots so the values gradually blend.

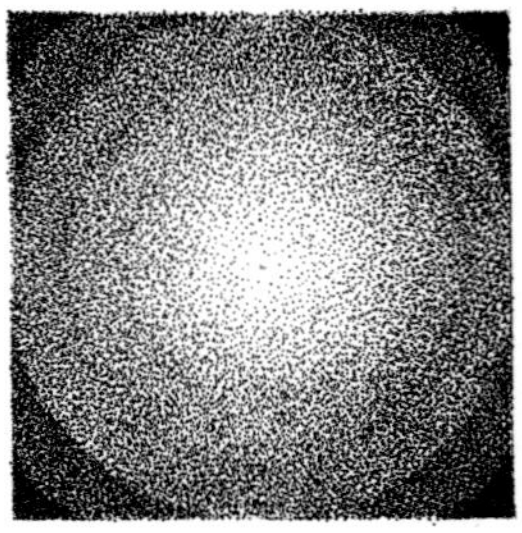

Step 10: Keep blending the values until the harsh lines separating the values from Steps 6 and 7 fade away. Observe and fine-tune until you're satisfied with the result. This is how we use the stippling technique for shading.

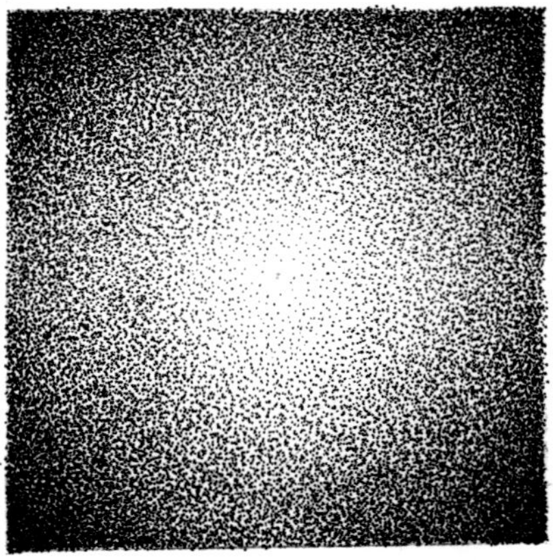

Let's Put It All Together

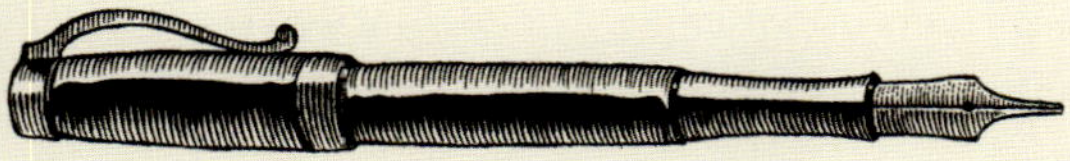

Stippling is a fascinating technique for creating shading and texture effects, and it can be used for a variety of subjects. Personally, I find stippling particularly effective for subjects with soft, natural structures. That's why, in this demo, we'll be drawing a rose together.

Complete Value Expression of a Rose

A rose can be more challenging compared to the simpler still life exercises we've done before due to the complex structure of natural subjects. Follow the step-by-step instructions below to achieve the result you're aiming for. However, don't worry if your drawing doesn't turn out exactly how you'd like! Practice is all about experimenting, gaining experience, and embracing "imperfection"—it's the best way to keep improving. For this drawing, let's use some basic pencils for sketching and fineliners in sizes 01 and 03 for shading. Let's get started!

Step 1: As always, the first step is sketching with a pencil. Determine the highest, lowest, leftmost, and rightmost points of the rose.

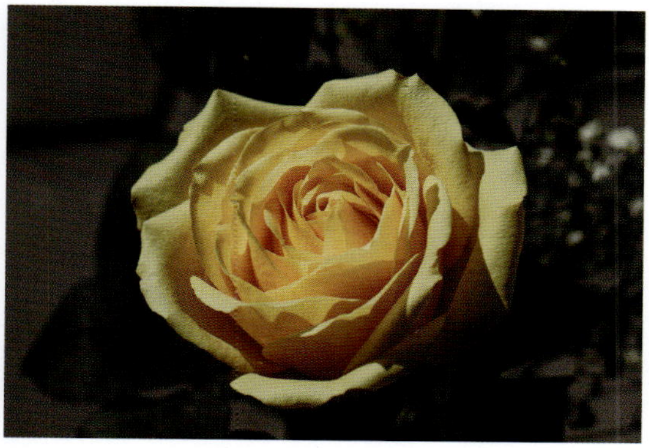

Step 2: As you can see, the rose is made up of multiple layers that curl toward the center. Identify the rose's central point with a cross. Then, determine the layers from the outer petals inward, and sketch these layers using simple strokes. You don't need to draw it exactly like the reference photo—you can simplify the number of layers and petals to make the exercise easier.

Step 3: Use simple straight sketch lines to define the shape of each petal based on the position of the layers you've identified. By now, you should have the overall shape of the rose. Feel free to make any adjustments if necessary.

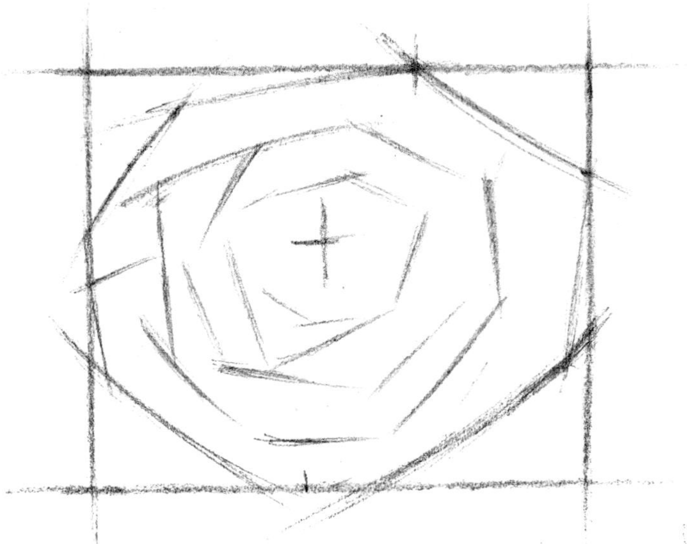

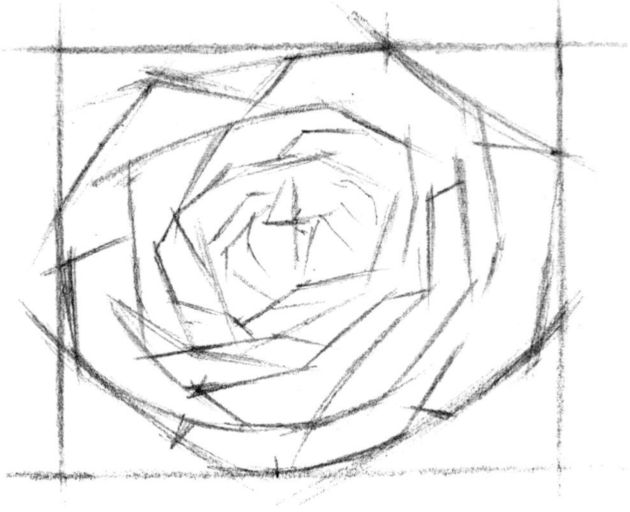

Step 4: Outline the rose using curved lines based on your observation and comparison with the reference photo. At the same time, identify the overall value by marking the light and dark areas with dividing lines, using a light pencil (H or HB) to shade the dark areas on the flower to express the overall value. The darker areas are usually found deeper within the petals, as light cannot reach these spots.

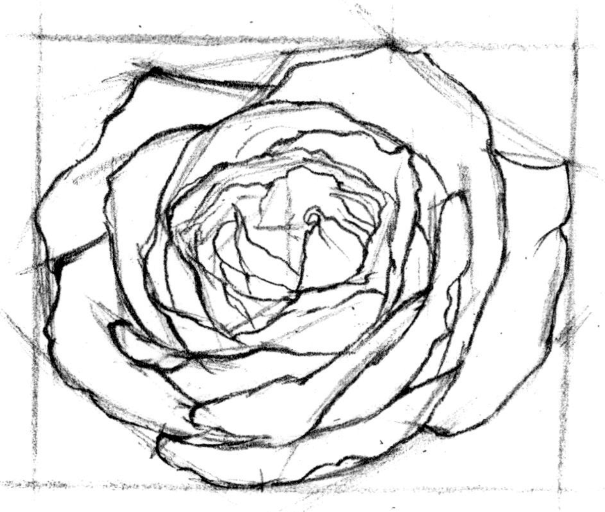

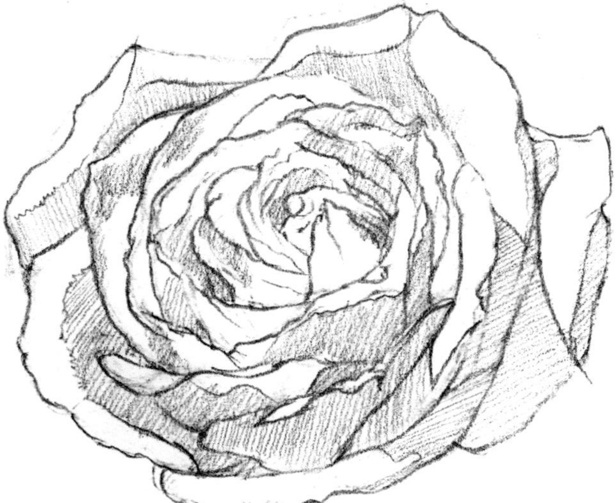

Step 5: Relax your hand, grab a fineliner, and start the "journey" of stippling. Begin by arranging countless tiny dots to cover the entire dark area, representing the overall value. Take your time—no need to rush, the book will always be there waiting for you. Keep adding dots until you create a neutral gray.

Step 6: Identify the very dark areas and the core shadows on the rose, which are usually located deep within the petals and in areas opposite the light source *(in this image, on the right side)*. Add more dots in these areas to shade them darker.

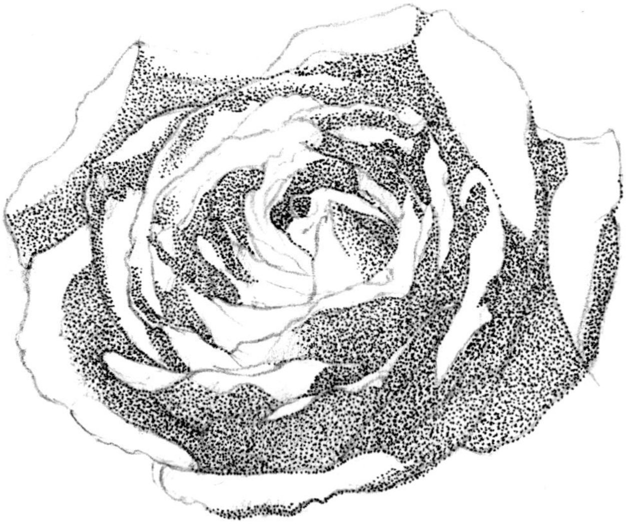

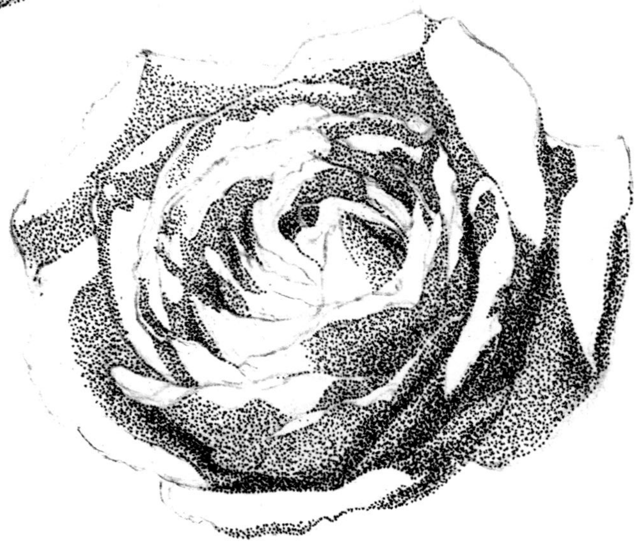

Step 7: Once you've finished shading the dark areas and the core shadows, apply the blending and value transition techniques you've practiced to depict the mid-tones and areas in direct light. You can either leave the highlight areas blank or use very sparse dots, as these are found at the top of the petals.

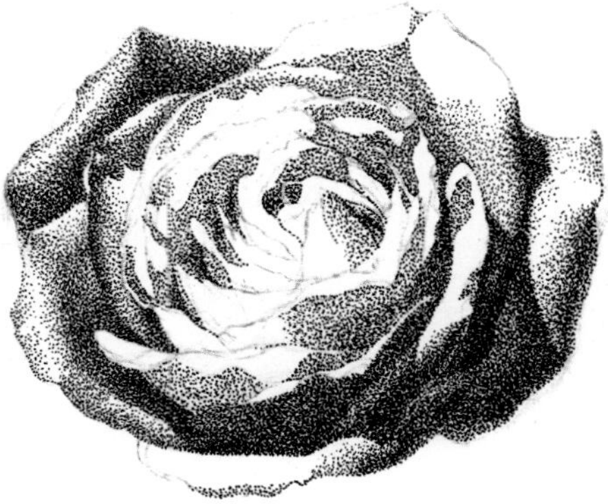

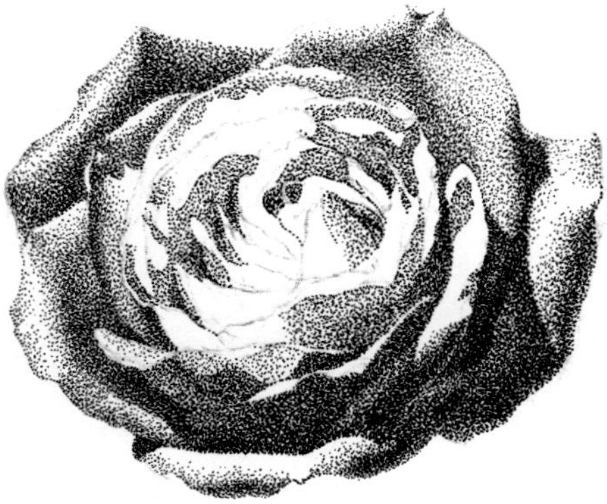

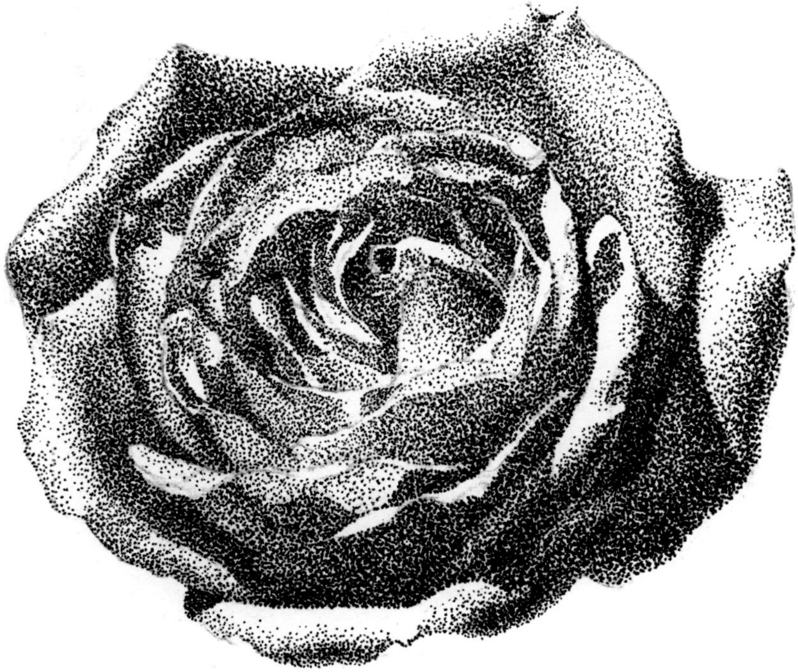

Step 8: At this point, the rose is nearly complete, with the values clearly defined. Take a moment to observe and compare with the reference photo once again, and start adjusting the values, adding background if you want to create more depth, increasing the contrast, and refining the drawing to make it more balanced. Finish it up, and you're done!

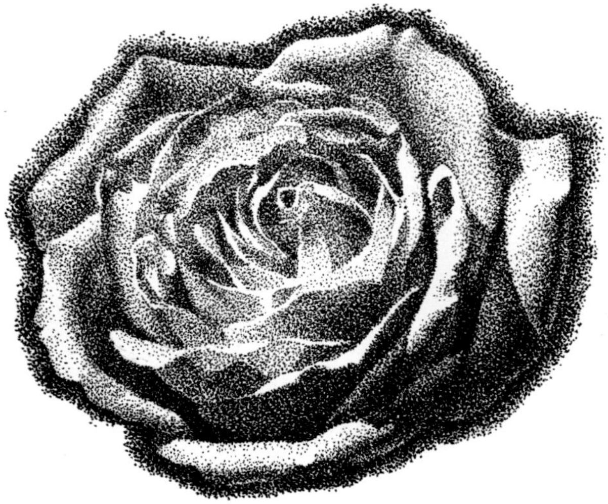

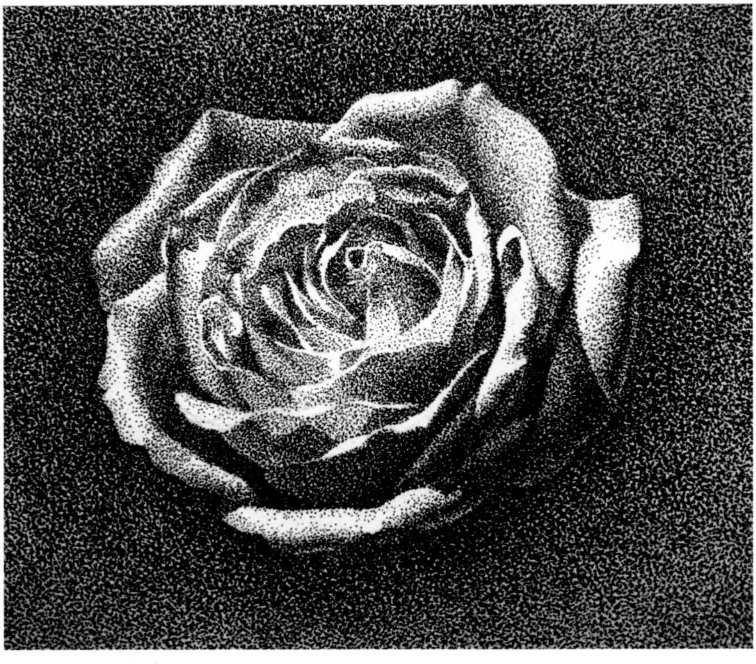

Make Your Drawing Look like an Engraving

In this section, we'll explore using cross-contour lines combined with varying line thickness to create drawings that resemble classic "engraving" techniques used in traditional printmaking. Through these techniques, you can represent the three-dimensional surface of a subject and achieve shading effects using parallel lines with adjusted thicknesses.

Cross-Contour

Cross-contour is a technique that uses parallel lines to create a 3D illusion for a subject without shading. By drawing simple lines that follow the surface and form of the subject, you can effectively depict the space and structure in a realistic way.

Cross-contour lines can range from simple straight or curved lines to more complex ones, requiring a good understanding of the subject's 3D structure. To get used to this technique, let's start with some basic exercises using simple forms.

Practicing Cross-Contour: Turning Basic Forms into Subjects

Step 1: Start by sketching basic forms like a cube, a sphere, and a cylinder with pencils, using basic geometric shapes to create the illusion of 3D forms. At this point, you just need to draw simple forms and not focus on perspective.

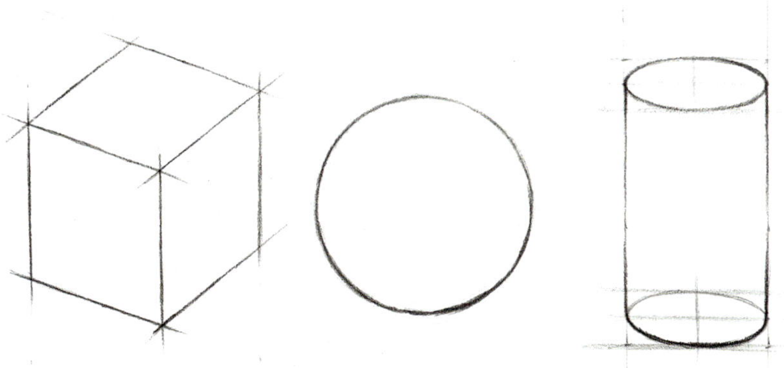

Step 2: Based on these basic forms, let's "distort" them a bit to make the exercise more interesting and to support the upcoming shading exercise.

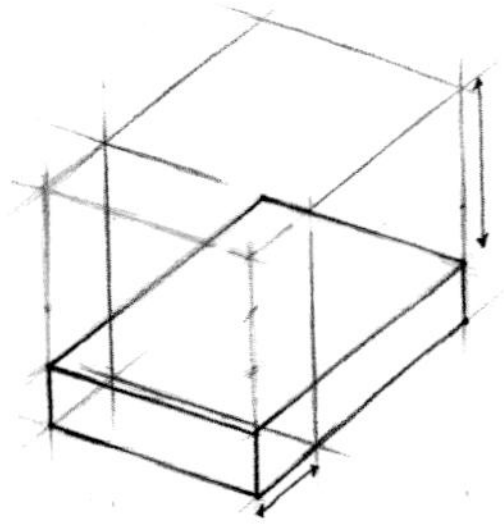

Cube: Reduce the height of the cube to 25% and increase the depth by another 25%. Now, the cube is transformed to resemble a book.

Sphere: Imagine this as a ball of clay, and you're using your finger to press down on the top of it. To represent this change, identify a point about one-quarter of the height of the circle, and draw a small, curved line bending downward as illustrated.

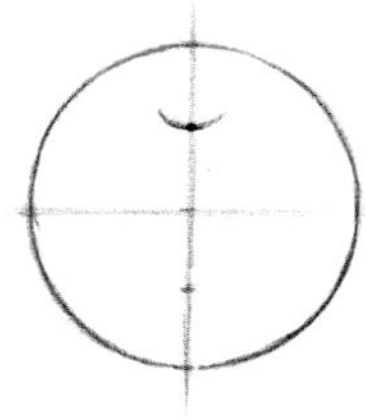

Cylinder: Divide the height of the cylinder into four equal parts. Taper the first part at the top to change the shape of the cylinder's upper surface.

Step 3: Imagine we're cutting these forms vertically. These cuts will create various straight and curved lines that follow the shape of the forms. Follow the instructions for each form described below.

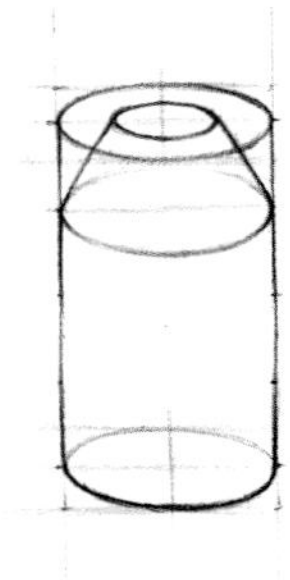

Cube: Draw a line in the center of the top face of the cube, parallel to the edges that slope down toward the right side. Then, extend this line to the side of the cube, and draw a vertical line to represent the thickness of the "book."

Sphere: Based on the concave surface created by the imagined finger press in the previous step, follow the cutting direction established in the cube and draw a wavy line that connects to the curved line, representing a deformed sphere.

Cylinder: Outline the top of the cylinder with a straight line like the cube, connecting to the angled line at the transition of the upper part of the body, and finally, draw a vertical line running along the side of the cylinder.

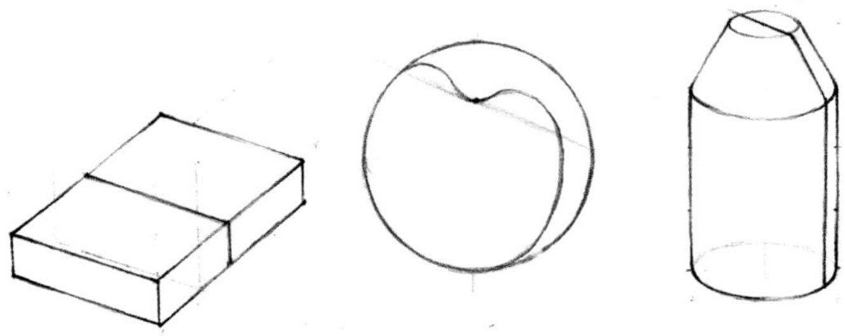

Step 4: After cutting these forms vertically, let's now cut them horizontally.

Cube: Draw straight lines parallel to the edges of the cube, dividing the height into two equal parts.

Sphere: Draw a horizontal curved line to represent a half-oval shape that matches the diameter of the circle.

Cylinder: Similar to the sphere, draw a half-oval shape that matches the width of the cylinder, positioned right in the middle of its body.

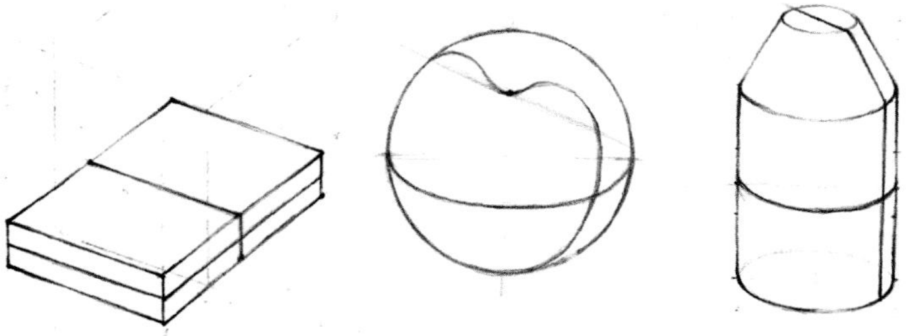

Step 5: Based on the lines you've drawn, create parallel lines to these cuts to represent cross-contours across the entire form.

Cube: Draw straight parallel lines on the top face of the cube that follow the cuts made in the previous steps.

Sphere: You can also add another vertical cutting line in the opposite direction of the first to clarify the form further. Continue by drawing curved lines parallel to the horizontal cuts. As these lines move toward the top of the sphere, the cut will transition into a complete oval shape instead of a half one.

Cylinder: Based on the horizontal cuts, draw the remaining parallel lines. However, the size of these lines will change at the top of the form according to the distortion.

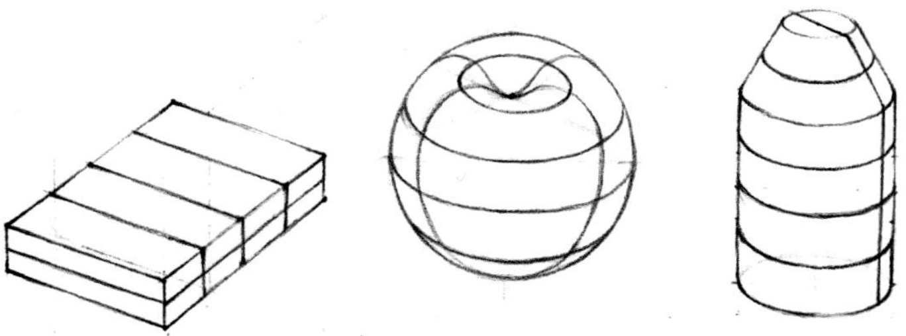

LINE THICKNESS

Line thickness (or line weight) refers to the thickness of a line. By varying the thickness of your lines thoughtfully, you can effectively use shading techniques combined with cross-contour to illustrate different values. Let's practice some exercises to deepen our understanding.

Create a Solid Value with Line Thickness

Step 1: Let's start by sketching two squares: For Shape 1, draw a basic square, and for Shape 2, draw a basic square but make the top and bottom edges curve upward.

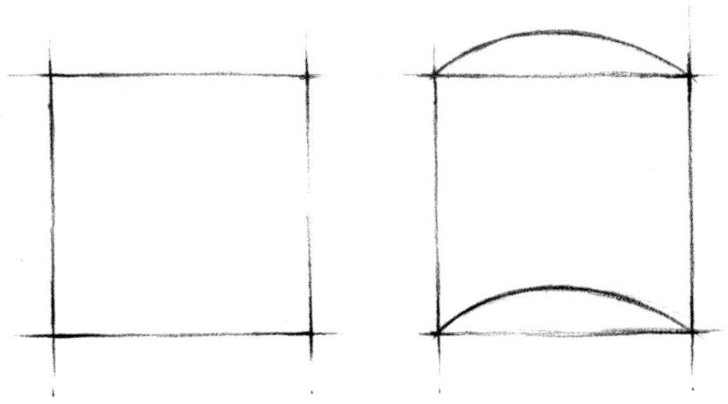

Step 2: Draw vertical and horizontal lines to divide these two shapes into equal squares (about 16 squares in each shape). For Shape 2, the horizontal lines will be curved, following the upward curves of the top and bottom edges.

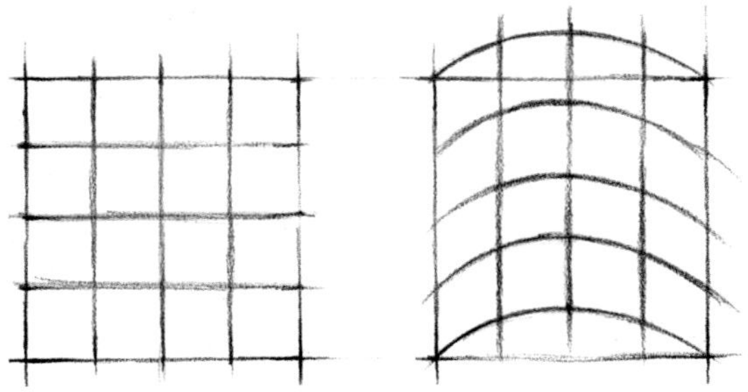

Step 3: Use pencils to create a thumbnail value scale at the top of each shape for reference when shading with pen and ink.

Shape 1: Create a value scale transitioning from dark to light from left to right.

Shape 2: Create a value scale like Shape 1, but make the far left side of the value scale a bit lighter to symbolize reflected light, and the far right side slightly darker to represent direct light. This way, we can illustrate the key shading components on the value scale.

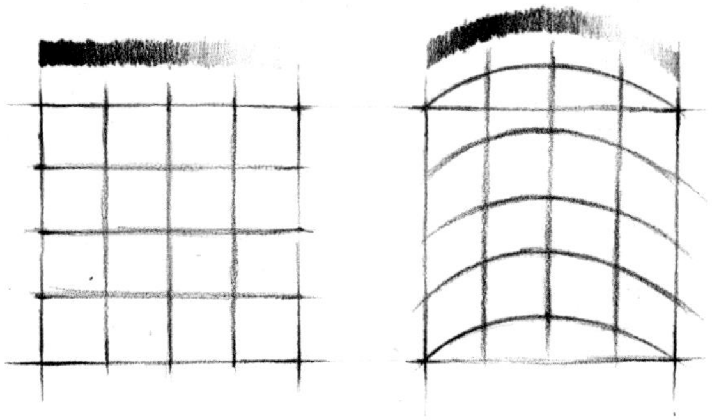

Step 4: Based on the horizontal cross-contour lines, draw parallel lines with a fineliner size 01, spaced about 1 mm apart. In light areas such as direct light or highlights, switch to dashed/broken lines to represent the value more accurately. With this technique, you don't need to move your hand as quickly as in traditional hatching; draw at a moderate pace to maintain better control over the lines. Keep drawing and complete the overall shading for these shapes.

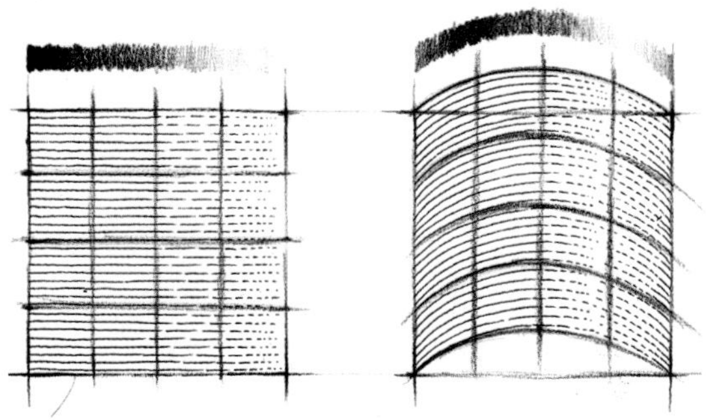

Step 5: Pay attention to the lines on the left side (the first column). Now it's time to make these lines slightly thicker. You can switch to a fineliner with a slightly larger pen tip, or simply go over the lines you've already drawn to build up their thickness. No need to make the lines too bold—just enough so you notice a difference compared to the rest of the drawing. Once you're finished, you can erase the pencil sketch to better see the correct values.

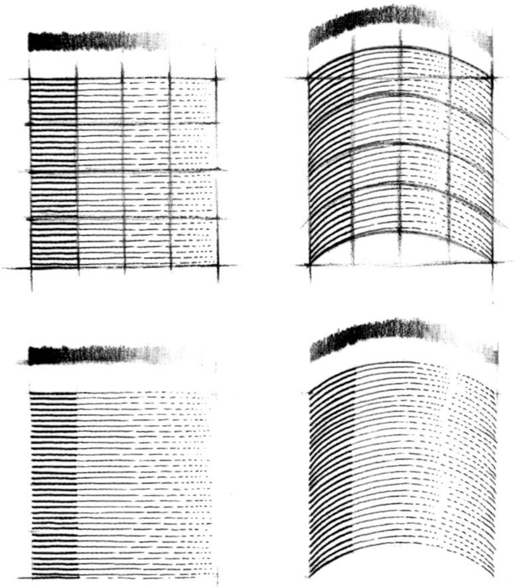

Step 6: In this step, continue to thicken the lines to represent the core shadow. However, there's a key difference between the two shapes you're working on.

Shape 1: Thicken all the lines on the left side, leaving only very thin white gaps between them.

Shape 2: Only thicken the lines where the core shadow is, as you identified in the previous step.

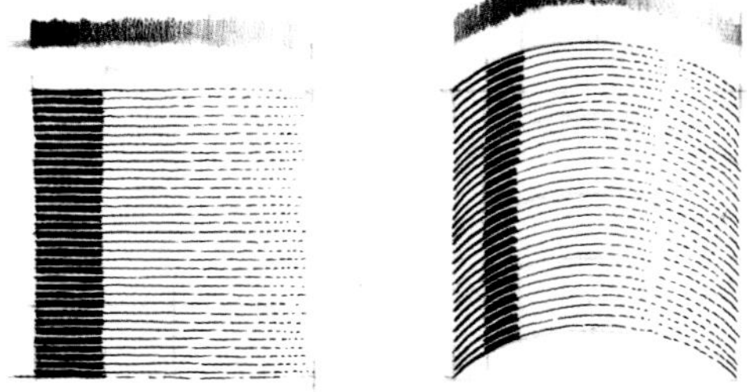

Step 7: In the mid-tone area (around the second column of the sections you've divided), make the lines thicker, but not as thick as the core shadow.

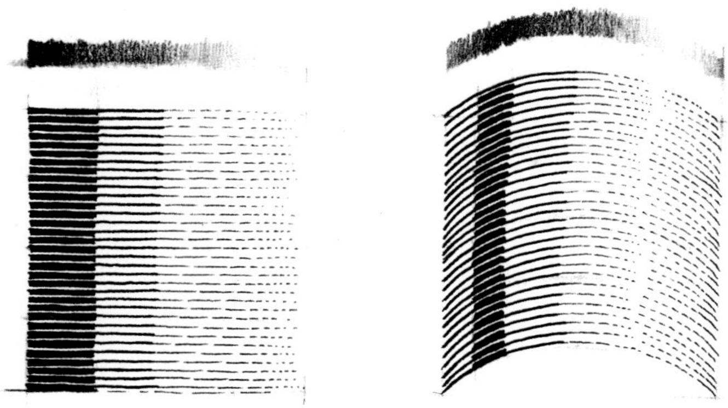

Step 8: Let's blend the divided sections to create a smooth transition of values. The method is to gradually make the lines thinner as they move from the core shadow to the other shading components, like the mid-tone and reflected light. You can use a fineliner with a small tip, such as 01, to achieve more precise control over the thickness of the lines.

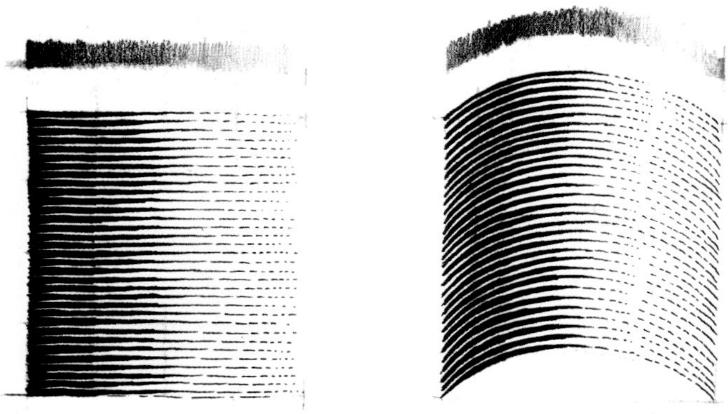

Step 9: If you prefer the look of parallel hatching lines, you can consider the exercise complete after the previous step. However, sometimes we can create more depth in the drawing by adding a layer of crosshatching using a similar cross-contour method. Give it a try!

Based on the horizontal hatching you've already drawn, add another layer of hatching at a 30-degree angle to the first layer (like the crosshatching technique). This will help increase contrast and create more depth in the values. While adding this second hatching layer, continue to combine solid and broken lines. You can also vary the thickness of the lines in darker areas, such as the core shadow, to further emphasize the value in those spots.

Shape 1: Draw straight, parallel lines.

Shape 2: Draw curved lines similar to the first hatching layer but in a diagonal direction.

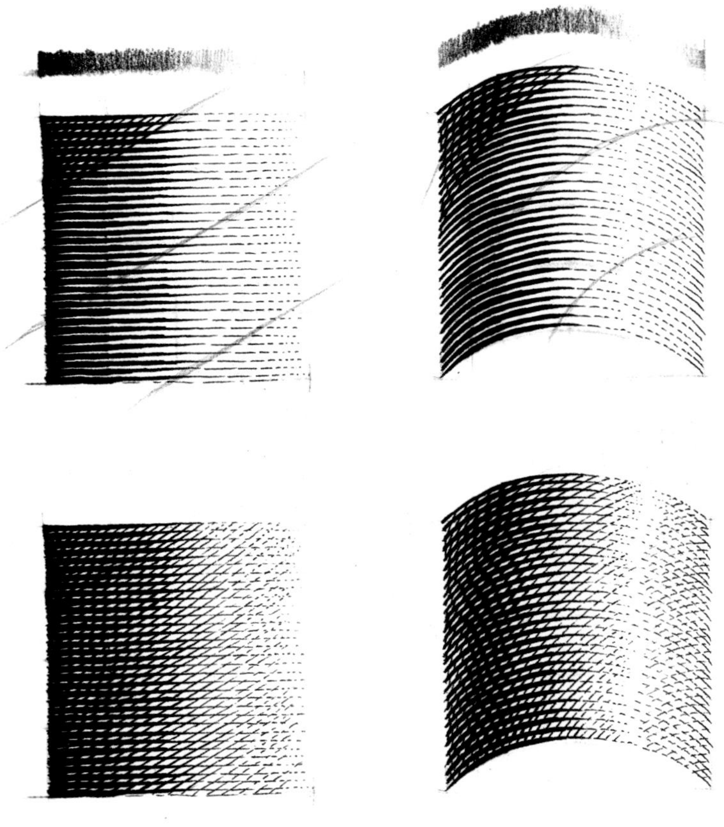

LET'S PUT IT ALL TOGETHER

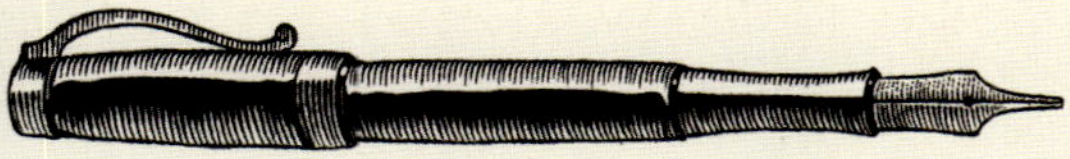

In this demonstration, we will apply the cross-contour and line thickness methods to the sketch we created earlier in the Constructive Sketching Made Simple section on page 48. The subjects in this composition are arranged to represent the three basic forms: a cube (the notebook), a sphere (the apple), and a cylinder (the vase). This setup will make it easier for you to apply the techniques we've covered in this section.

Cross-Contour

Step 1: Starting with the notebook, draw cross-contour lines parallel to the corresponding edges of the notebook's surface, just like in the cube drawing exercise from earlier. To show the thickness of the notebook's cover, add short vertical lines. You can also add more in-between lines to make shading easier in the later steps.

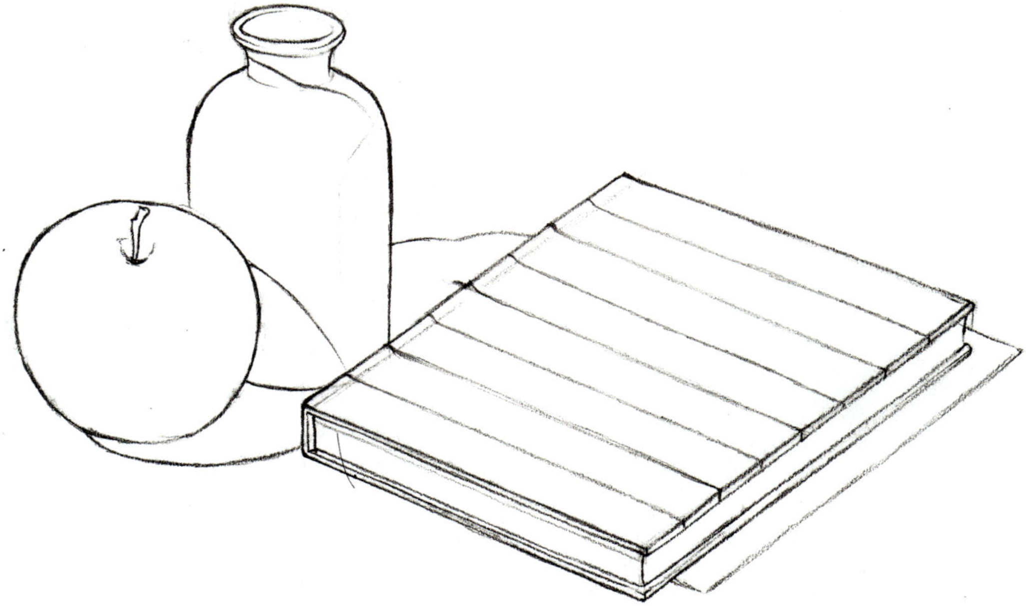

Step 2: Move on to the vase. You'll notice this object looks like the cylinder form we practiced. Draw cross-contour lines as half-oval shapes along the body of the vase. For the inside of the vase's opening, draw curved lines that arc upward to give a sense of space.

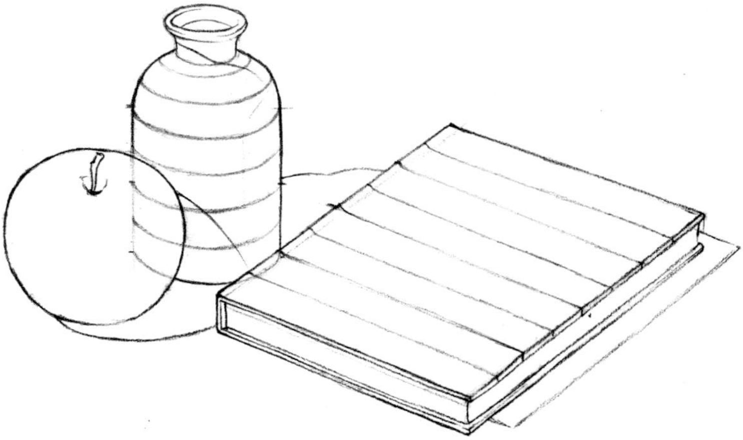

Step 3: Analyzing and drawing the cross-contour lines for the apple is similar to drawing a sphere. Start by drawing curved half-oval lines, and as you move toward the top, the cross-contour lines should transition into a full oval shape.

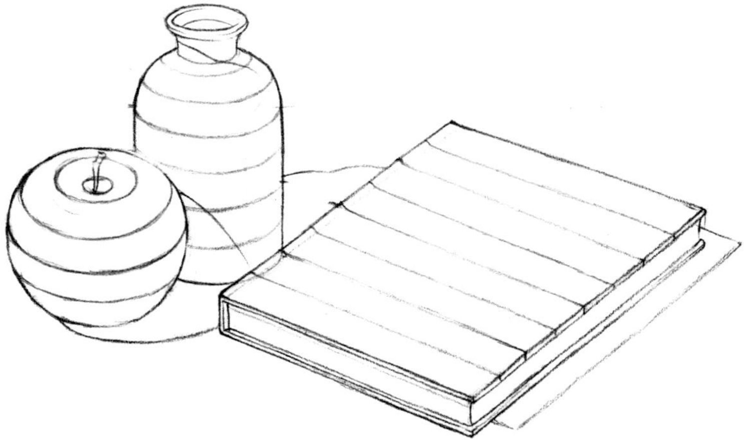

Overall Value

Step 4: Based on the reference, identify the key shading components using simple lines. You don't need to shade with pencils; just draw the dividing lines. In this demonstration, we'll focus on the objects and not include the background.

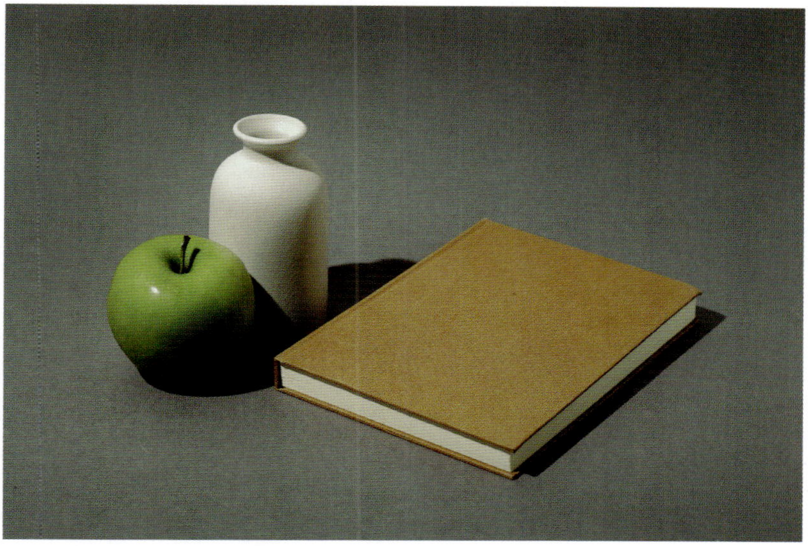

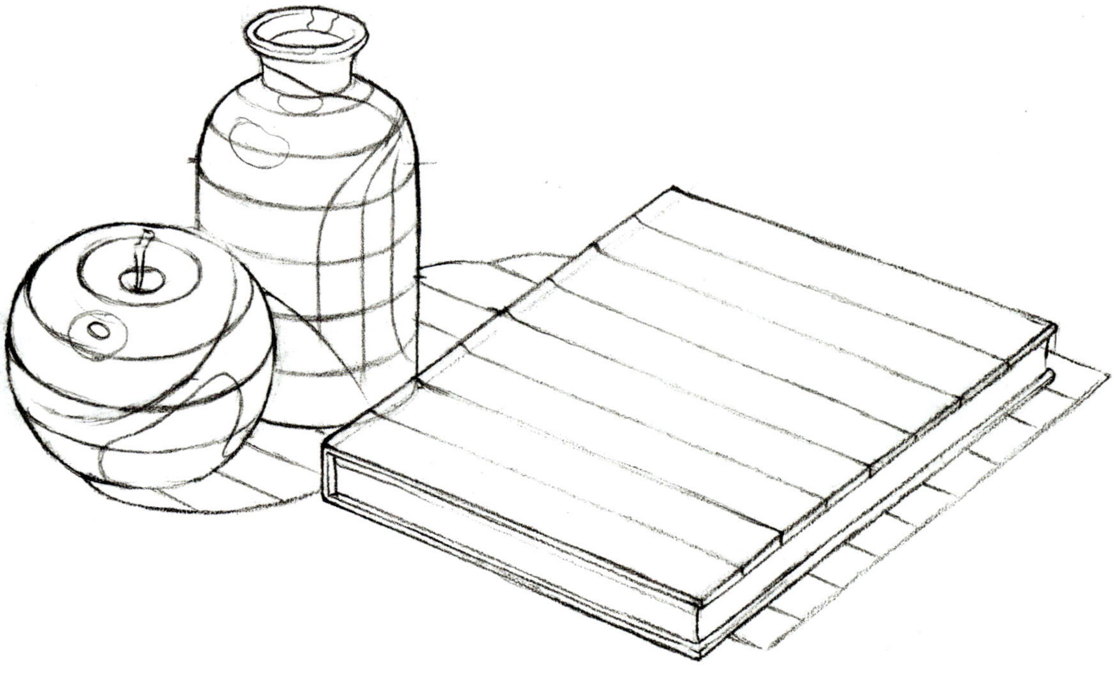

Step 5: To complete the overall shading on the notebook: Using a 01 fineliner, start by drawing straight lines spaced about 1 mm apart, parallel to the cross-contour lines that cover the entire top surface of the notebook. You can add a small, curved line on the left edge to represent the spine of the notebook.

Next, draw vertical lines along the thickness of the notebook to depict the detailed structure of these parts.

To show the layers of paper, draw thin parallel lines along the corresponding edges. You can also use broken lines in the lighter areas to prevent the values from getting too dark. Additionally, keep the lines closer together to create a more realistic texture for the paper layers.

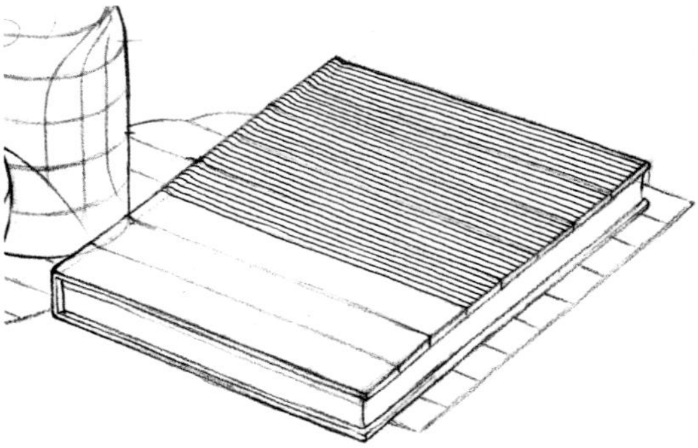

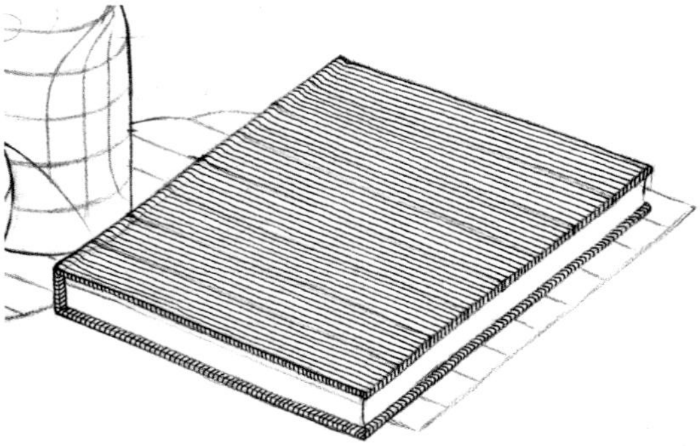

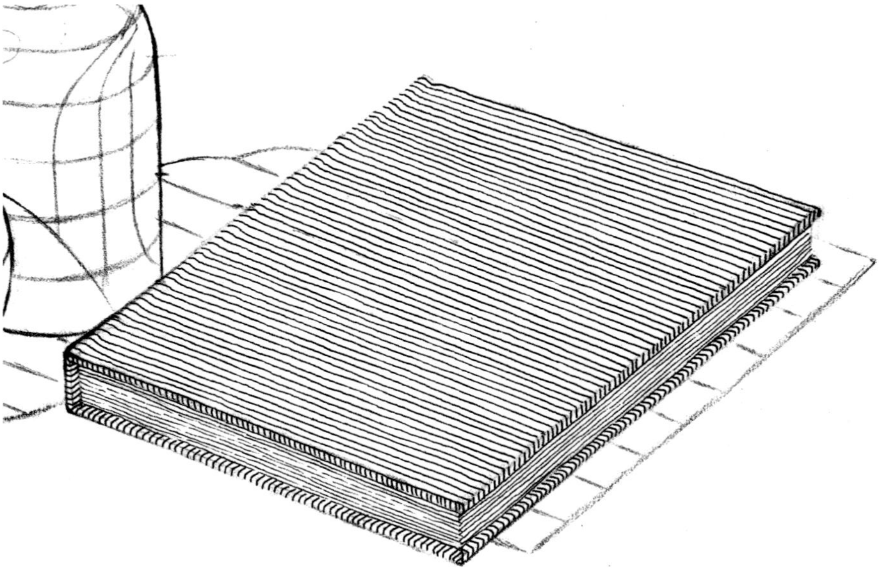

Step 6: To complete the overall shading on the apple: Based on the cross-contour lines, continue using a fineliner with a pen tip of 01 to draw curved lines that run parallel to each other, covering the entire apple. In areas of high value with direct light, switch to using broken lines. Leave the highlight area blank, without adding any further lines.

Step 7: To complete the overall shading on the vase: The lines will be similar to those used for the apple, with values represented by curved lines that combine both solid and broken lines, depending on the position of the shading components you've identified. It's good to mention again that for the inside of the vase's opening, the lines should curve upward to accurately represent the structure of the subject. If you're unsure whether to draw solid or broken lines in certain areas, feel free to use broken lines. It will be easier to convert them into solid lines later if needed.

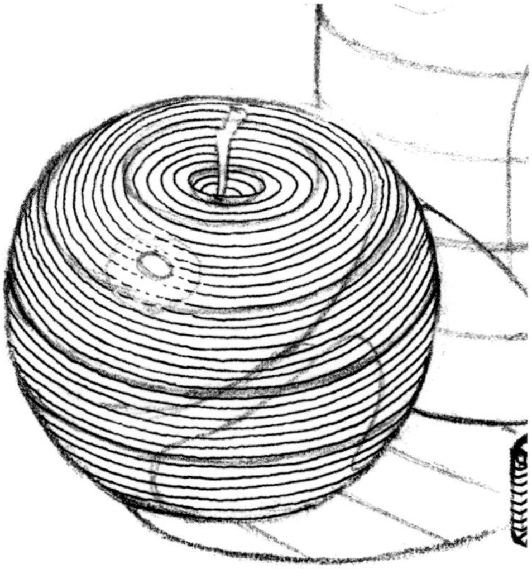

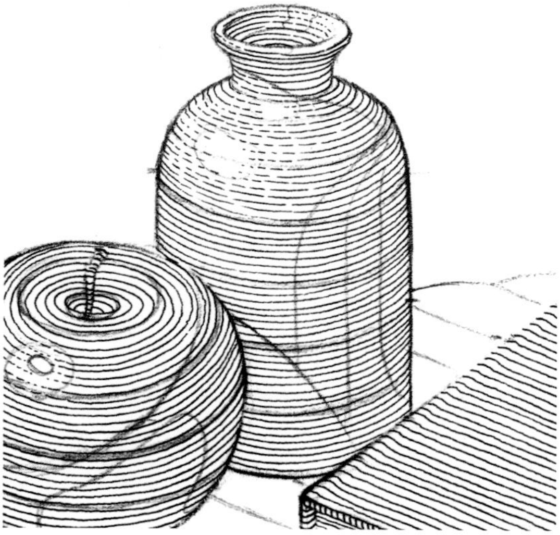

Step 8: Complete the overall shading by drawing straight parallel lines in the cast shadow areas. You can draw them in the same direction as the notebook's top surface cross-contour.

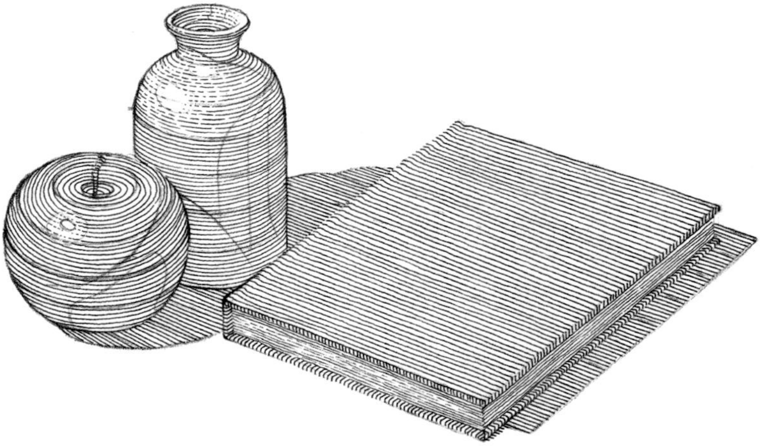

Shading

Step 9: Based on the key shading components you've identified and the overall value, determine the positions of the core shadow and cast shadow, and thicken the lines in these areas. However, you don't need to achieve the exact value you want; just make them thick enough to differentiate the specific light and dark areas. Once you're done, erase the sketch lines to present the values more accurately.

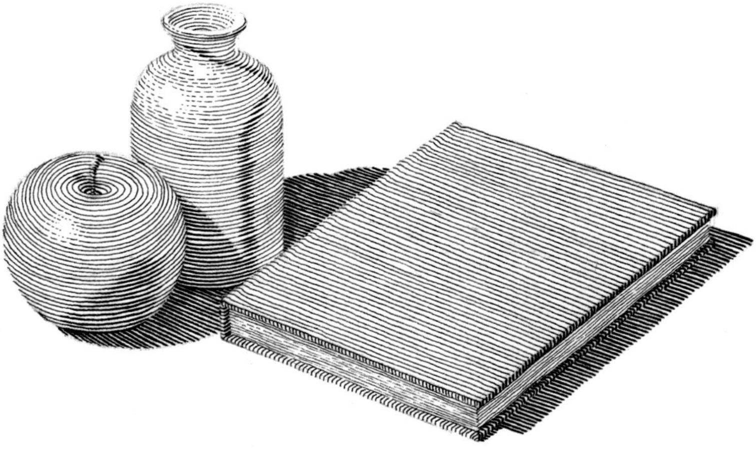

Step 10: Using the core shadow as a reference, create a smooth transition of value by thickening the lines in the mid-tone and reflected light areas. Apply the blending value technique from the exercise on page 56, ensuring that the lines gradually get thinner from the core shadow position to the bright areas. Additionally, darken the cast shadow area to emphasize the overall value of the composition. Continue to adjust and balance the values for a harmonious look.

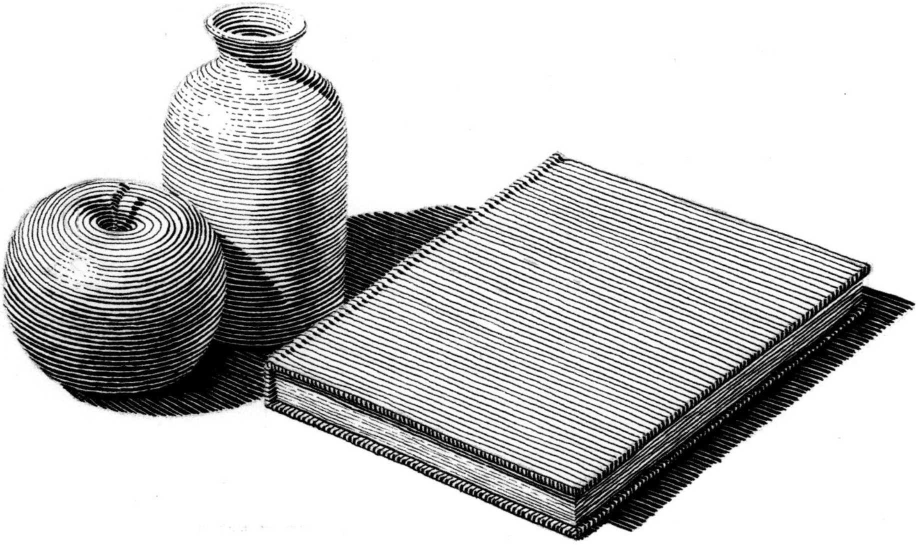

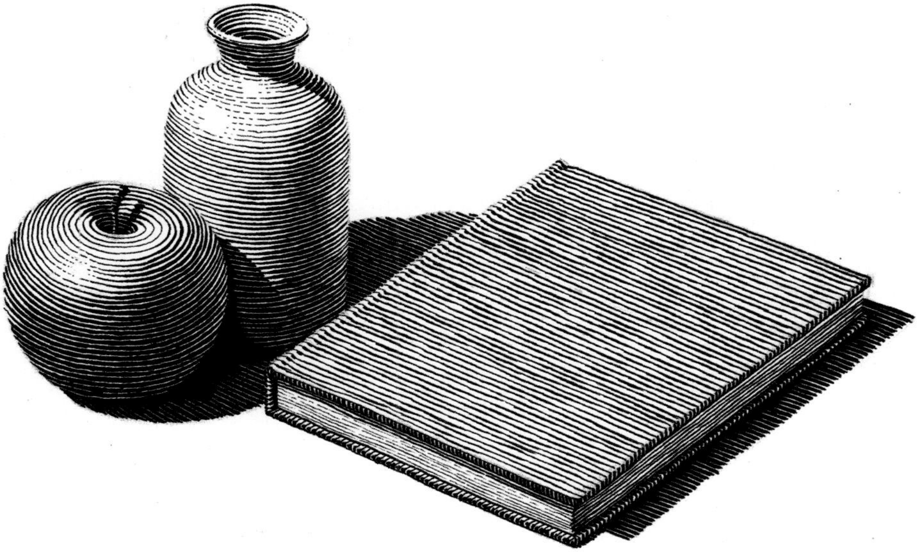

Step 11: To emphasize and add depth to the drawing, apply the crosshatching technique that we learned on page 75. Draw parallel lines like the previous hatching layer, but change the direction at an angle of about 30 degrees. The lines can be straight or curved, depending on the subjects and the lines from the previous layer. Combine solid and broken lines, and vary the thickness of the lines to highlight the dark areas and balance the values.

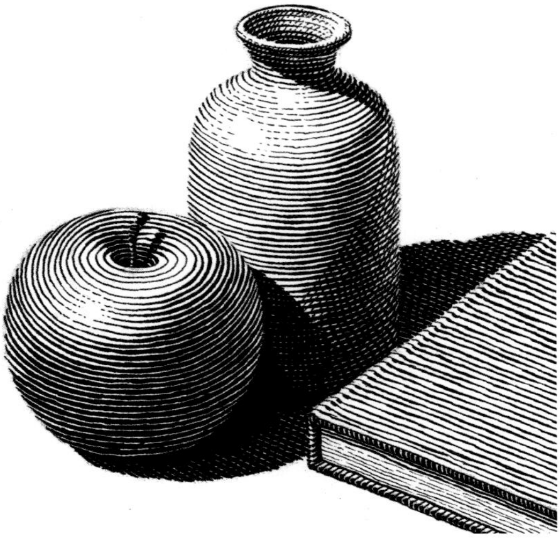

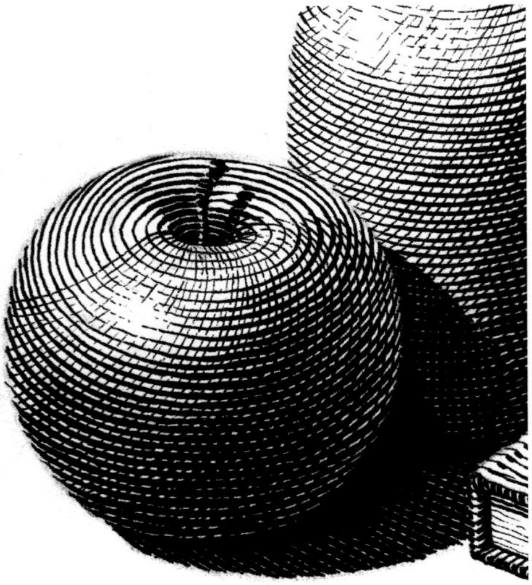

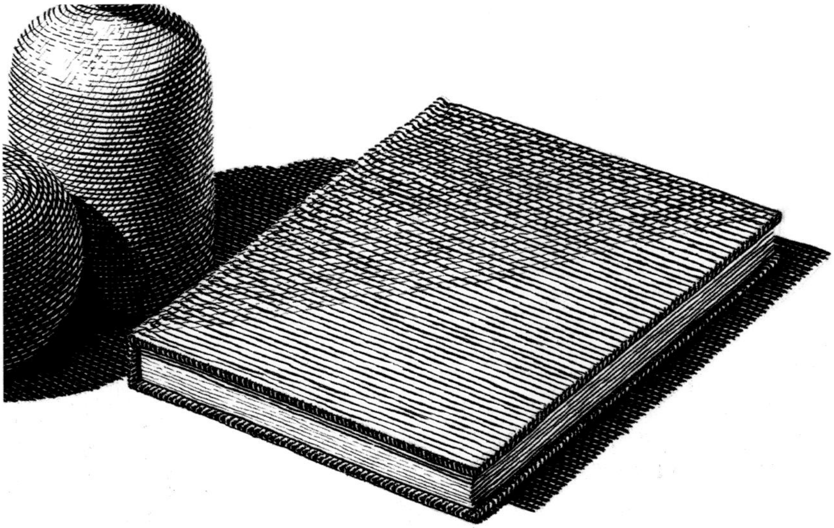

Step 12: Observe the reference photo, compare your drawing to it, and adjust the value until you're satisfied with the result. You've completed a still life drawing and made it look like a classic engraving work!

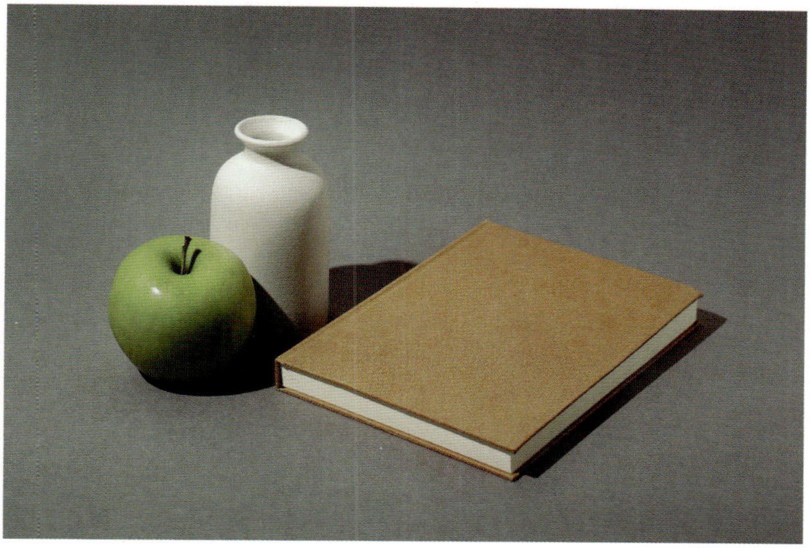

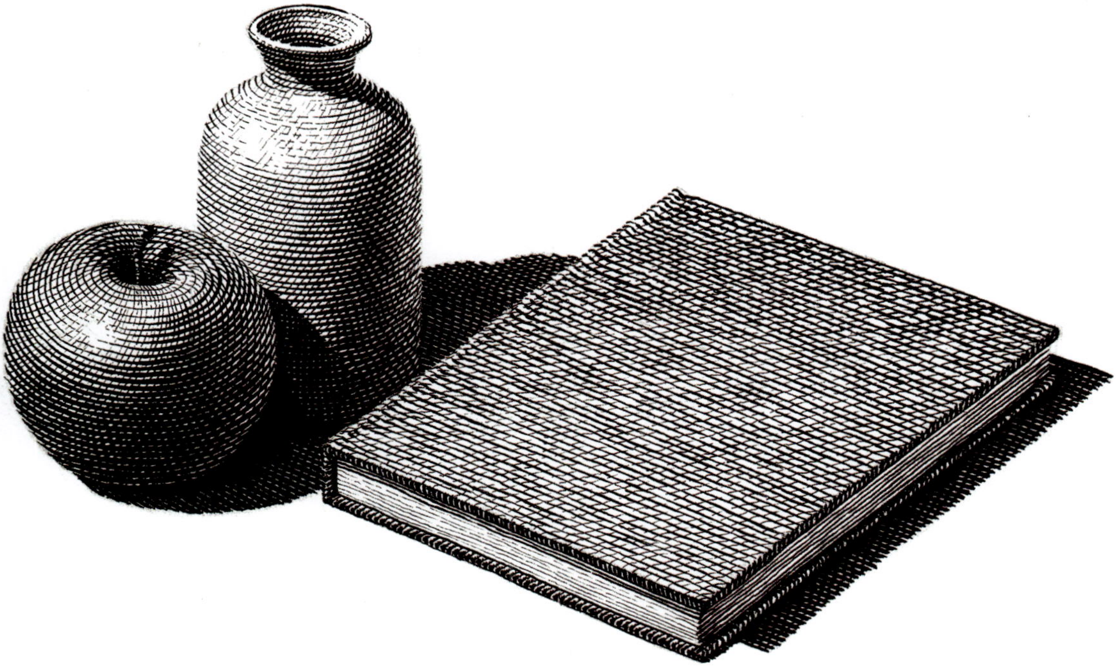

How to Draw Materials and Textures

To diversify the ways of expressing and shading with pen and ink, in this section, we will experiment with some additional shading techniques along with methods for depicting materials and textures. These techniques will help you draw a variety of subjects, like still lifes, people, animals, and nature, with a richer shading approach.

The Beauty of Nature

The world of nature is incredibly beautiful and vibrant, and drawing is one of the most engaging ways to capture this beauty. In this section, we will learn how to depict natural elements and their textures, from trees and clouds to rocks and water surfaces. In addition to the shading techniques we've learned, I will also share some additional techniques to help you portray these subjects more vividly.

Tree

Step 1: Similar to any other subject, a tree trunk can also be simplified into basic shapes. Use an HB pencil to sketch spheres for the basic form of the tree's foliage and cylinders to represent the tree trunk and branches. At the same time, identify the positions of key shading components (review the key on page 59 if you need a refresher on the key components).

Step 2: Tree foliage is made up of small leaves. You can draw random, wavy strokes to represent the leaves. For the tree trunk and branches, use curved and wavy lines to create a natural shape and form.

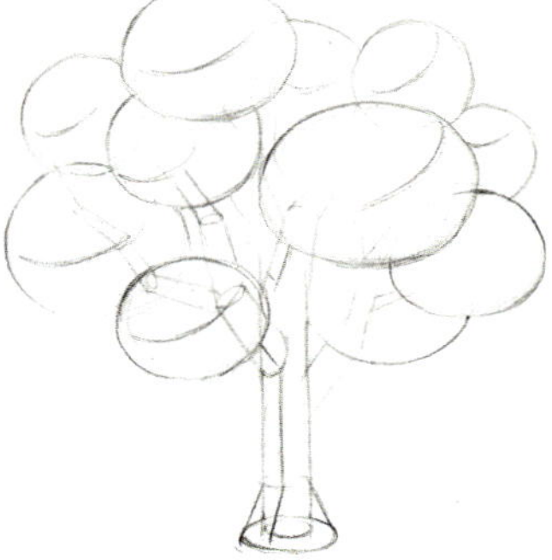

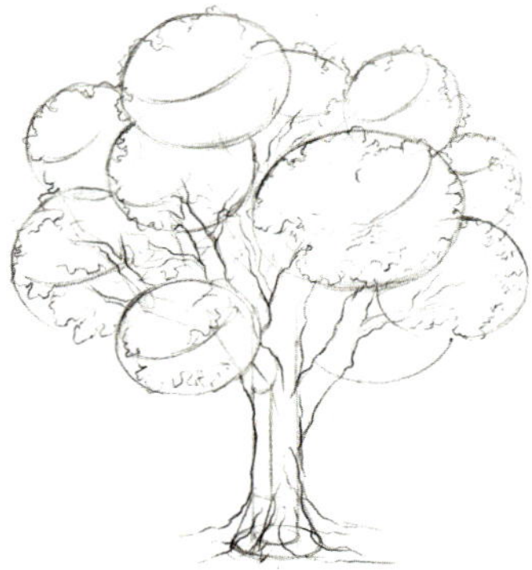

Step 3: To shade the overall value for the foliage, we can apply a technique called scribble. This involves using random, free, and unstructured strokes to create loose marks that reflect the natural texture of the subject. The more you scribble in a particular area, the darker it becomes.

Step 4: To shade the overall value for the tree trunk, apply the hatching technique following the direction in which the trunk grows. This technique will help you depict the natural wood grain and the movement of the tree.

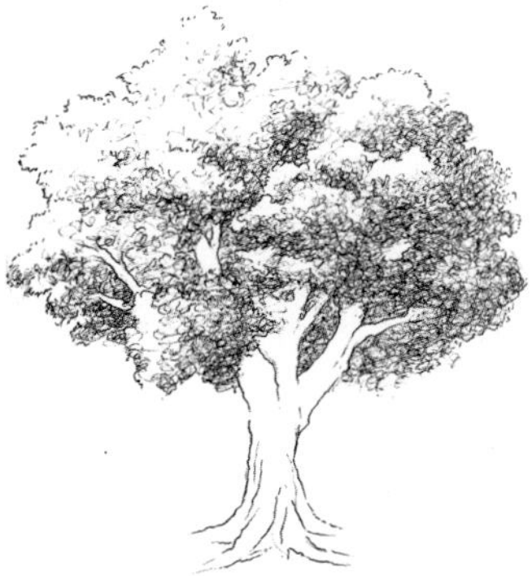

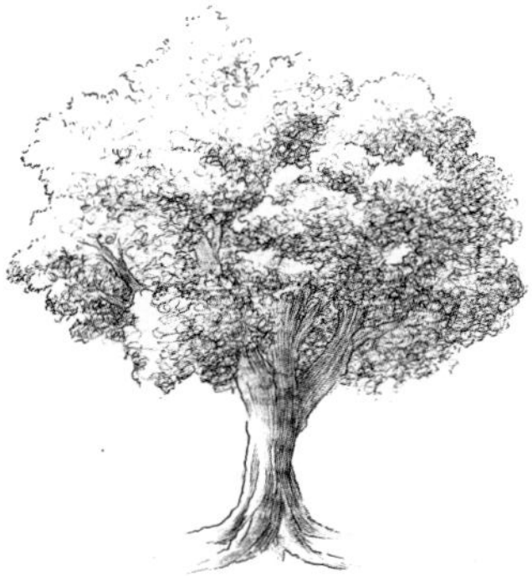

Step 5: Find the very dark or almost black areas on the foliage, trunk, and branches and shade these areas. You can use a brush for shading in solid black areas. Apply the same scribble technique to represent the foliage and use hatching to illustrate the tree trunk.

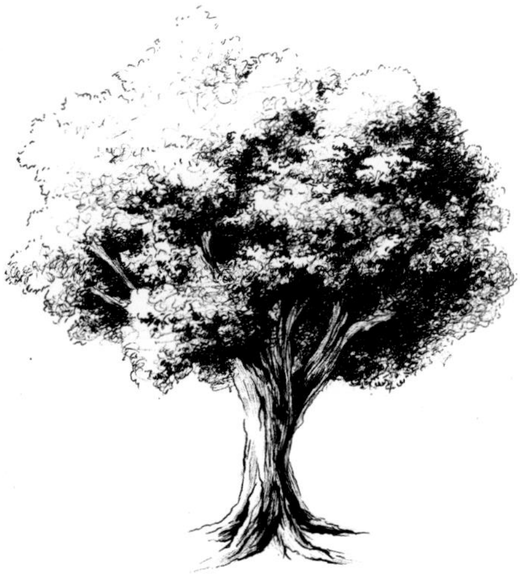

Step 6: Using the key values you've established, begin shading the mid-tone and lighter areas. For the foliage, you can create the sense of small leaves without drawing each one individually by using very short, curved hatching lines that follow the natural form. For the tree trunk, keep using the hatching technique in the high-value areas. You can add crosshatching to enhance contrast in the core shadow of the tree trunk.

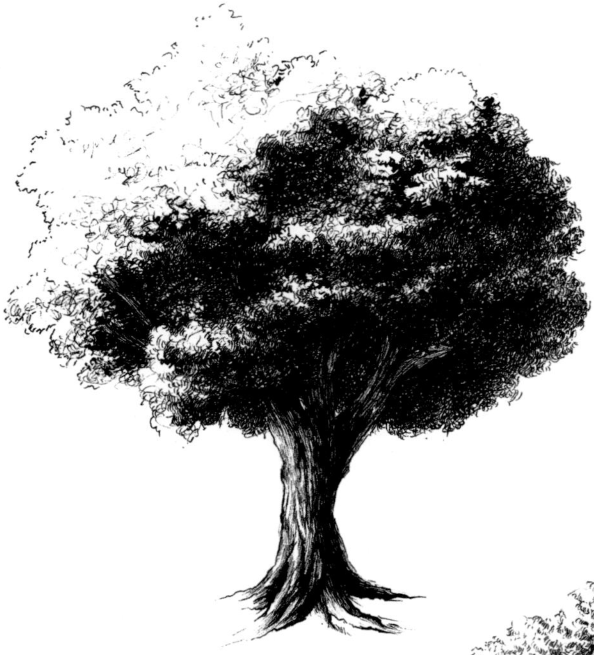

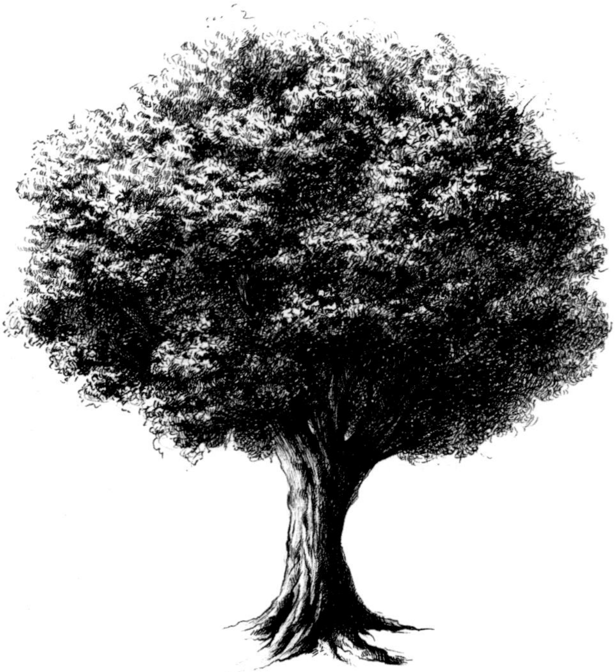

Step 7: Take a step back and observe the overall drawing. Balance the values, and add small details like the texture of the bark, individual leaves, and tiny branches around the foliage—and you've just completed your tree drawing!

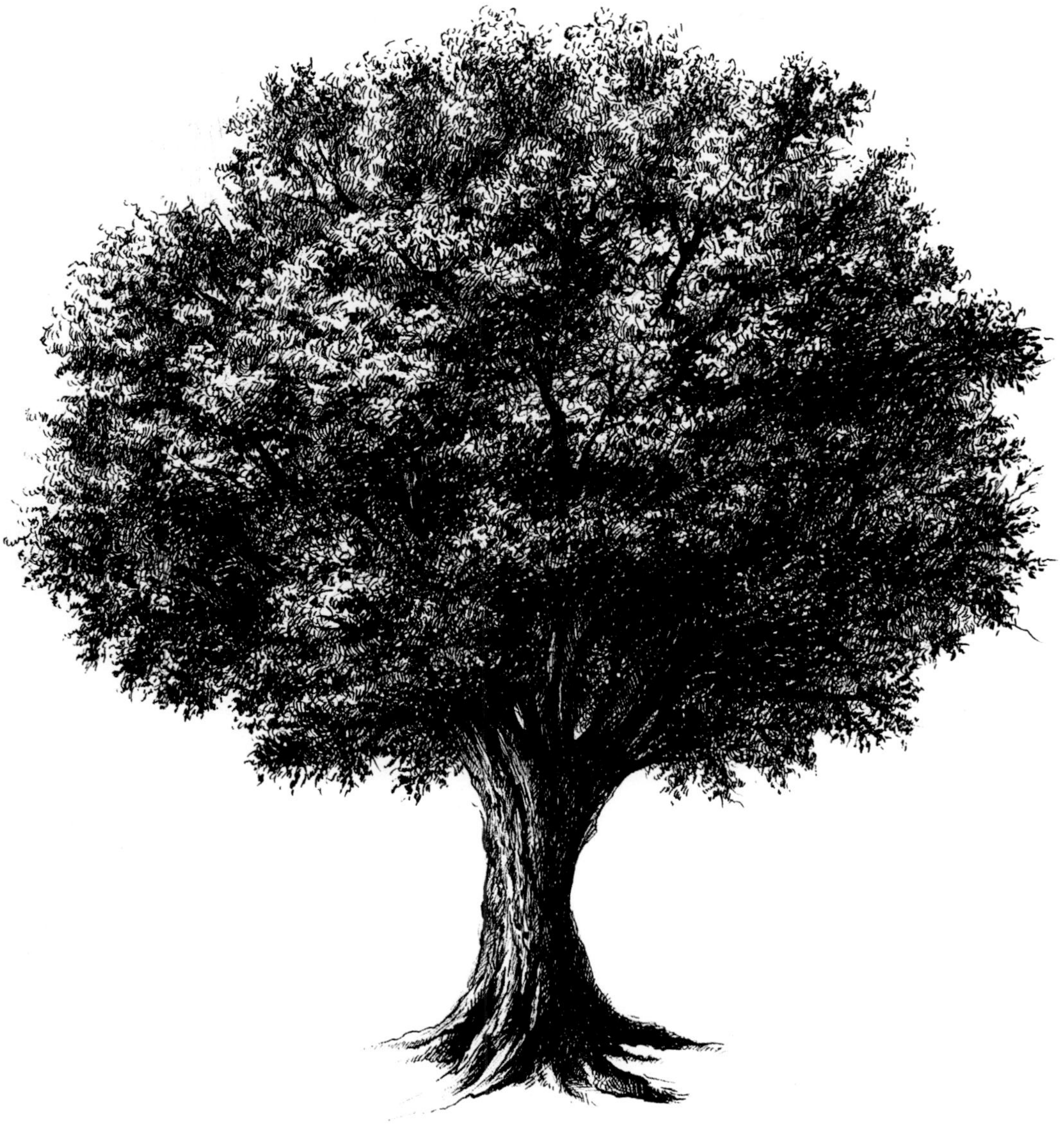

Rocks and Water Waves

Step 1: Start by outlining the overall shape using the constructive sketching method (page 48). Draw the larger structures of the rocks and waves, then work your way to the smaller details. Once you've created a rough sketch of the overall scene, use a light pencil, like an HB, to shade in the overall values of the drawing.

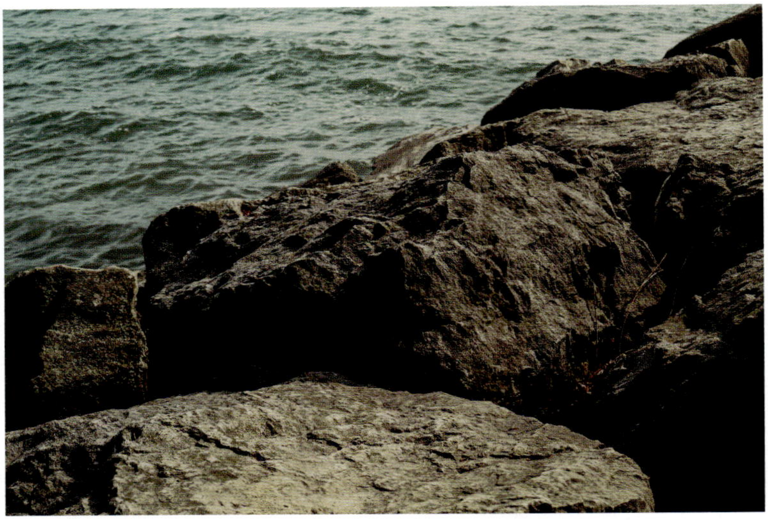

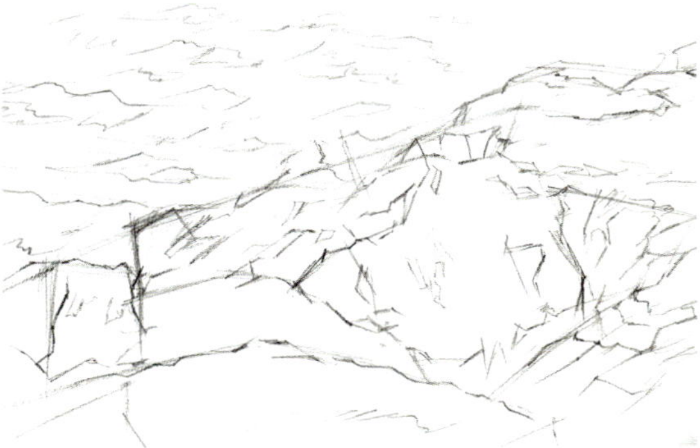

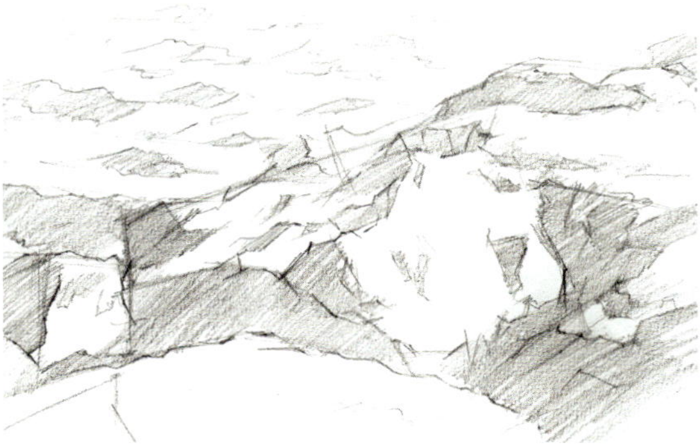

Step 2: One interesting shading technique that can effectively depict stones, rocks, or mountains is short-line hatching. Draw short hatch lines, about a few millimeters long, forming a small cluster. Then, change the direction of the hatching and draw another cluster next to it. Pay attention to the sharp edges of the rock; drawing parallel hatching lines along these edges will help you capture the natural structure more effectively. Continue this process to create a layer of short hatches in different directions. For the waves, use hatching lines that follow the direction of the wave movement. Once you're done, you'll have completed the overall shading values for the drawing.

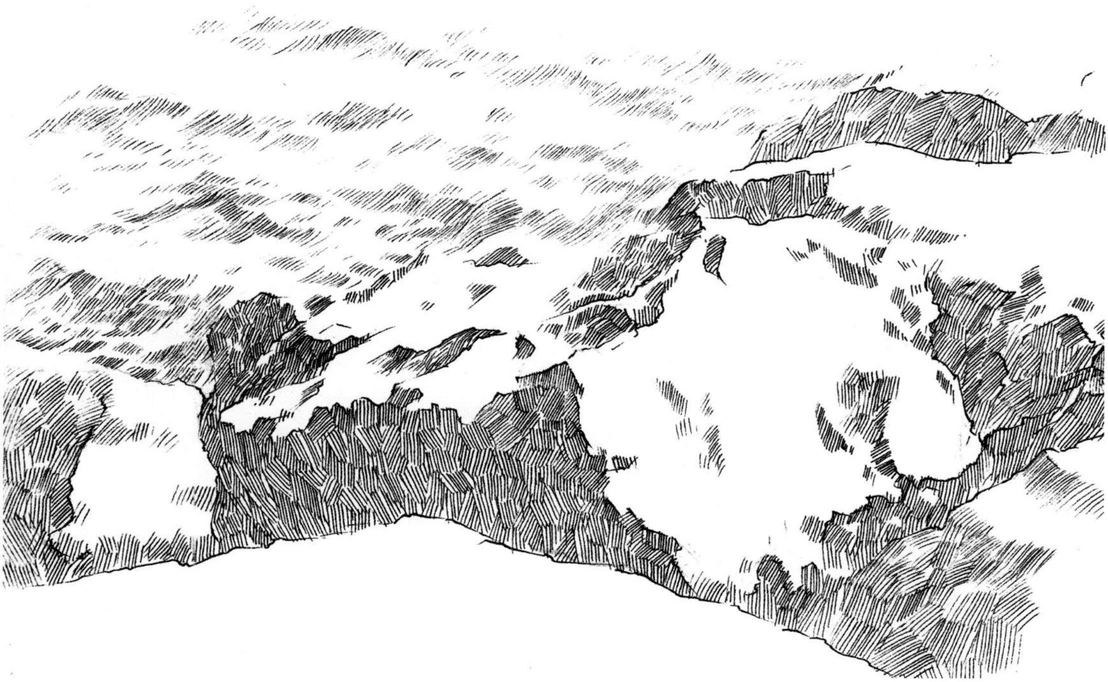

Step 3: For now, set aside the water waves and focus on the rocks. Identify the very dark or black areas on the rocks and shade these sections. You can use a brush pen for solid dark areas, but be sure to follow the direction of your hatching lines to maintain the natural texture of the rocks.

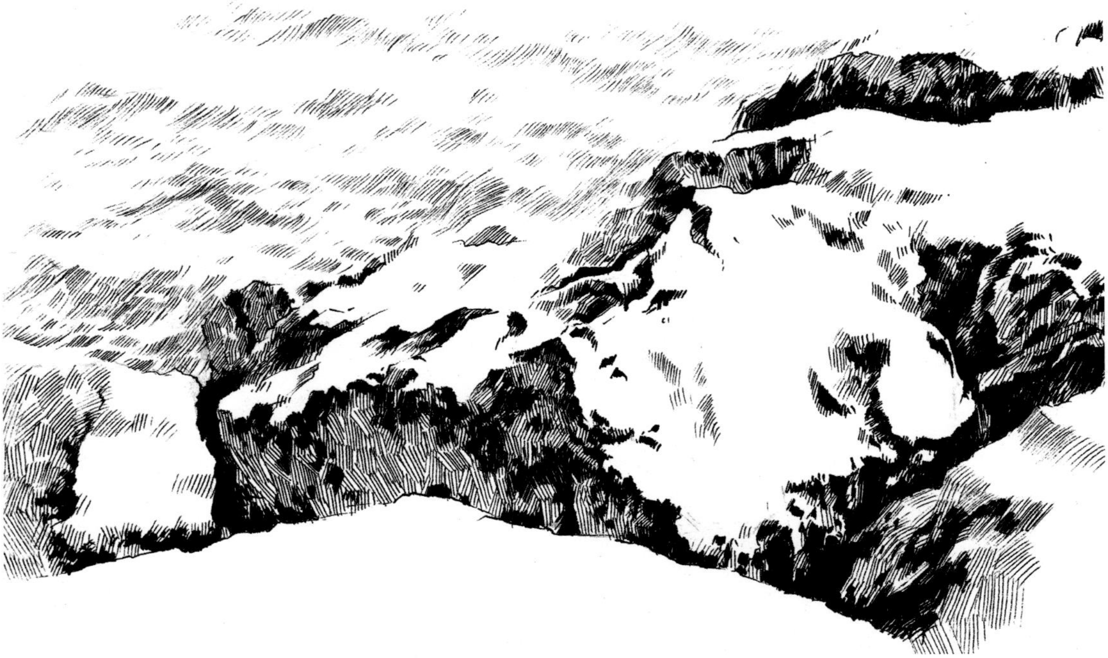

Step 4: In this step, we will depict the rough and uneven surface of the rock using the short-line hatching technique. With this technique, you can divide the rock's surface into small patches and apply the hatching technique (not crosshatching) in different directions within each section.

In this illustration, you can see that the natural light comes from above. As a result, when the light hits the rock, shadowed areas, such as the lower or left side of the rocks, will appear darker. These are the areas where you will apply this technique. Based on the position of the core shadow, use this technique in the darker areas while keeping some areas slightly lighter than the core shadow, to create the effect of reflected light. Stick with the short hatching strokes, layering over previous hatching to adjust values as needed. Once completed, you will notice that the separate hatching sections placed closely together create the illusion of an uneven rock surface.

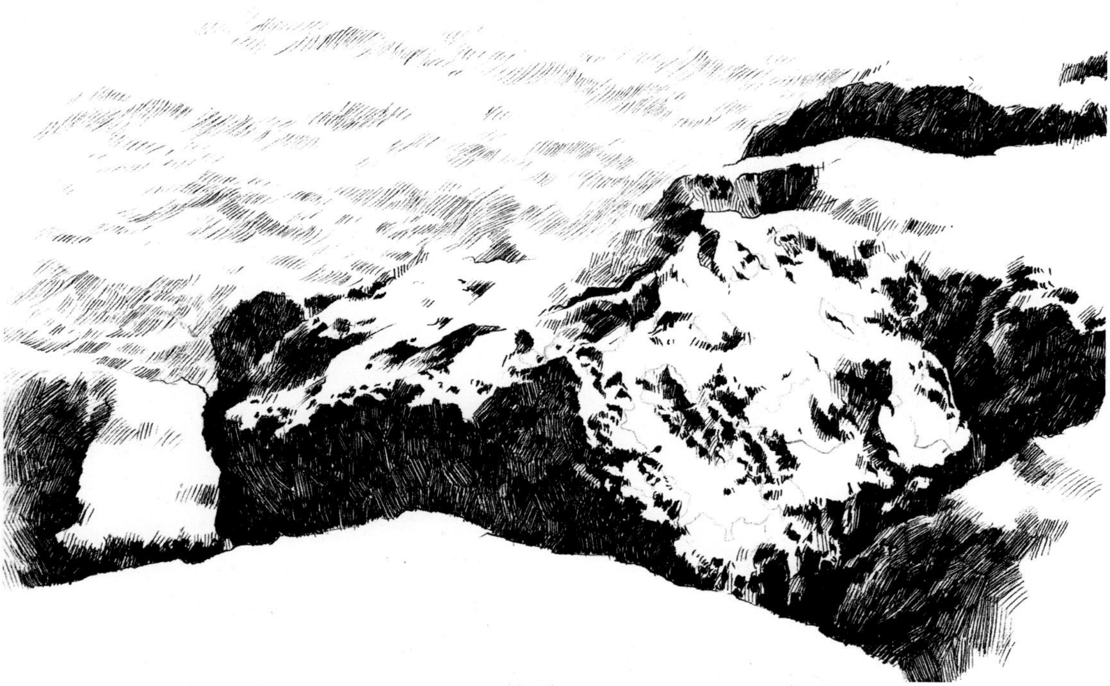

Step 5: Moving on to the lighter areas, use short hatching strokes to express the mid-tone, direct light, and highlights, following the rock's texture. To further depict the details and texture, you can reapply the short-line hatching technique from the previous step. Drawing small hatching patches in random directions at different areas of the rock will enhance the details, making the rock appear more realistic and natural. In selective dark spots, you can also apply crosshatching to fine-tune the value balance.

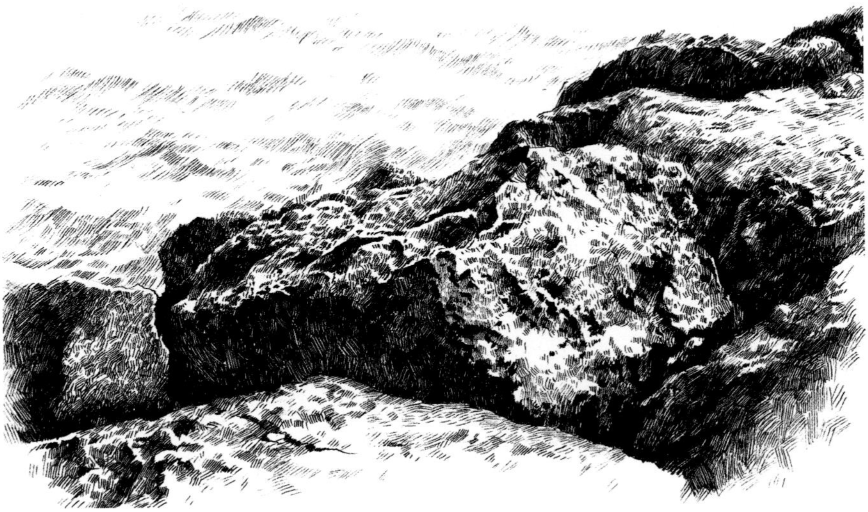

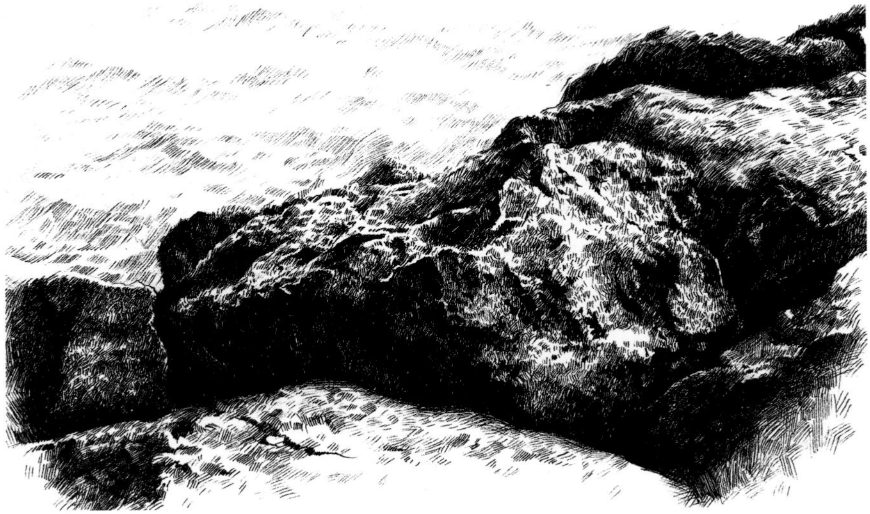

Step 6: Now that the rocks are complete, let's move on to the waves. Shading water presents certain challenges due to water's complex surface structure and movement, but there's a way to make it easier to depict! Imagine each wave as a "pyramid." When light interacts with the water, the core shadow typically appears at the transition point between light and dark, near the peak of the wave. Based on this position, you can use the hatching technique to indicate the direction of the wave's movement. Near the wave peak, apply multiple overlapping layers of hatching to define the core shadow, gradually fading it out as it connects to the next wave.

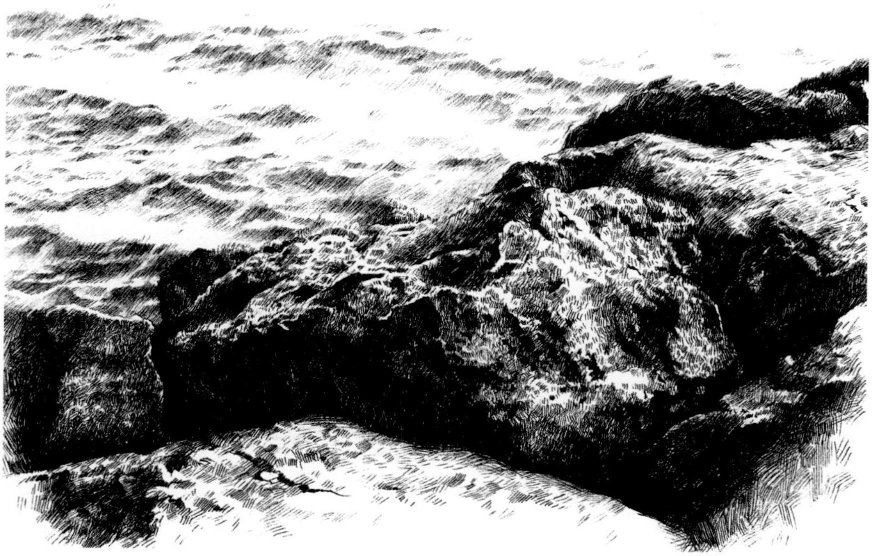

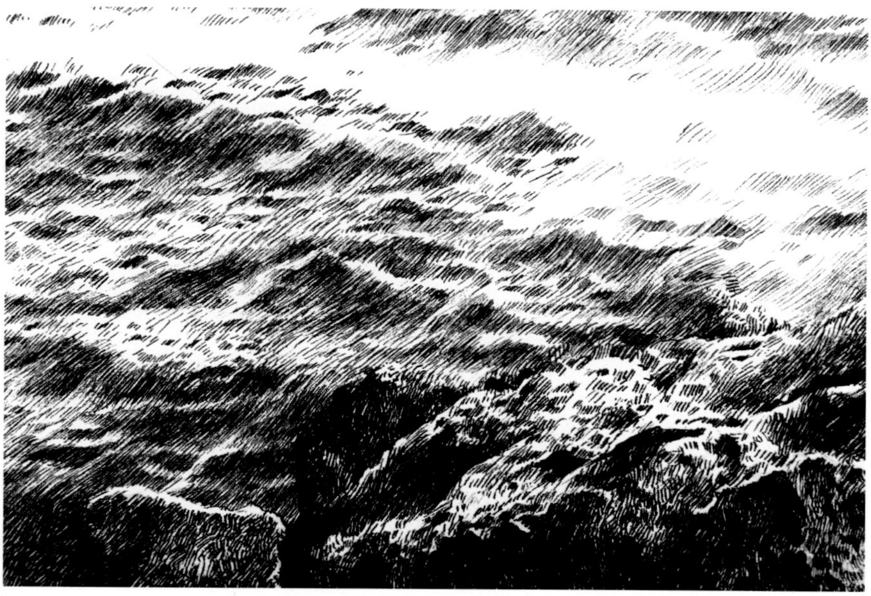

Step 7: At this point, our drawing is nearly complete. However, to capture the finest details and enhance its realism, we'll add a few final touches. First, let's focus on the rocks. In the lighter areas, add small, dark strokes to create subtle textures, such as rough spots or cracks, making the rocks look less uniform. In the core shadow areas, emphasize contrast by adding crosshatching where necessary to deepen the shadows.

For the water, there are currently too many white and highlight areas. In reality, water reflects the color of the sky and is not entirely bright white. To balance this, add hatching strokes in the direction of the water's flow in the lighter areas, leaving only a few small white sections to represent highlights.

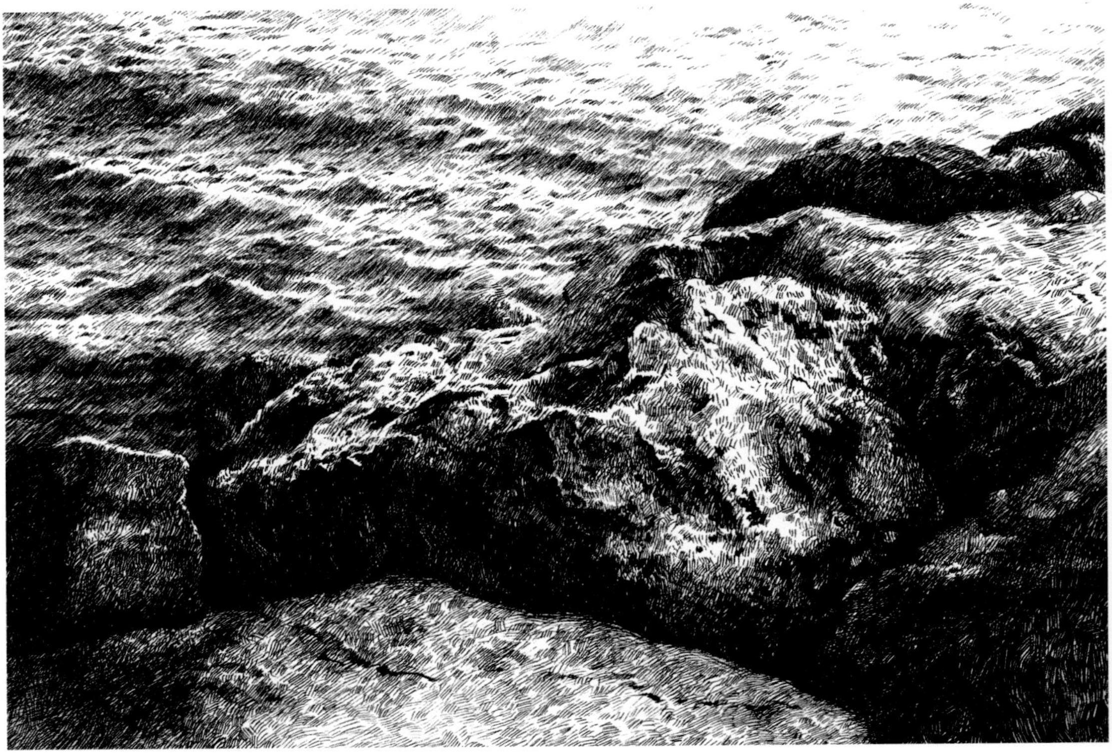

The Uniqueness of Metallic and Transparent Subjects

Every day, we use many different artificial objects, such as kitchen utensils, a teapot, a car, a camera, and more. Each object is made from various materials, creating distinctive textures. But what makes these materials so special when we depict them in pen and ink?

Metal: Think of shiny metal like a mirror—it reflects everything in the environment around it on its surface. However, the difference is that metal objects don't always have flat surfaces, so the reflections on them will be distorted according to the object's form and surface structure. When drawing a metal sphere, reflections will appear in a fish-eye perspective.

Transparent: The most distinctive feature of transparent subjects is that we can see through them, and everything behind or in the background is visible. These subjects could be made of glass, clear plastic, or even water. Additionally, you'll notice that when light passes through these objects, it also affects both the surface on the opposite side and the cast shadow.

Metal Ball and Glass Cup

Step 1: Begin by sketching the shapes of each subject using constructive sketching (page 48). The metal ball will be a sphere, and the glass cup will take a cylindrical form. Refine the shapes as we have practiced in previous exercises. At the same time, sketch lines to divide the overall light and dark areas. In this illustration, I draw my subjects on a fabric tablecloth, but you can draw any background you prefer. The purpose of drawing the background is to create a context that helps you demonstrate the transparency of the object. Draw lose lines to depict the fabric background and edge of the table.

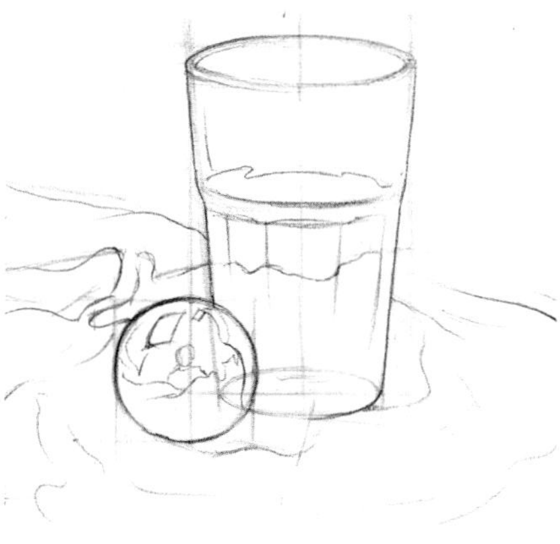

Step 2: For this drawing, I'll use hatching and crosshatching techniques for shading. Start with an overall value shading by applying a layer of hatching over the shadowed areas of each subject and part of the background to capture the transparency of the glass. The background wall is dark, which will come through in the glass. The metal ball will reflect a light source coming from the left. And the table will have a draped texture, which requires definition around the glass and ball. For the metallic sphere, you can use your imagination to recreate the reflection of the surroundings (for example, your room or your self-portrait) and distort this space to follow the curved shape of the sphere.

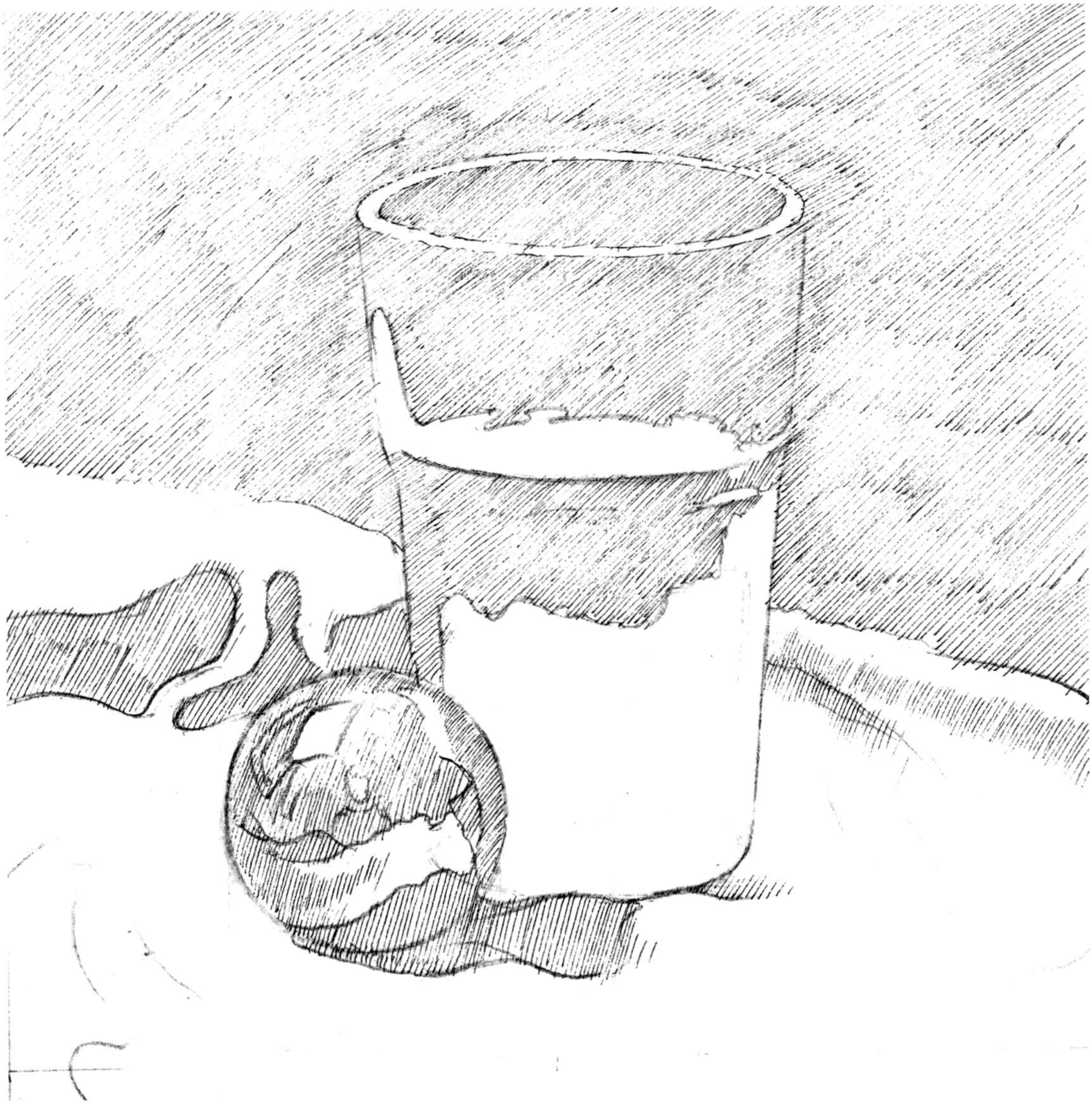

Step 3: Shade the dark areas and core shadows. As you'll notice, the dark background will also be visible within the glass due to its transparency. For the metal ball, the surrounding environment (including myself) will be reflected on its surface, so shading the sphere will feel like creating a mini drawing. My (or your) reflection will be in the center, with highlights on the top, bottom, and right.

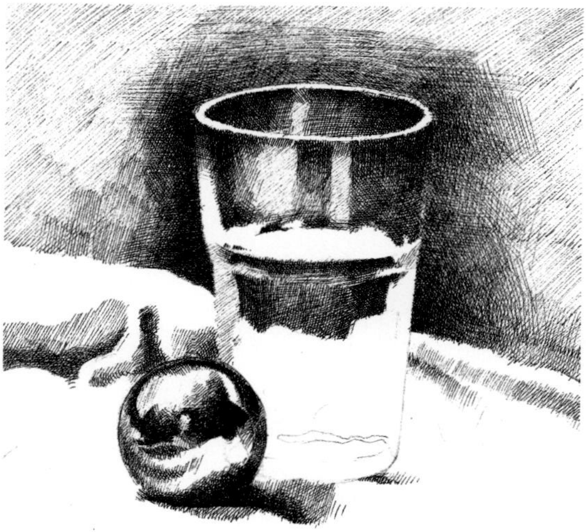

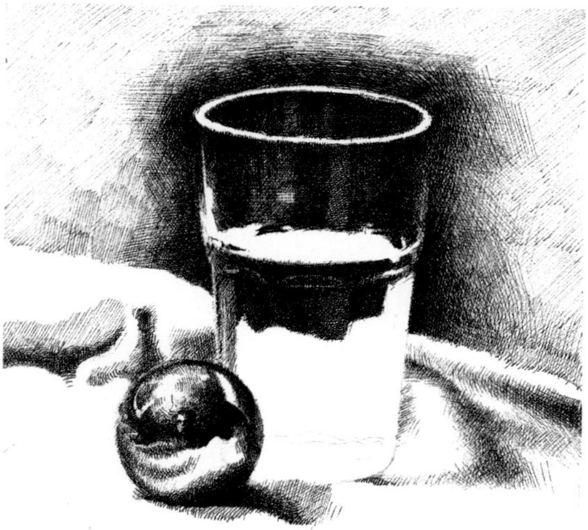

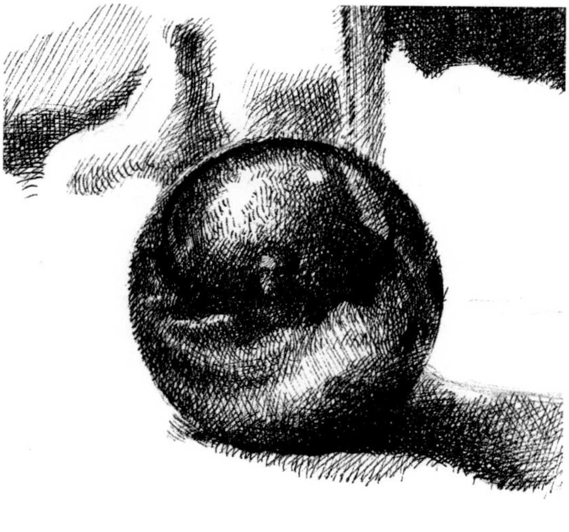

Step 4: Once the darkest key values are in place, add mid-tones, highlights, and direct light. Depicting value in transparent objects like water or glass depends on the background behind them. As you can see in this illustration, the background is very dark, so most of the glass and water also appear dark. However, certain highlights will still affect the glass. Typically, the brightest areas are found along the edges of the glass, around the rim, and in small highlight spots where the light directly hits. To accurately capture these details, you can refer to my illustration or take a real glass, place it under a light source with a dark background, and observe how the light and shadows interact.

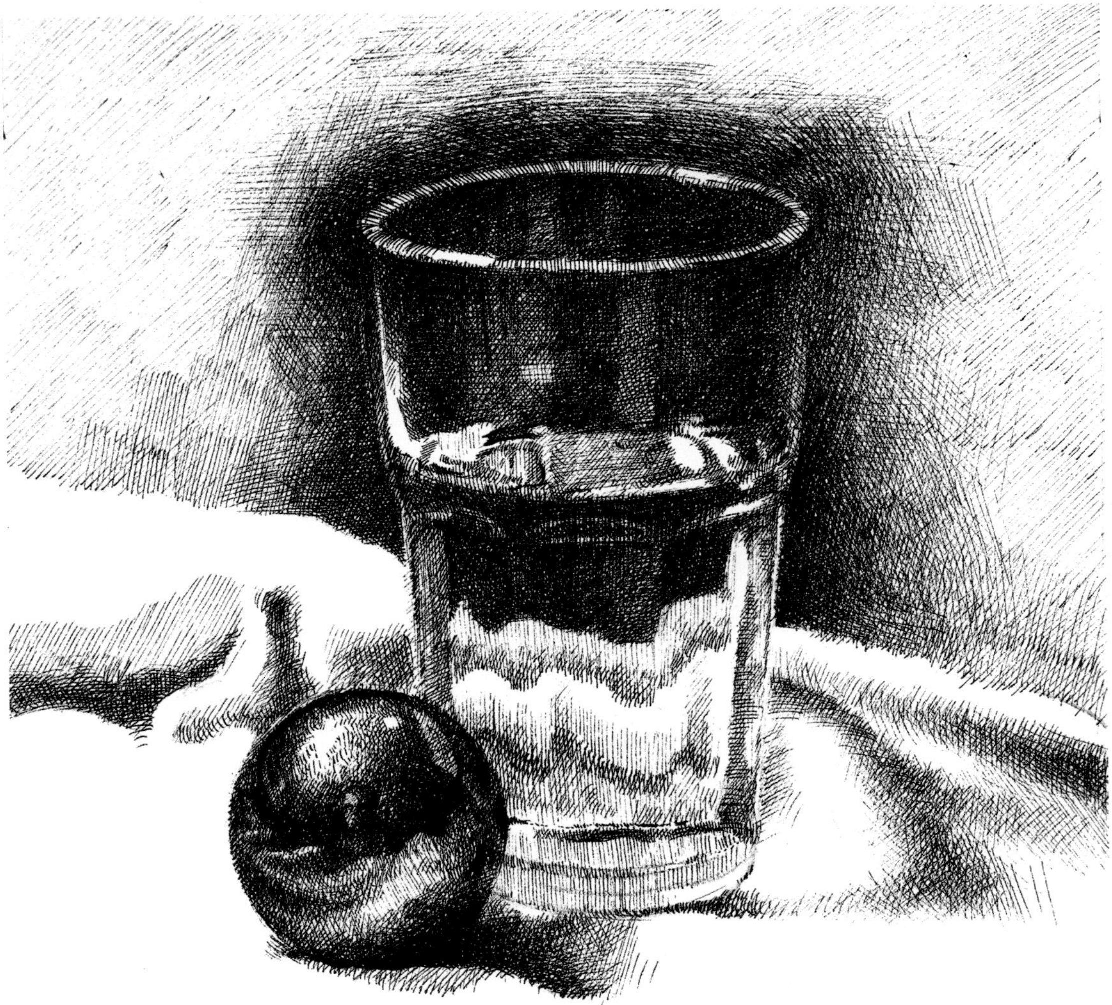

Step 5: To better establish the context and environment of the drawing, you can also work more on the background, particularly the dark wall behind the transparent glass. Depict it with heavy crosshatching.

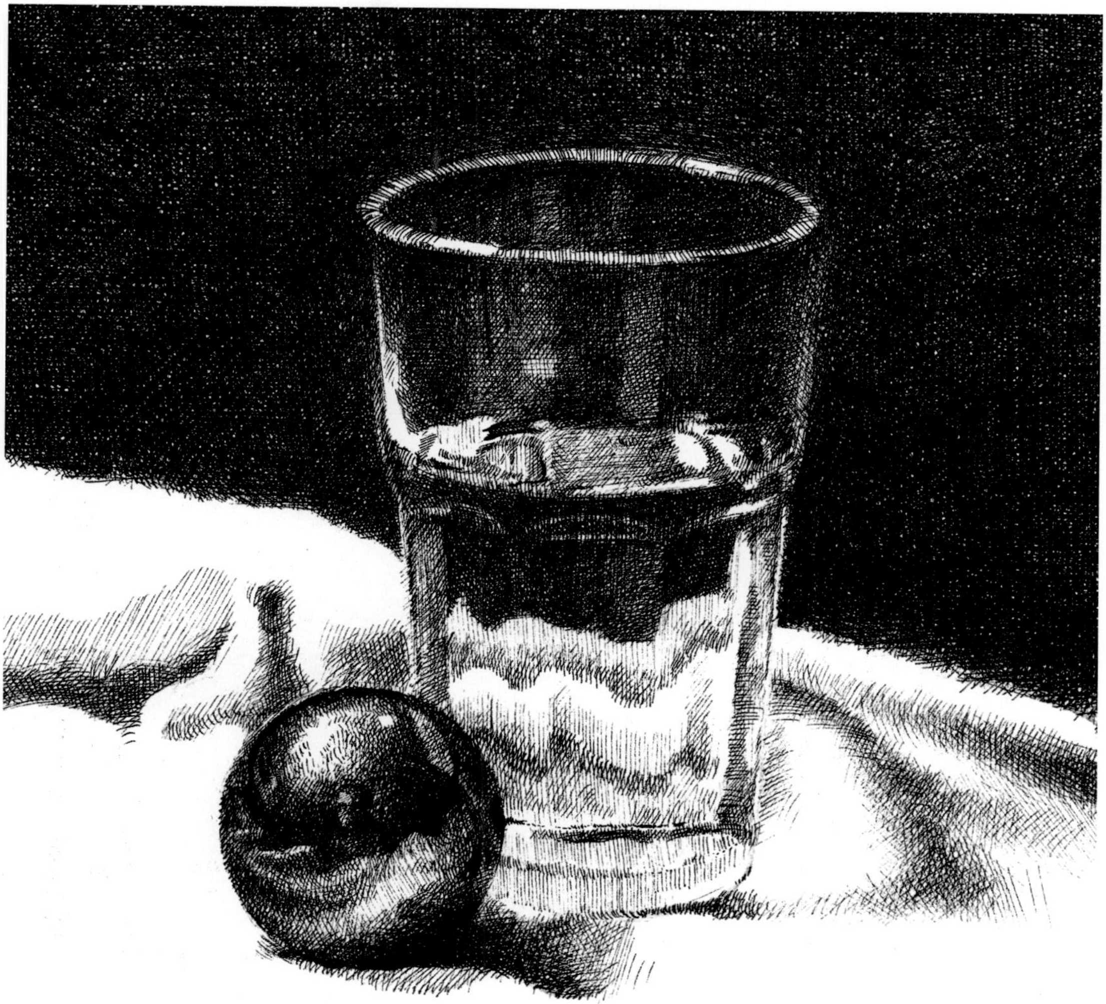

Step 6: For the final touches, let's enhance the highlights and slightly reduce the brightness in the direct light areas. This will help convey the realism of the lighting and the depth of the background. Specifically in this illustration, the highlights that need to be emphasized are the areas right next to the cast shadows of the metallic sphere and the glass. These spots receive strong light, making them essential for defining the scene's lighting. The rest of the fabric should be slightly darkened using crosshatching with light, delicate strokes to capture the texture and prevent it from becoming too dark.

Additionally, you can apply more crosshatching in the very dark areas of the background to enhance the overall contrast of the composition. Moreover, your feeling plays a key role in art: Take the time to observe, reflect, and add small details where necessary to refine the drawing.

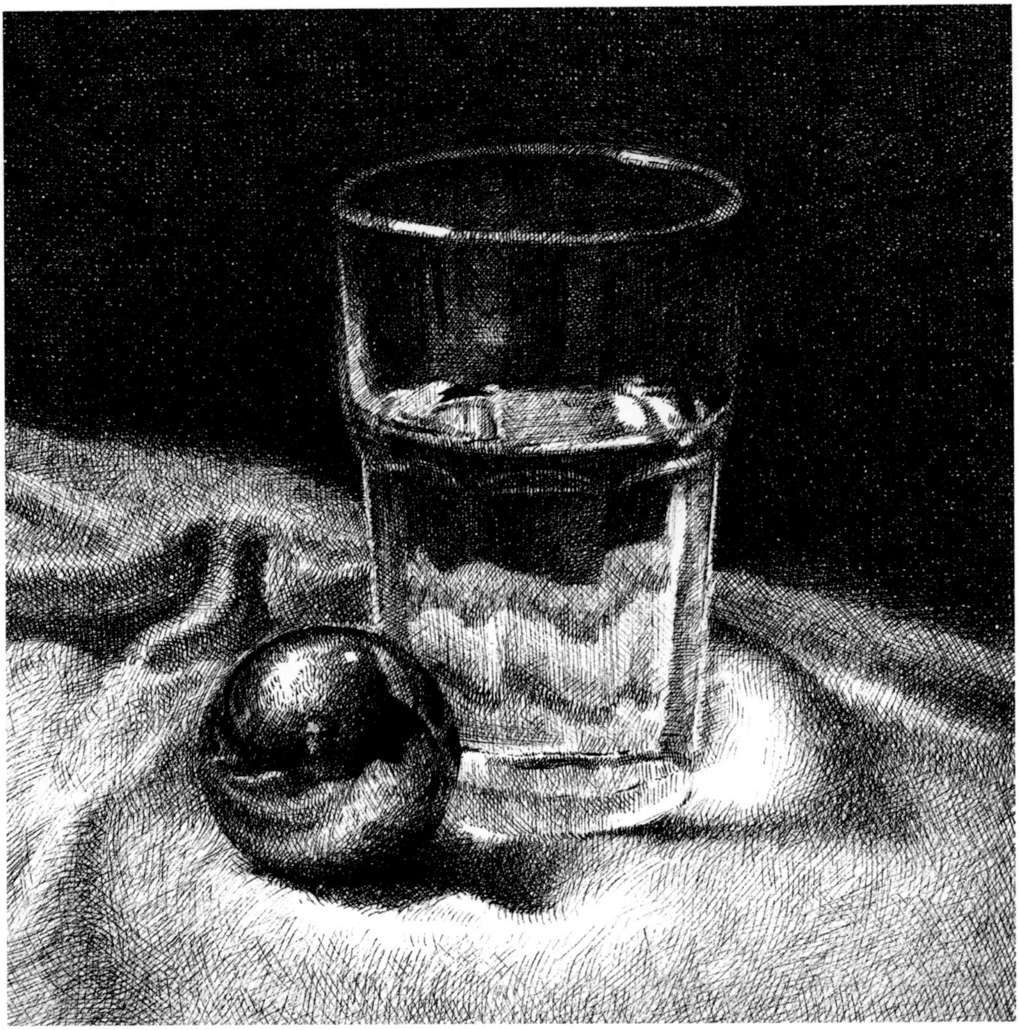

DEPICTING ANIMAL FUR

Drawing animals is an incredibly inspiring and interesting subject matter. For animals with fur, the shading technique can be a bit challenging due to the fine details and the unique texture. In this demo, I'll draw a cat to demonstrate how to approach fur. You can use this method as a reference for drawing any furry animal you like! If you have a pet like a dog or cat, that's fantastic! We can draw together.

Black-and-White Cat

Step 1: As usual, start by sketching the cat by simplifying the head into basic shapes, defining the facial features positions and proportions, and using constructive sketching (page 48) to outline the shape of the cat's face.

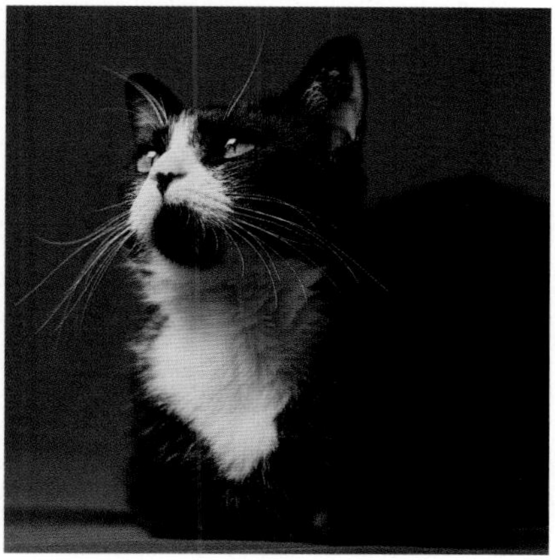

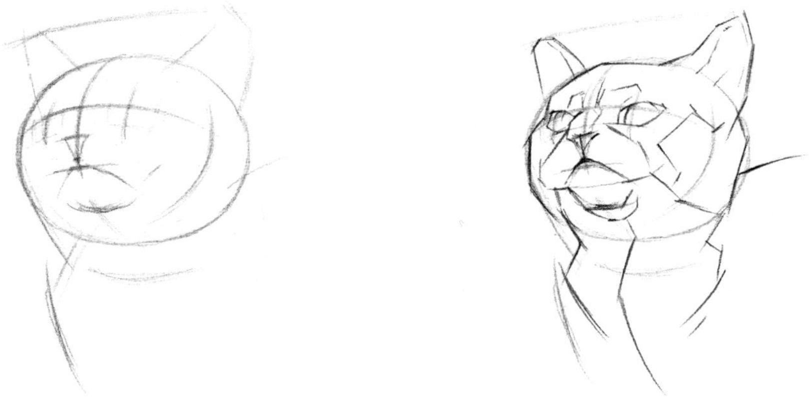

Step 2: Fur grows in specific directions and follows the cat's body form. Identifying the direction of fur growth is essential to capturing its natural texture and movement. Based on your sketch, use a 005 fineliner to outline the cat's actual shape. Be sure to use short hatching strokes that follow the direction of the fur growth, as mentioned, to convey the natural texture.

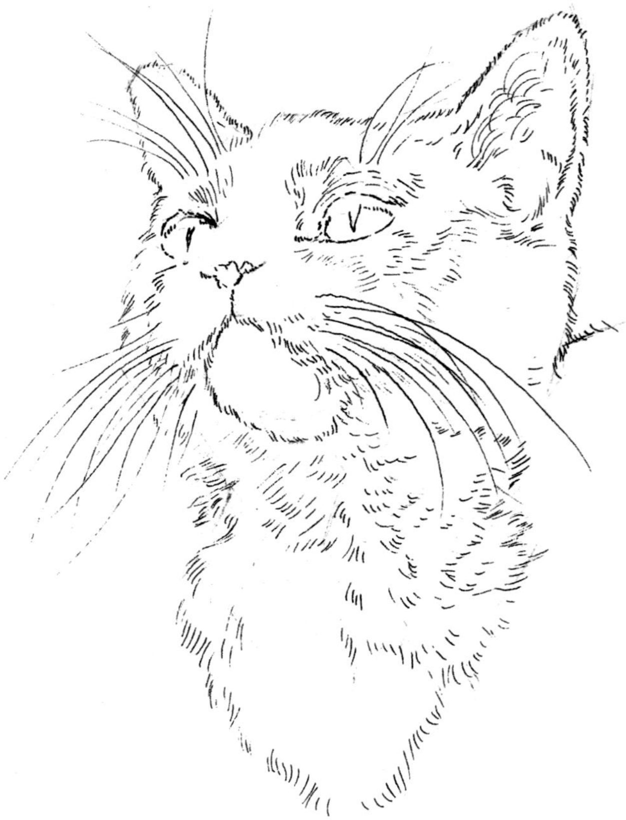

Step 3: Apply shading to the darker areas first. For animals with dark fur (like black or chocolate tones), you can start by shading these areas first to establish a foundational value. For animals with lighter or neutral-colored fur, focus initially on very dark details, like the corners of the eyes and nose, without shading the fur just yet (keep it for the next step). For our cat, begin with the right side of the fur, the rounds of the eyes, and the nose and mouth.

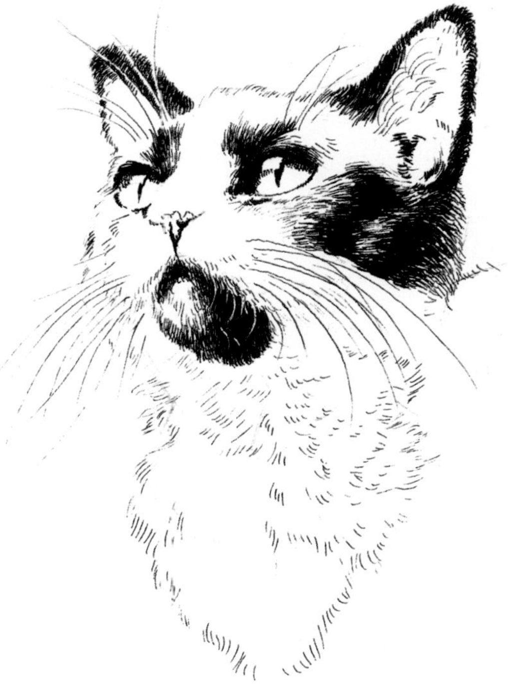

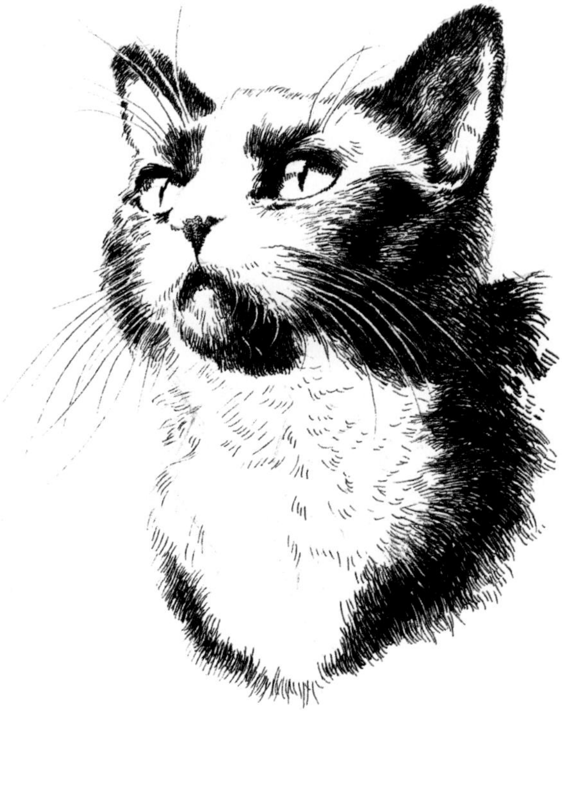

Step 4: Apply overall shading to the neutral or light fur areas using short hatching strokes that follow the fur's direction. At the same time, identify the darkest spots in these areas and shade them to show the core shadows. I used the hatching technique, drawing in the direction of the fur's growth to represent both the value and the texture of the cat's fur.

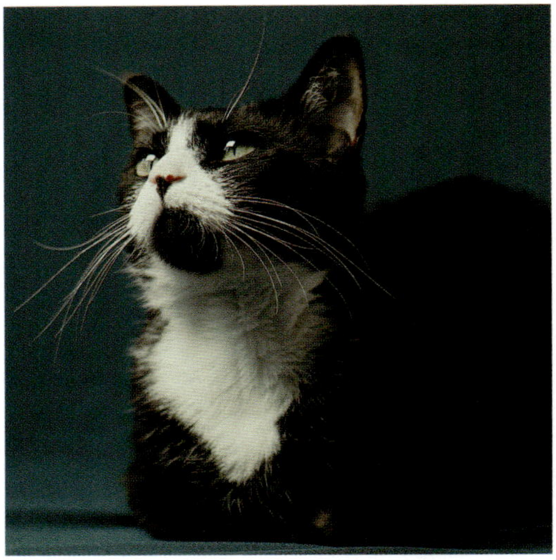

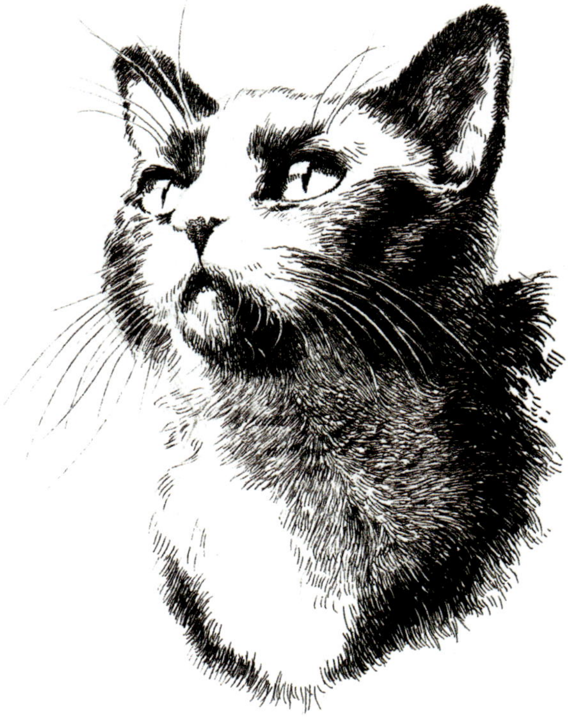

Step 5: Building on the key shading components (page 59), add shading for the mid-tones, highlights, and direct light using similar hatching techniques. In some areas, let the fur flow in a slightly more random direction to create a natural, realistic look. Add some stippling details to the eyes, making sure to indicate an iris and a highlight.

Step 6: Before finishing, take a step back to observe, adjust the values, and add any small details for balance. After observing, I noticed that the white fur under the cat's neck appeared uniform and lacked depth. To address this, I added shading to the darker areas using the hatching technique, similar to the previous steps. Additionally, I applied shading in some transition areas between the white and black fur, such as on the cat's cheek, to blend these sections more smoothly and create a more natural look.

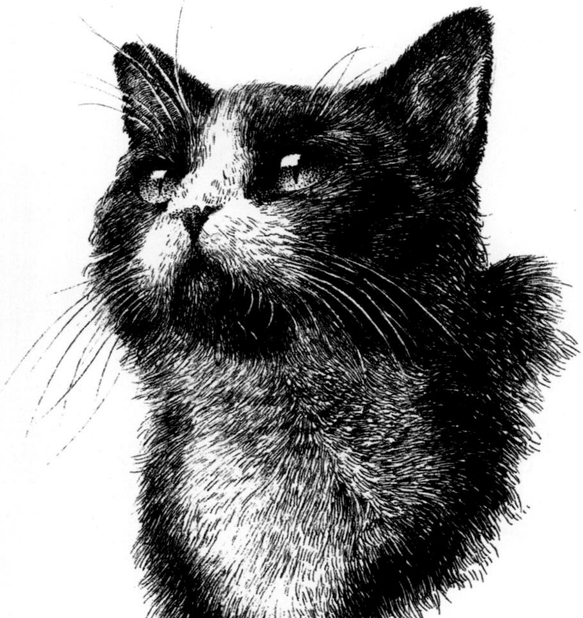

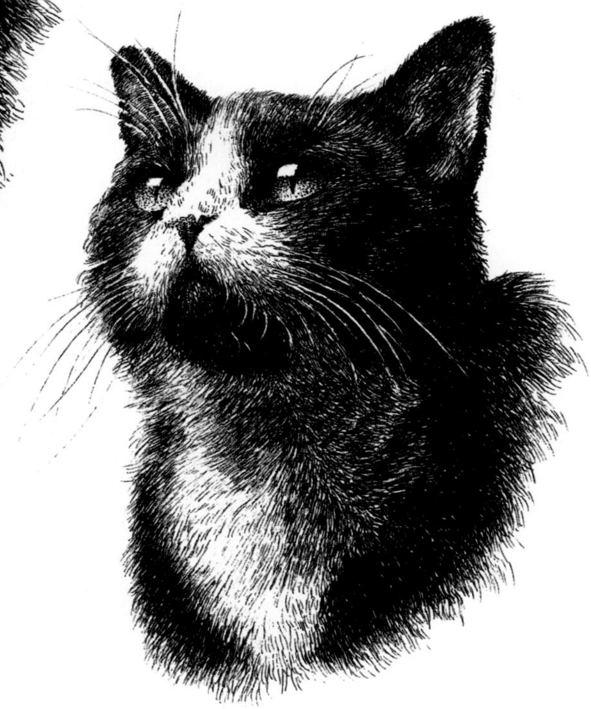

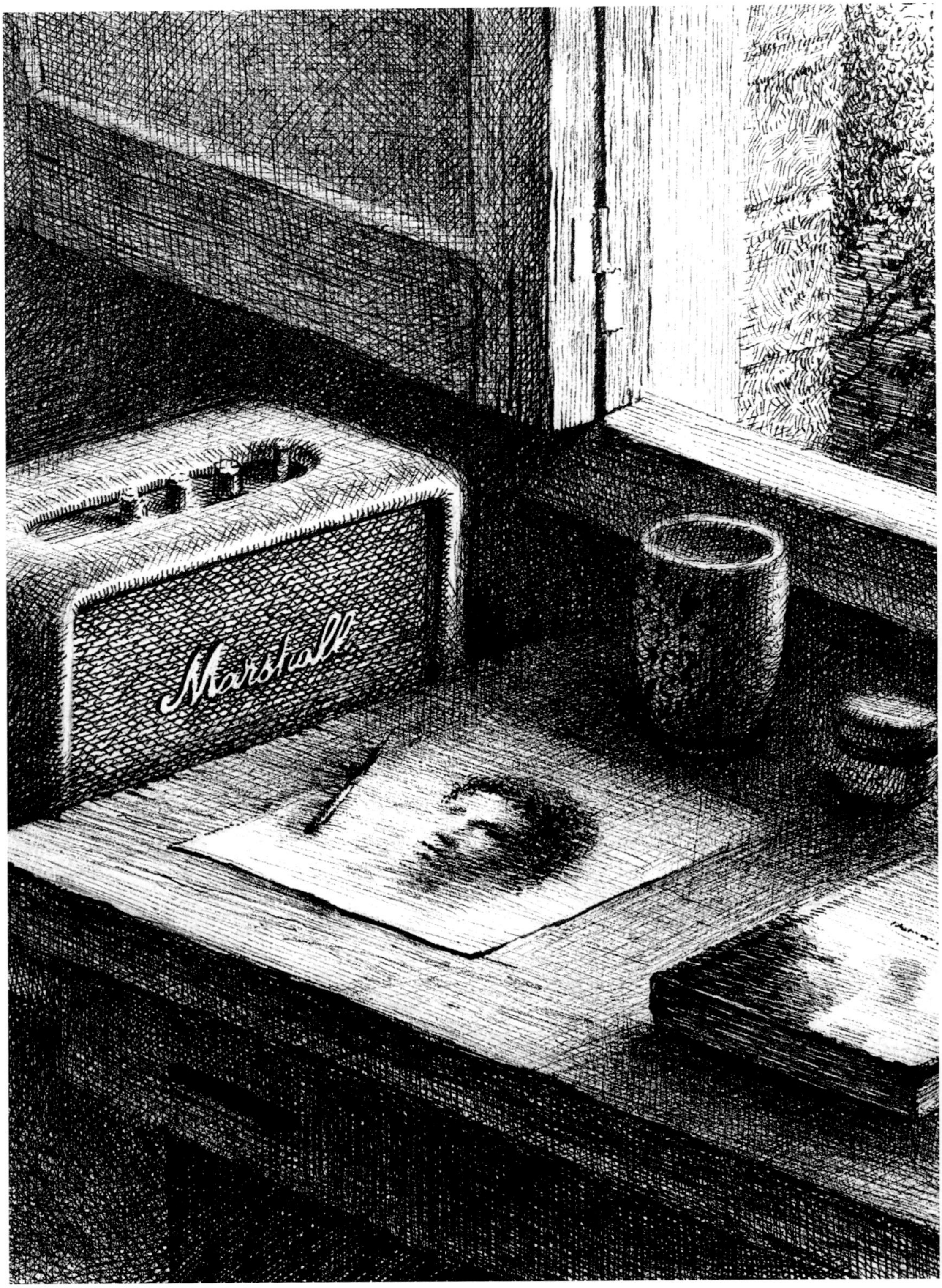
Marshall

Chapter 6
Going from Idea to Completed Artwork

In this chapter, we'll dive deeper into the process of creating an artwork. Through this, we'll not only apply the techniques we've learned but also express your ideas, style, and personality through your work.

Shape Up Your Idea: What to Draw

In addition to creating your artwork (*which is more than just a technical exercise*), it's important to define the content and concept of your piece. Here are some factors to consider to help you come up with an idea that resonates with you.

Why Do You Want to Create This Artwork?

Every individual has a different purpose when creating art. Some make art to express their emotions and thoughts, others to capture moments in life, or simply because they love the process of creativity. Regardless of the reason, identifying it will help you better direct your initial idea development for the artwork.

Which Style Best Reflects Your Desires?

Artistic styles and art movements are developed to meet the needs of expressing a work in a complete, satisfying, and emotional way. There are many different styles, and you can choose one or more that you feel most comfortable and satisfied with to shape up your idea. You might want to create a realistic depiction to capture a beautiful moment, or use abstract and random shapes to express your emotions. Whatever style brings you joy in creation, go for it, or even better, you can develop your own unique style! Here are some suggested styles you might consider:

Realism: This style aims to accurately represent what you see in reality, emphasizing the true appearance of the subject.

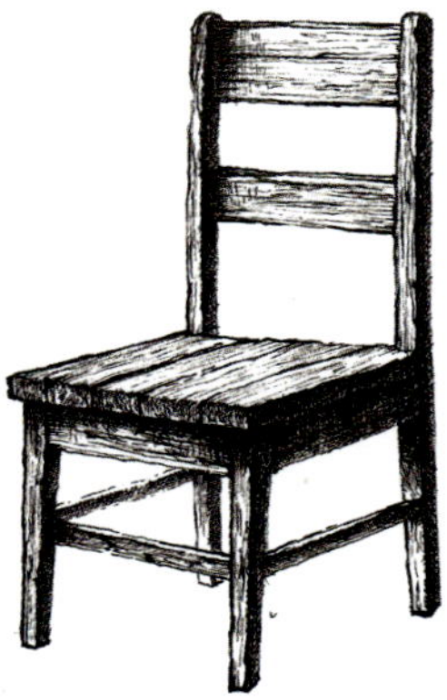

Cubism: Famously associated with Picasso, this style was developed in the early twentieth century, characterized by geometric shapes to depict lines, space, and movement of subjects.

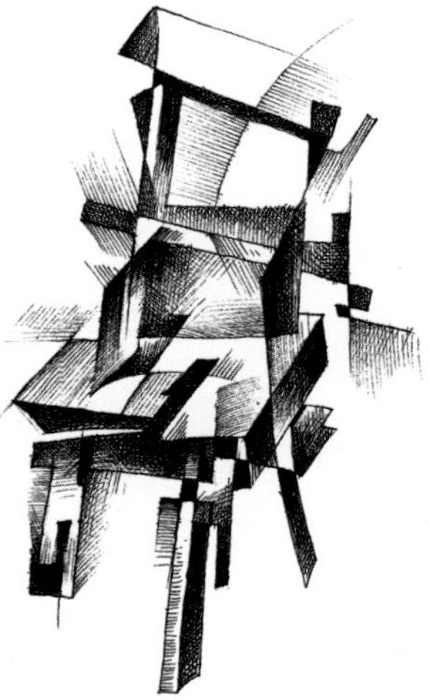

Surrealism: Surrealism offers a dreamy, unconventional escape from reality and logic to express inner thoughts and emotions.

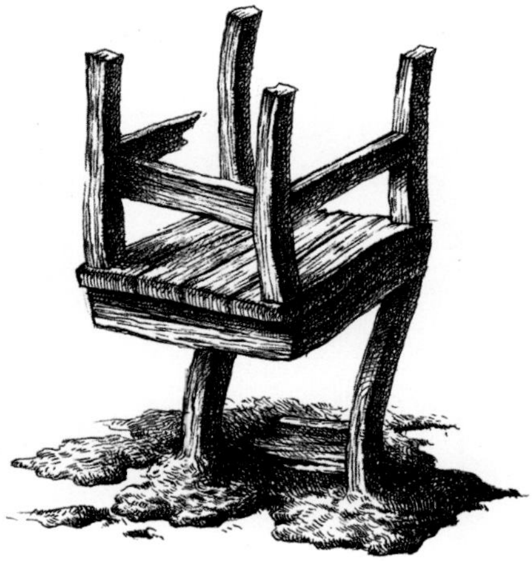

Postimpressionism: This style focuses on capturing moments quickly, highlighting personal emotions and perspectives, with a free and distinctive technique.

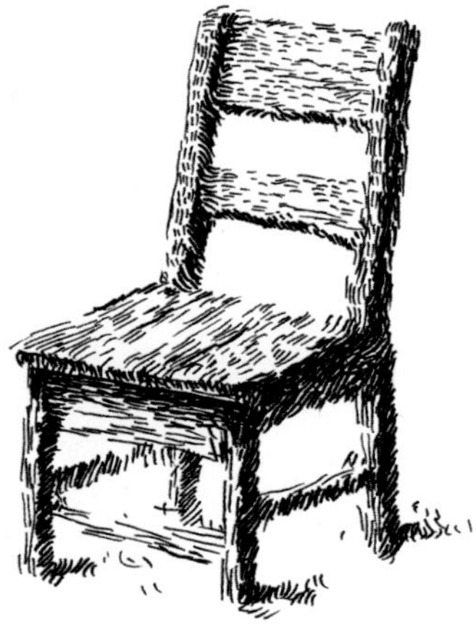

Abstract: This art style uses abstract subjects to convey thoughts, messages, and emotions, rather than depicting clearly defined and recognizable forms.

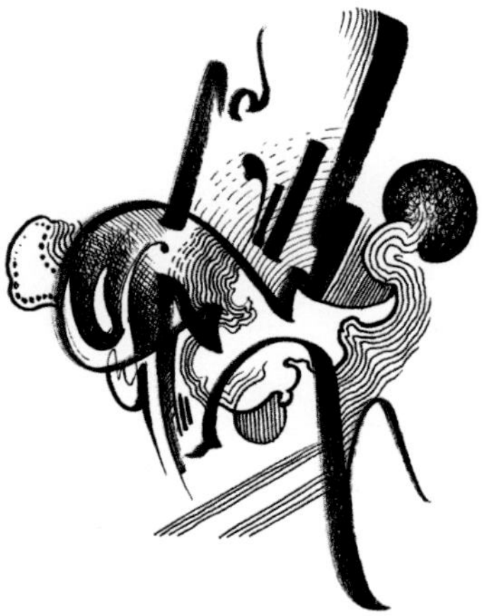

What to Draw?

Choosing subject matters is essential for shaping your artwork. Depending on your chosen style, your subjects can vary. You might depict an object of personal significance, a portrait of a friend, subjects that metaphorically represent your thoughts and feelings, an animal, or even imagined imagery. Choose visual subjects that effectively convey the idea you want to express. Here are some subject suggestions you might consider:

Geometric Shapes & Forms: Simple shapes and forms can be very powerful in conveying your idea. They can also be both a mindful drawing habit and a great way to practice your shading within large, simple shapes.

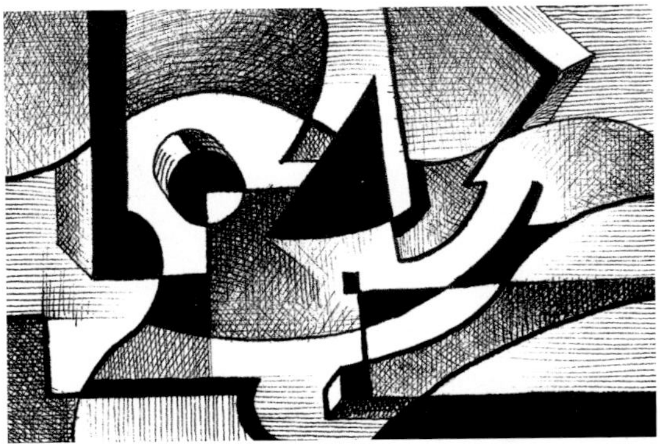

Still Life: Still life drawings typically feature stationary subjects, like everyday objects you use. These are great for capturing the everyday objects you love and turning them into works of lasting art.

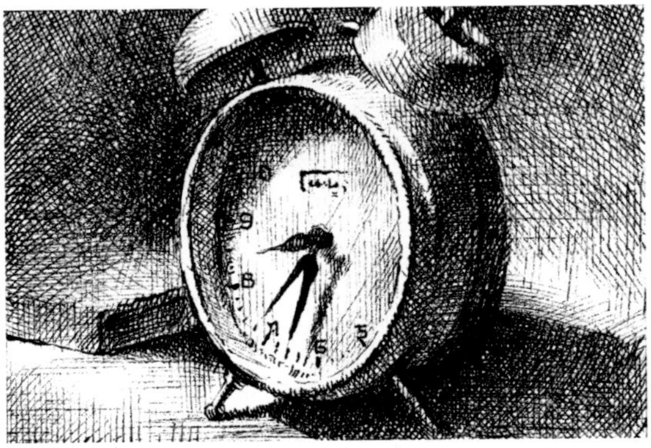

Landscape, Nature & Animals: The vast and majestic natural world can be a great source of inspiration. Forests, seas, trees, skies, and animals are all wonderful subjects and a rich landscape for texture, shadows, and depth.

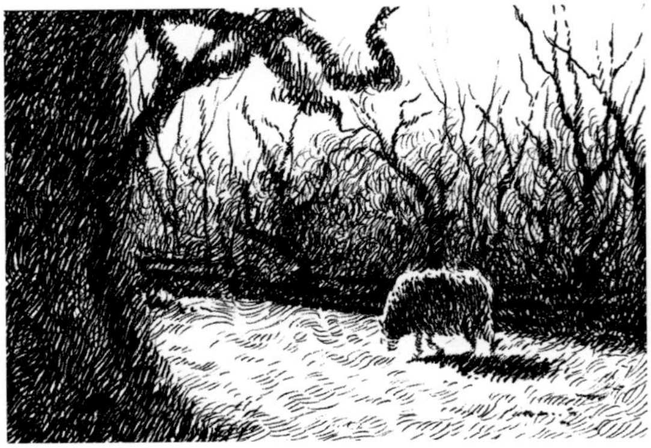

Urbanscape: The bustling and developed cityscapes with closely packed buildings and people on the streets reflect modern human life. In addition to that, they are perfect for playing with perspective.

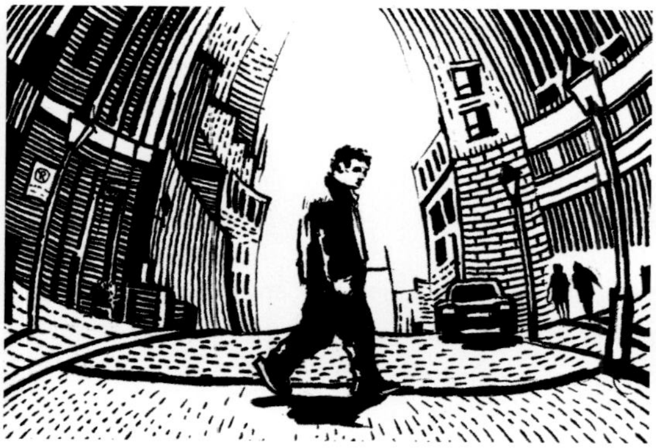

Figurative & Portrait: Humans are often depicted in art with various stories and personalities. It is a special privilege to capture friends, family, and fellow humans in pen and ink. Just as faces all have a unique look, so is each artist's interpretation of that face.

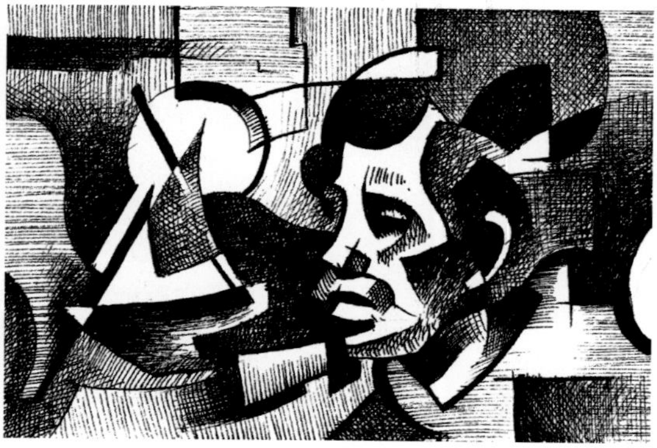

Imagination: We never stop imagining. Let your imagination run free with whatever you come up with. It could be a mythical creature, an invention that doesn't exist yet, or a scene from a dreamy and poetic land.

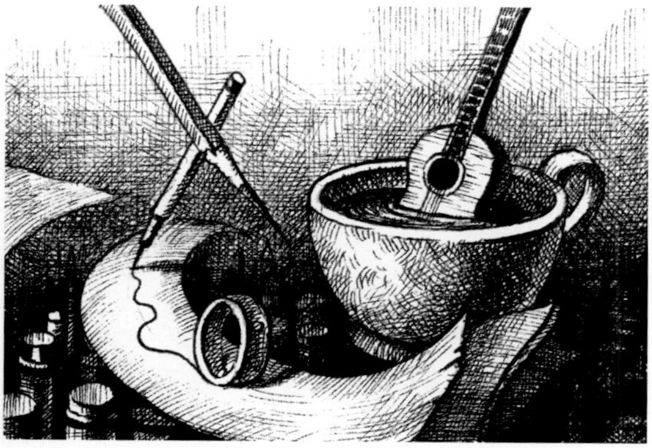

Reference, Visual Composition, and Sketching

Once you have your direction, idea, style, and subject matters, let's discuss the process of bringing these ideas to paper.

References

References are resources such as images, information, books, articles, or any other materials that help you visualize your subject matters and assist in the drawing process. In this section, we'll focus on **visual references**, which help you to visualize your subject matters. Essentially, we have two main approaches:

Ready-Made References: These are photos or materials created and available from various sources. Currently, reference photos are quite diverse and can be found through websites (free or paid), photographers/models, and other reference sources. Some reference stock photo websites I use are unsplash.com, pexels.com, and pixabay.com. The advantages of ready-made references include convenience and a wide range of options and perspectives. However, the drawbacks are that you may not find a reference that exactly matches your idea, and there can be issues related to copyright and creative ownership. Therefore, this type of reference is often used for practice and studies.

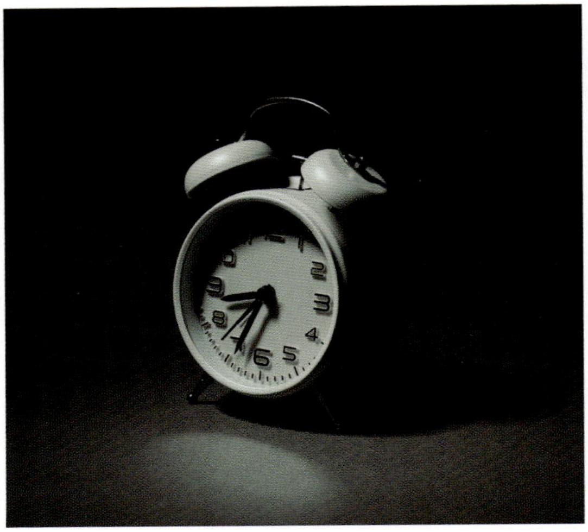

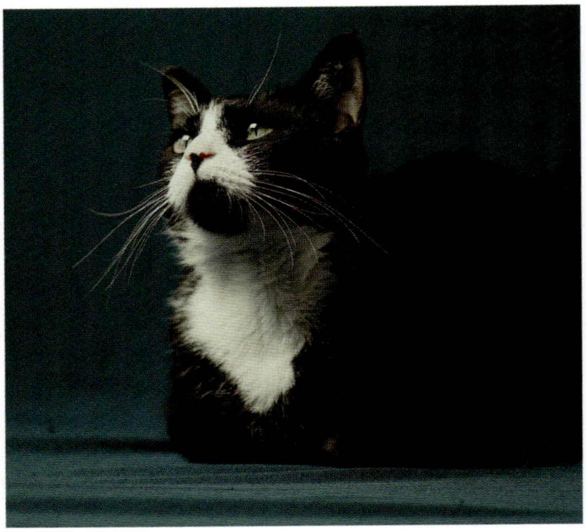

Your Own References: If you capture a beautiful scene during an autumn stroll by taking a photo or sketching it directly, that's your own reference. This type of reference, whether a photo you took or a life drawing, offers purity in idea, creativity, and emotion. You can achieve exactly what you want to depict in your artwork and personalize your piece. The downside is convenience and variety. Capturing a majestic and epic snowcapped mountain with surrounding clouds can be quite challenging for some of us. However, this is still the type of reference I always encourage people to use for creating original works.

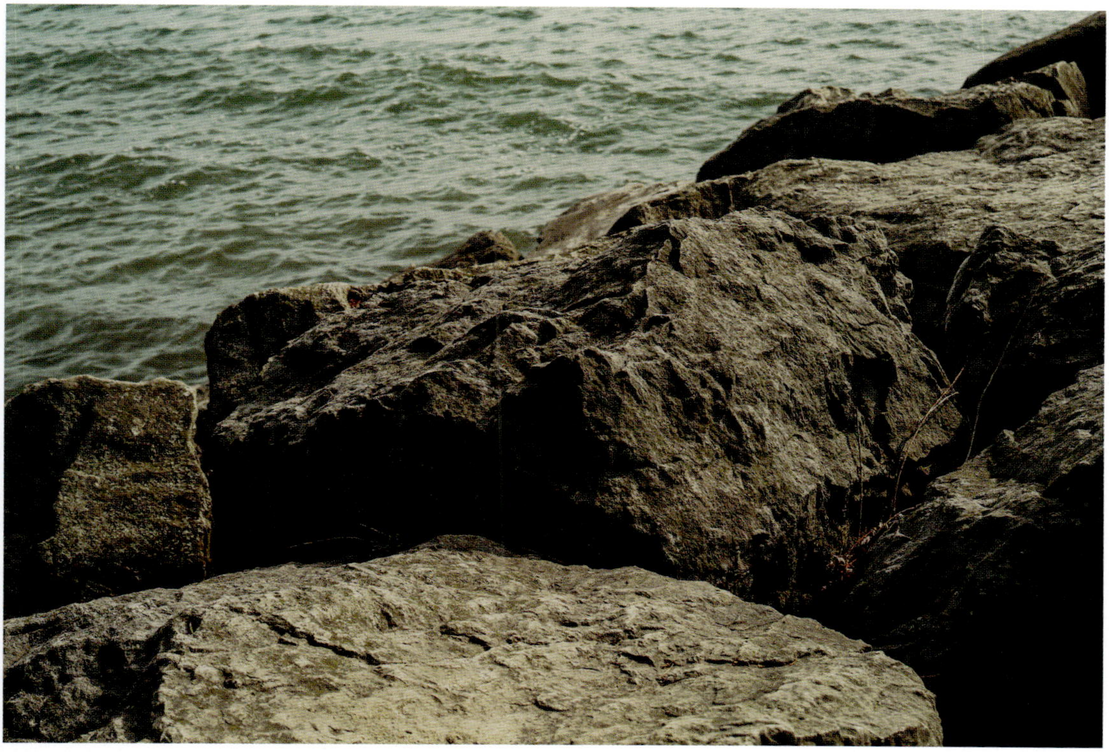

Visual Composition

Composition is how you arrange elements and subject matters in your artwork to convey your idea and concept. There are many principles of composition in visual arts and drawing. Here are some suggestions to enhance harmony in your artwork:

Focal Point: This is the area you want to highlight the most, drawing the viewer's attention and serving as the centerpiece of your artwork. Here are some methods to consider for creating an effective focal point:

- *Center Point:* The center of the artwork naturally draws the most attention. Placing your focal point here can make it the primary focus.
- *Rule of Thirds:* Divide your canvas into nine equal parts using two horizontal and two vertical lines. The intersections of these lines are known as the "one-third points." Placing your focal point on one of these points creates visual harmony.
- *The Golden Ratio:* Based on the Fibonacci sequence with a ratio of 1.618, the golden ratio is considered a pleasing proportion in visual art. This sequence creates an attractive spiral, with the center of the spiral often used as the focal point.

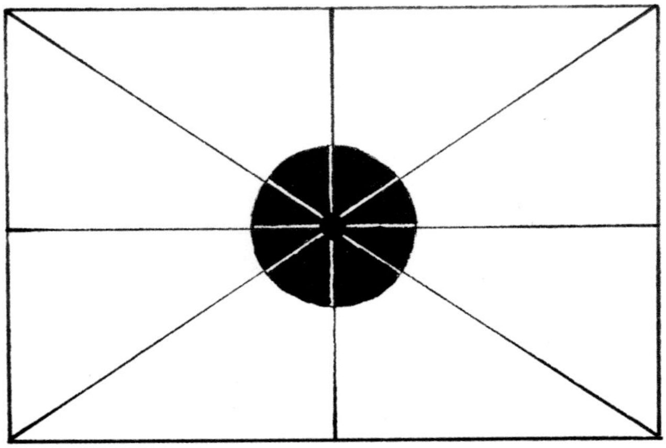

Center Point

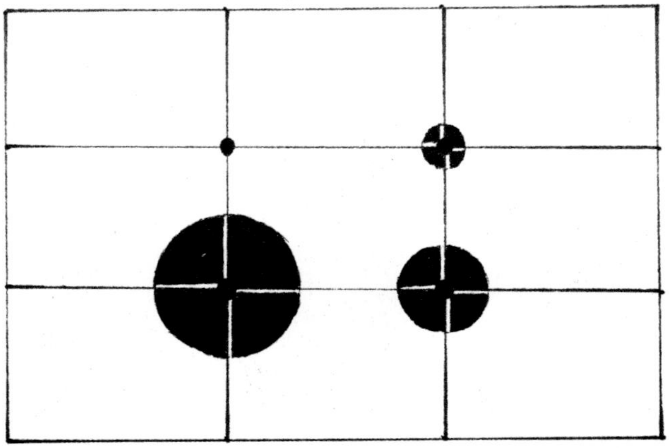

Rule of Thirds

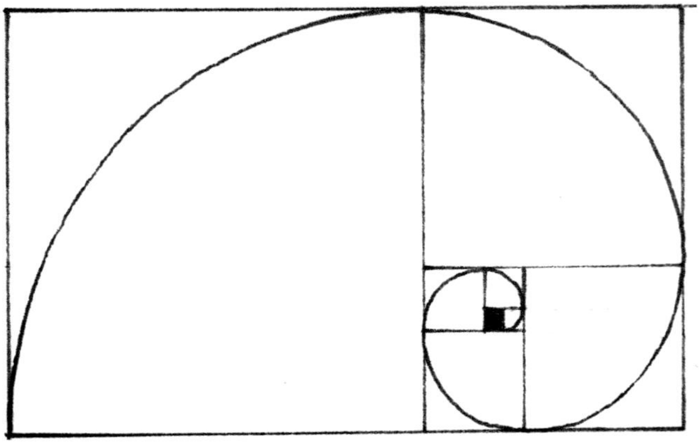

The Golden Ratio

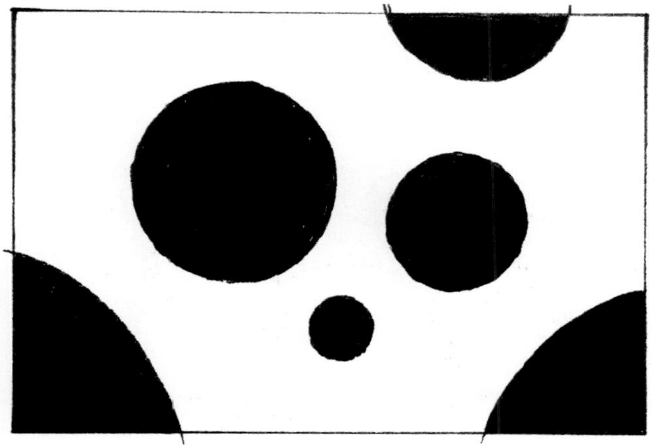

Balance & Imbalance: Balance is essential for creating harmony in your artwork. It involves not only the physical size but also light, rhythm, emotion, and how elements complement each other. Imbalance, on the other hand, can evoke feelings of instability and tension, used to convey emotions or create a striking visual effect.

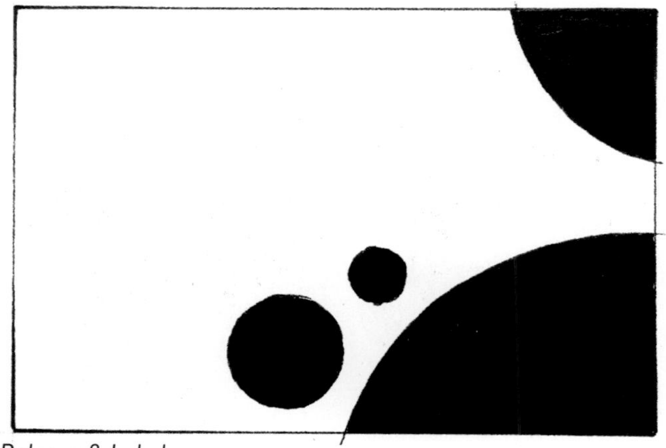

Balance & Imbalance

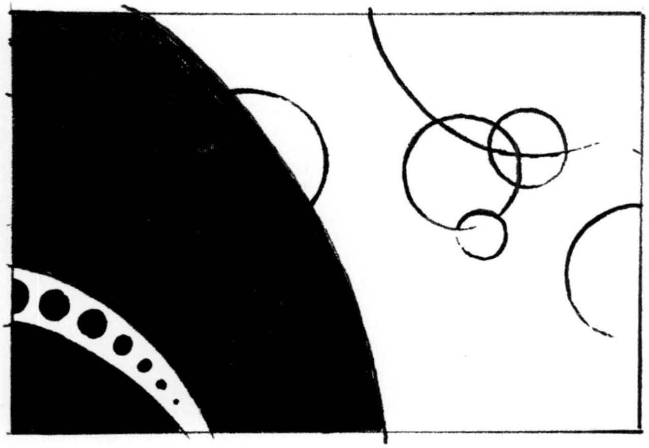

Contrast & Harmony

Contrast & Harmony: Contrast emphasizes and dramatizes how the artwork is presented. It involves differences in light and size (large/small), subject complexity (simple/detailed), movement (static/dynamic), and mood (bright/dark). Harmony, in contrast, reduces emphasis by creating similarity among elements, often seen in background details or nonfocal areas.

Unity & Variety: Unity creates a sense of harmony and coherence through repeated elements and similarities. Variety introduces richness, change, and contrast, highlighting the unique characteristics of each subject.

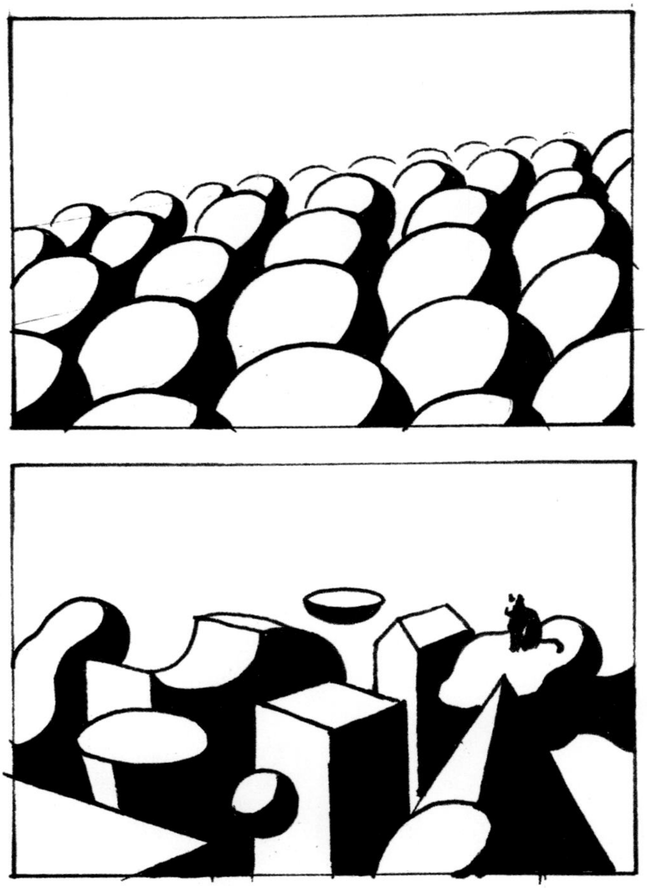

Unity & Variety

Tips for Sketching

After discussing and understanding the previous sections, you likely have clearer ideas and images in your mind. Now, to bring them to life on paper with a pencil sketch and ensure your sketch accurately reflects your vision, consider these tips:

Thumbnails Sketching: This is a small-scale version of your planned sketch, like a quick way to explore your ideas and layout with mini sketches about 2–3 inches (5–8 cm) in size. You might create multiple thumbnails to find the best option for your composition.

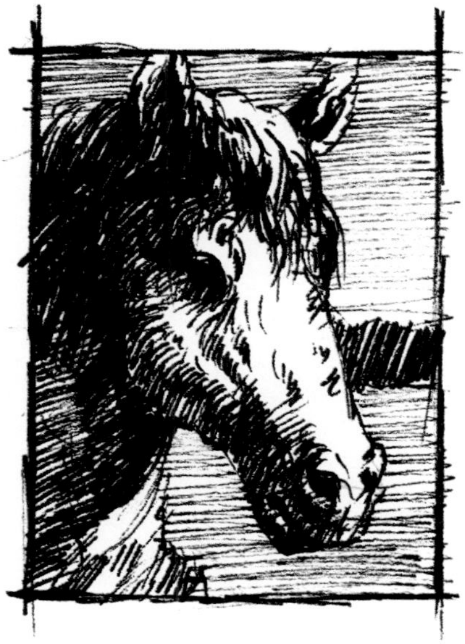

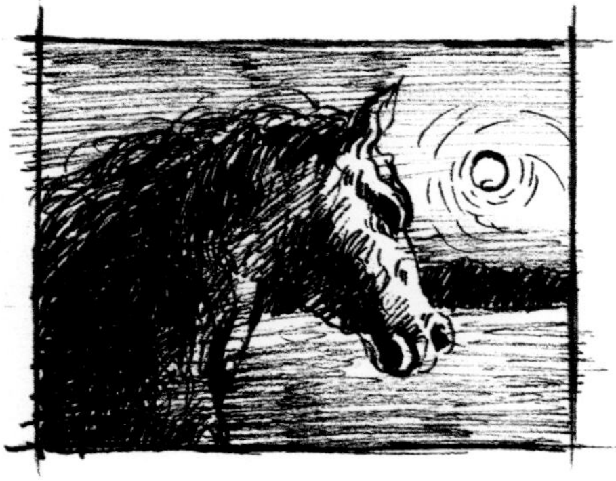

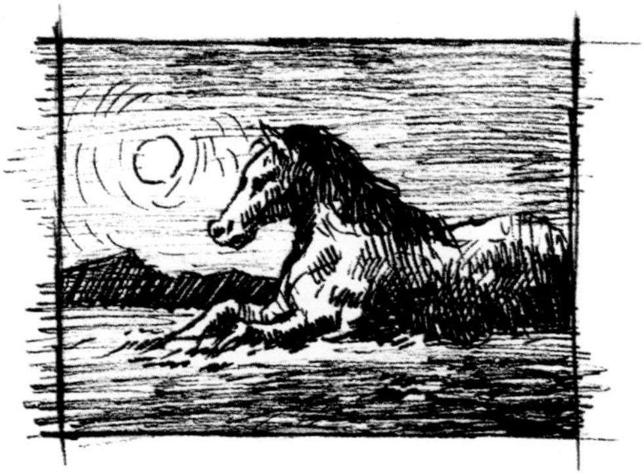

Constructive Sketching & Simplified Forms: As discussed in previous exercises, identify the placement of subjects using geometric shapes, simplify these subjects into basic forms, and represent their shapes and features with simple lines like straight or curved.

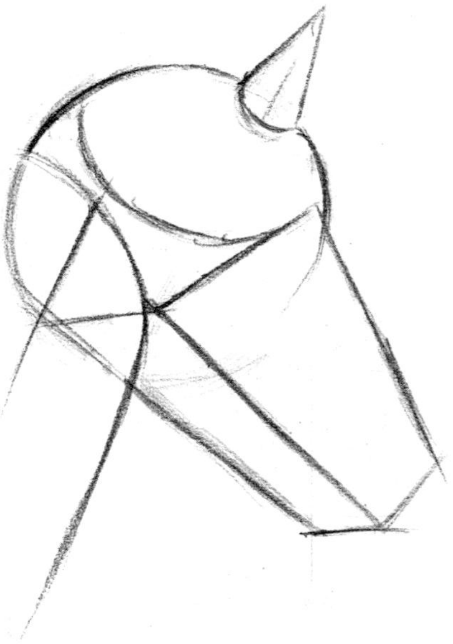

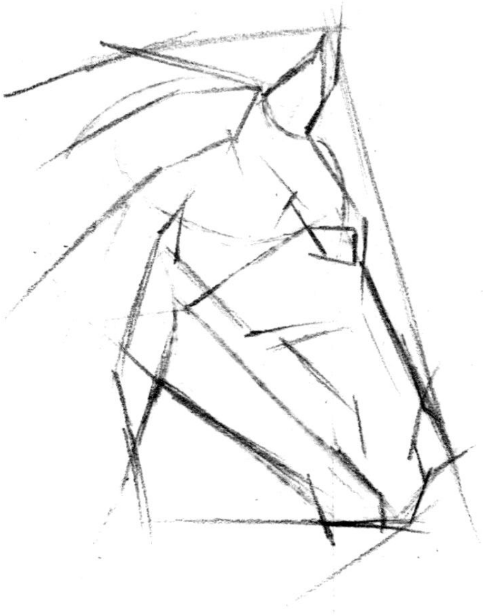

Grid Method: This technique helps you transfer your thumbnails onto your main sketch using vertical and horizontal lines (grid). The small squares from the grid make it easier to position subjects and layout by comparing and enlarging the thumbnails onto the final sketch.

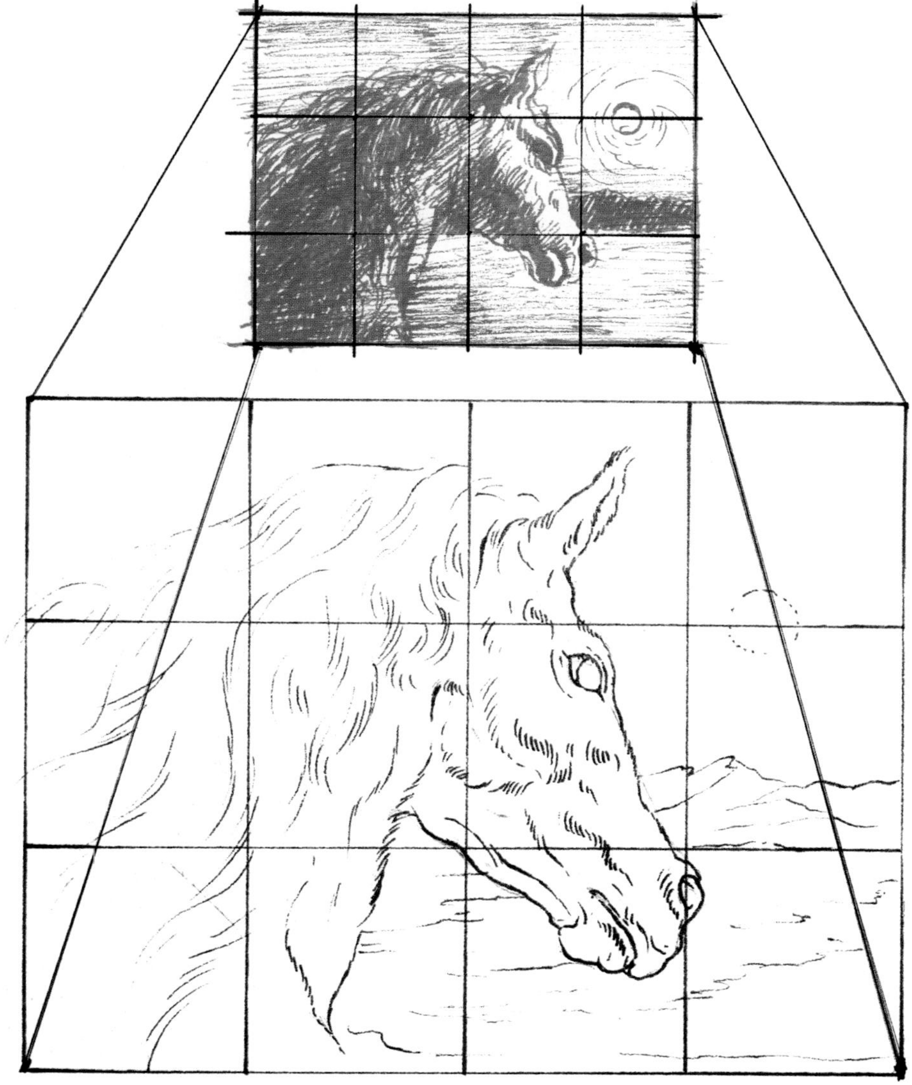

Take a Break

Taking a real break is very important in the process of making art. Drawing for hours straight can hinder your observations and judgments. Call a friend, have a coffee, take a walk around the street, gaze at the sky, or enjoy a nice meal. After a few hours (or even a day), come back and look at your artwork again—you might notice a lot of differences.

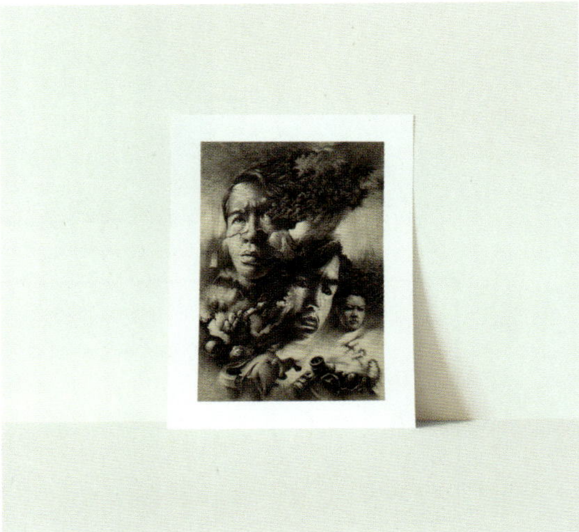

In addition to a typical break, you can also review your own work. Evaluate, analyze, and plan your next steps. Here are some specific suggestions to try:

View from a Distance: Place your artwork in a convenient spot or hang it on a wall. Step back 5–7 feet (1.5 to 2 meters) and observe. By viewing your piece from a distance and in a smaller size, you can easily assess the overall composition and layout. This perspective helps you spot any general flaws that you might want to improve or adjust.

Change Your Perspective: One interesting method to evaluate your work is to change your perspective. Show your artwork to a friend or family member, and listen to their feedback. Alternatively, you can view your artwork in a mirror or through a reversed reflection. This method helps you notice strengths and weaknesses that might be hard to see from a direct view. Another approach is to photograph your artwork and review it on different electronic devices. This allows you to analyze and evaluate your piece through the "camera's perspective." These methods will help you observe and analyze your artwork, giving you a clearer direction for any necessary changes in the next steps.

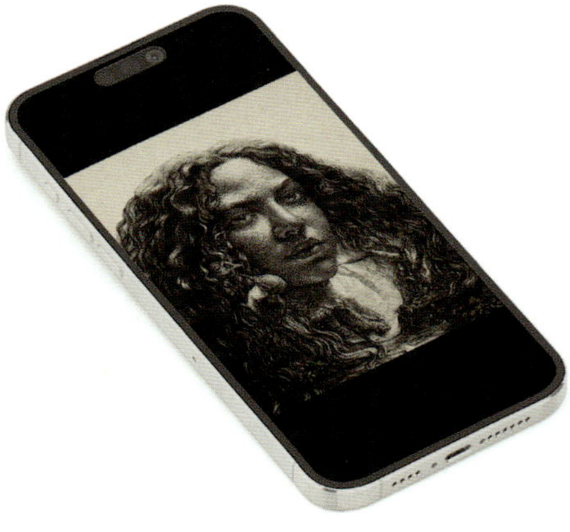

Your Creativity

Each of us has our own way of being creative. It's difficult to say that anyone can teach you "how to be creative." However, some specific techniques and methods can serve as tools to support you in finding inspiration and ideas.

Distortion: This is a term I use for artworks where the subject doesn't show its real shape but is changed according to the artist's perspective. Distortion can be shown in many ways, such as: altering the subject's shape, drawing the subject as geometric shapes (like cubism), drawing a subject abstractly, creating blurred lines to show movement and motion, adding or removing parts and details, and many other methods. With this technique, you can freely express your ideas without being limited to a realistic depiction.

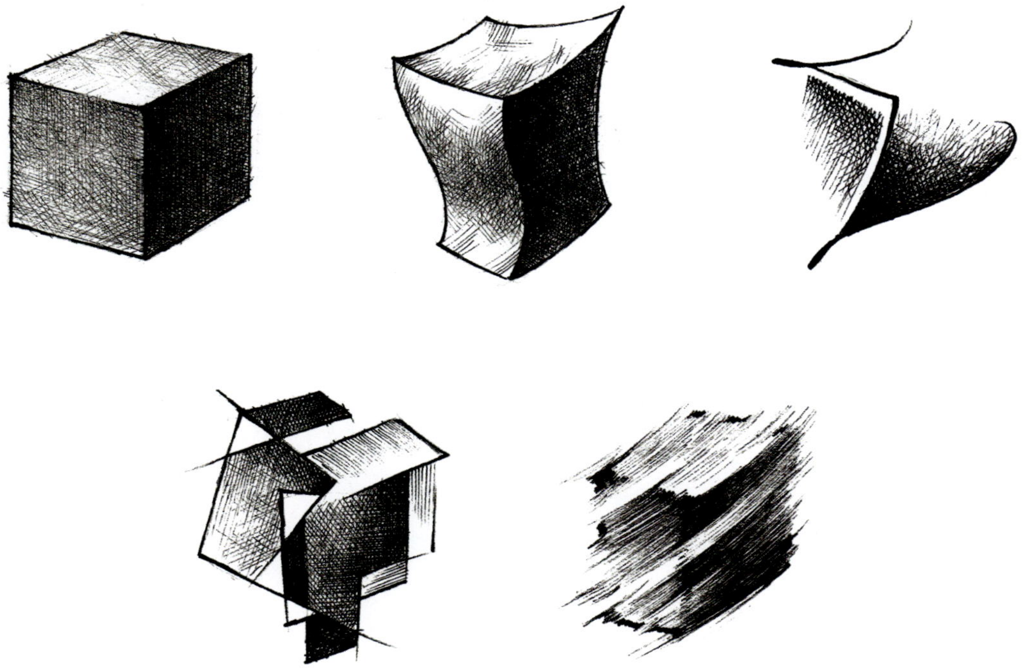

Inspiration from Art Styles & Movements: Art styles and movements are the results of ongoing creativity throughout art history. Explore different art movements—you might find inspiration there!

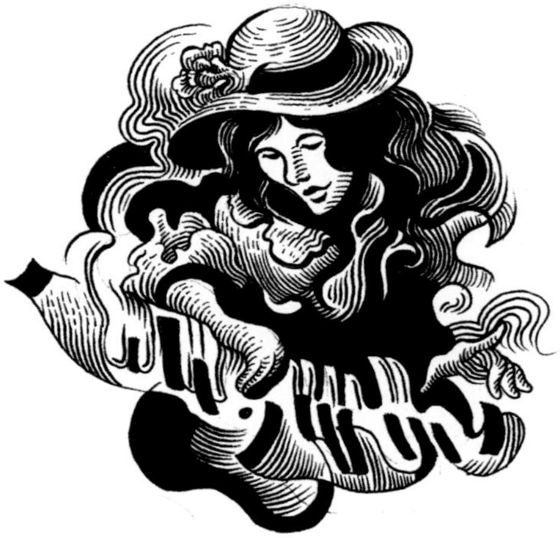

Alternative Subjects: Sometimes, using different images or subjects can help you convey your ideas more effectively. Instead of drawing the subjects you first think of, you can use metaphor or symbolism to represent the message or emotion you want to express. For example, to convey "freedom," you might draw a bird or a cloud in the sky. To show the opposite, you could draw a cloud floating in a locked room. Explore your creative power!

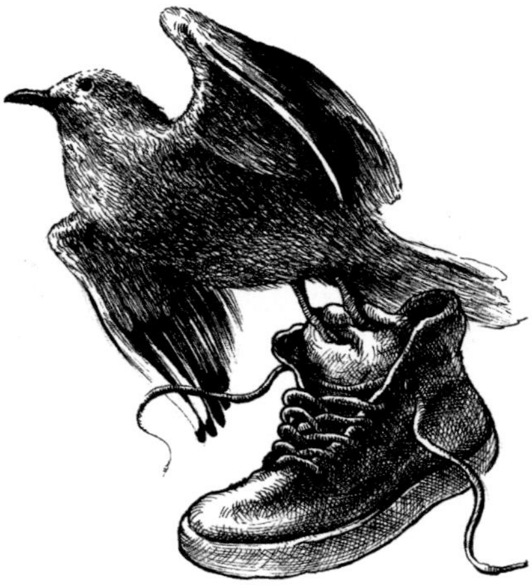

Subconscious & Automatism: Letting your thoughts flow naturally is another interesting way to boost creativity and imagination. Try drawing random things that pop into your head. These could be clear, realistic images or abstract subjects. You can also try automatism writing, a method to express your subconscious reactions. Through this, you can shape ideas based on your true and honest thoughts.

The Kalimba read a book yesterday
and decided to plant a tree,
despite losing its own voice.

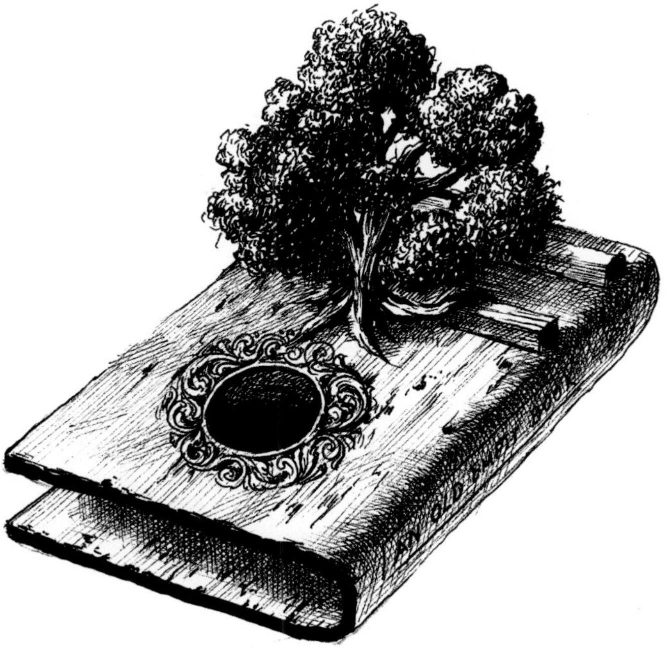

Let's Draw!

In this section, we're going to work on a series of pen-and-ink drawings not only to review what we've learned in the book so far but also to explore and express the world around us and our inner selves. We'll start with familiar subjects like a cozy room and an outdoor scene, but these will be unique to you. Pick your favorite cozy room or your favorite outdoor space and draw them using my tutorial as a guideline; the exact details will be different depending on what you pick. Are you ready? Let's get started!

Start from Your Cozy Place

Your cozy place is where you study, work, and create every day. It also reflects a part of your personality, interests, and who you are. Find a suitable spot, choose a favorite corner of your space, and pick up your pen to start drawing.

Choosing the Angle to Draw: Pick a corner of the place that you find most inspiring, and set that as the focal point of your drawing based on the composition principles we've discussed (page 146). You can try life drawing or taking a reference picture in this step.

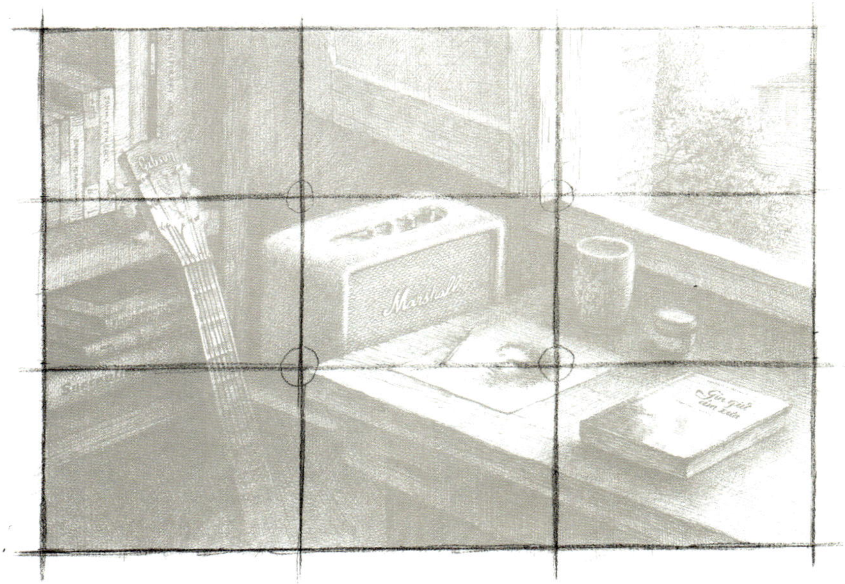

Linear Perspective: To arrange subjects easily, start with the overall context. Pay attention to wall edges, the floor, window frames, and basic room structures, and place them into a linear perspective by drawing simple straight sketching lines using an H or HB pencil. This will help you sketch the room's general space more effectively.

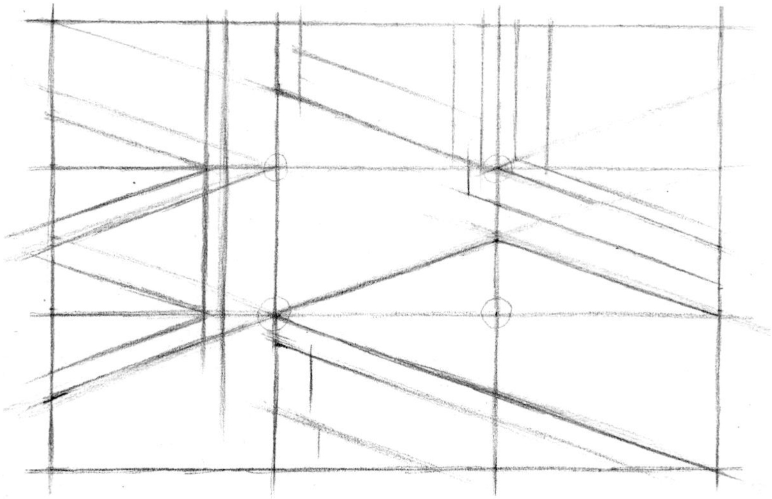

Sketch the Larger Subjects First: Identify and simplify the forms of large subjects, like the cupboard, bookshelf, desk, or bed using the constructive sketching method (page 48), and place them within the established perspective. These subjects will be easier to portray based on the room's structural lines that were sketched earlier.

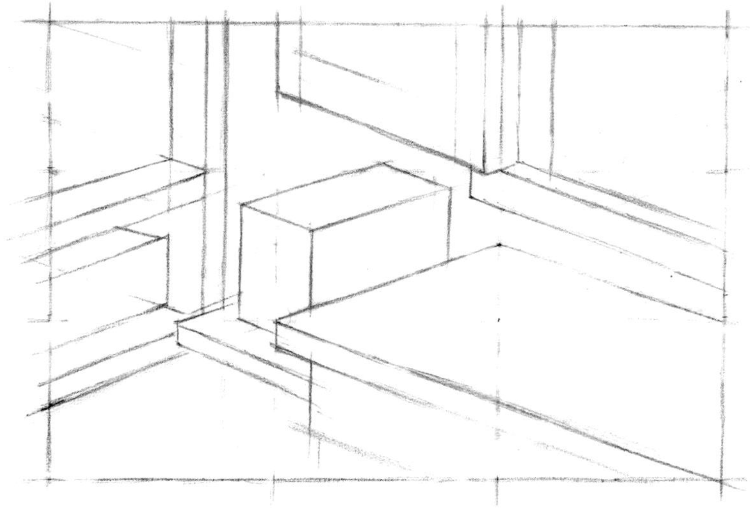

Sketch the Smaller Subjects: After sketching out the larger subjects, you'll get a better sense of the space and can start drawing the smaller ones based on the perspective and composition. You can include things like the computer, books on the desk, or decorative items on the shelf. Keep in mind, we're only focusing on drawing the overall shapes using the constructive sketching method at this stage, so there's no need to worry about the small details just yet.

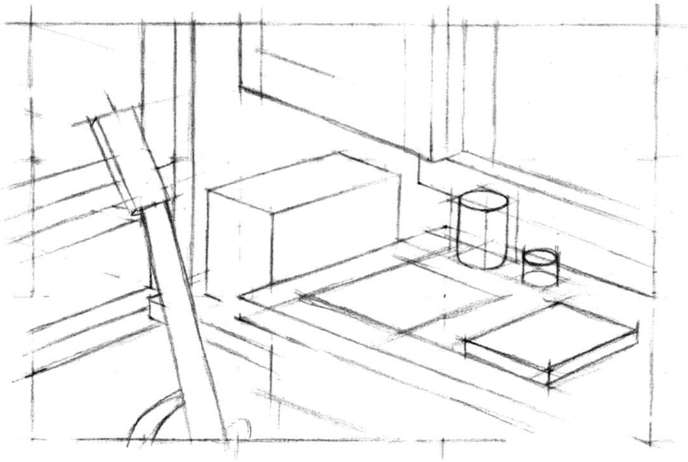

Outline Drawing: After completing the overall sketch and feeling satisfied with it, draw the outline of all the subjects in the picture to show their actual shapes, such as the neck of a guitar or curve of a candle. At this stage, use a darker pencil, like a 2B or 3B, to make the outlines more visible. Once you're done, you can erase any unnecessary sketch lines from earlier.

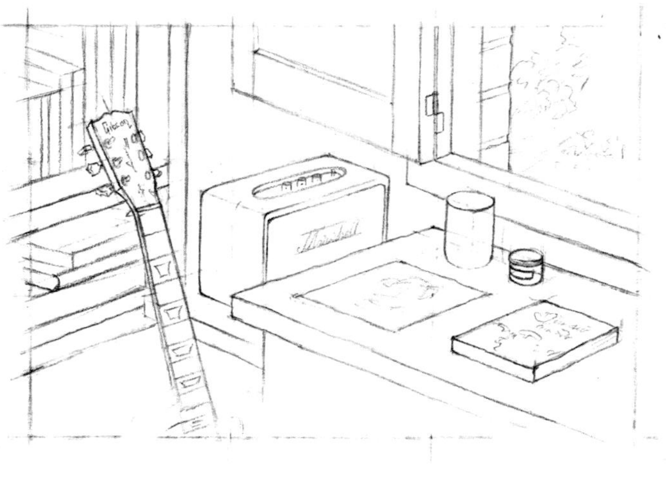

Key Shading Components: Observe your reference photo (or the space directly if you do life drawing), squinting slightly to better identify the overall light and dark areas. Then, start mapping out key shading components like the core shadow and cast shadow (the very dark areas), highlight (the brightest part), direct light (light areas), as well as reflected light and mid-tones by using a light pencil. There's no need to shade with the pencil yet, so the drawing will be easier to erase after finishing the sketch.

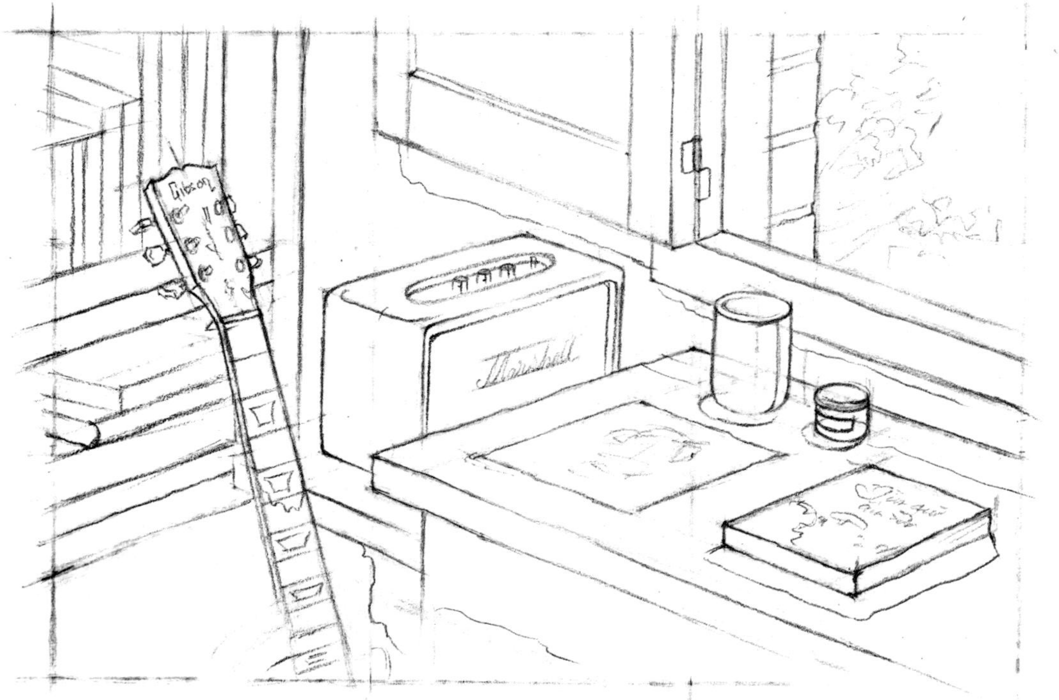

Overall Shading with Pen and Ink: Once the key shading components are defined, let's use pen and ink with any techniques you prefer to apply a light gray tone on the dark areas including core shadow, reflected light, and cast shadow. If you're unsure about the lightness or darkness of certain areas, squinting at your reference can help you determine the values. In this demonstration, I used multiple pen-and-ink techniques to express a variety of subjects in the drawing.

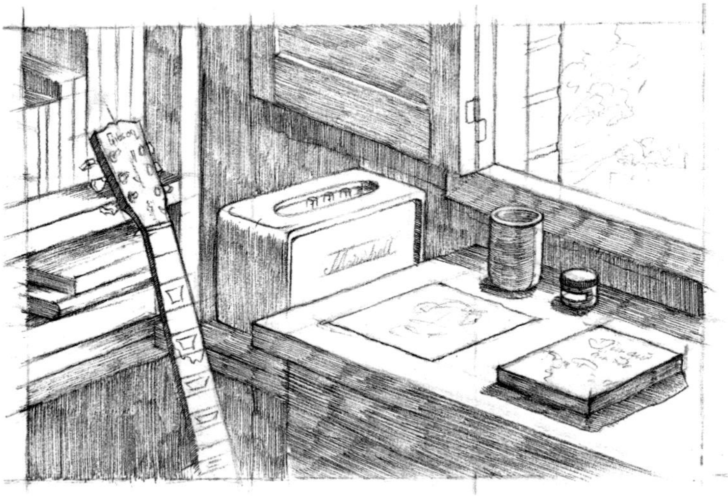

Find the Darkest Areas: As always, locate the darkest areas such as the cast shadow and the core shadow, and start shading those areas. If you want the focal point to stand out more (like the high-contrast areas or main subjects, like the guitar or cup), you might choose to emphasize the darkest areas in this spot first to balance the values in the following steps.

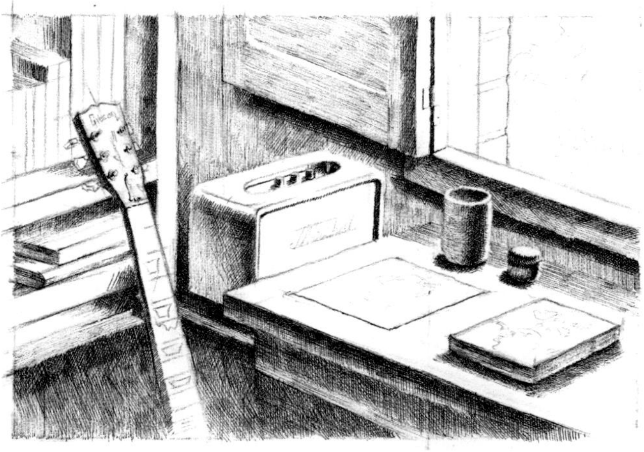

Blending the Value: Once you have the overall values and the darkest areas in place, start blending the values, and make a smooth transition between light and dark areas by shading the mid-tone. Focus more on the composition and overall lighting rather than small details or textures. At the same time, emphasize the values in the direct light and highlight areas to enhance the contrast.

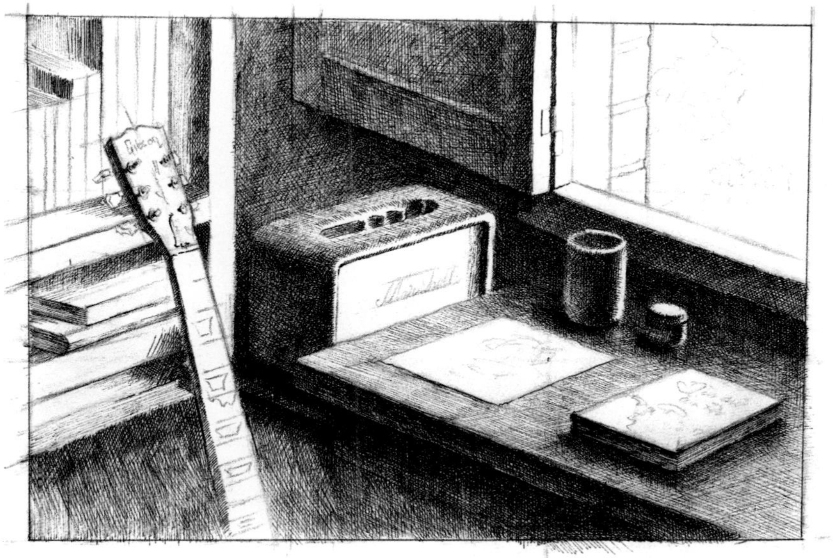

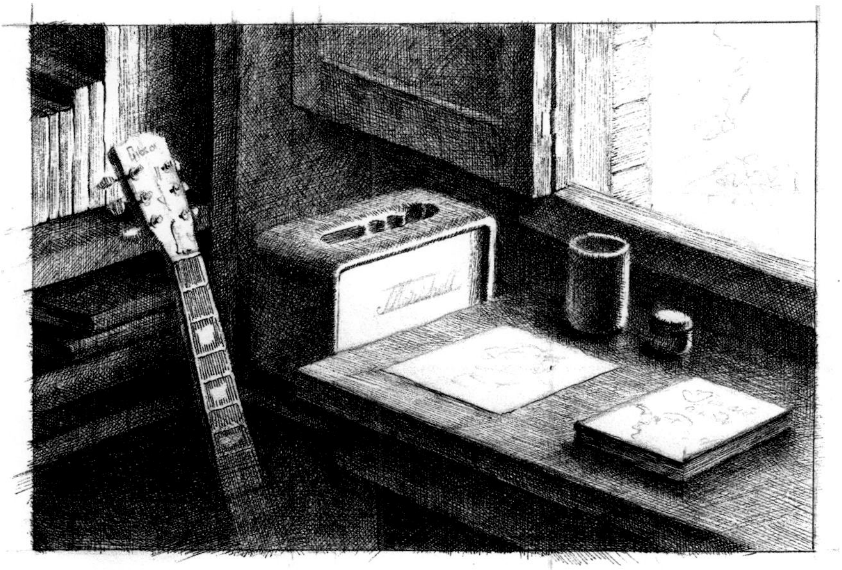

Final Touch: Take a break and step back to observe and compare your work with the reference before you begin balancing values, making adjustments, and adding details. This is the stage where you'll work on the finer details and textures—like the lettering on the cover of a book on the shelf, a pen, or a small decorative object. Use different techniques to capture the materials and textures of the subjects, bringing your drawing to life. Congratulations! Take a moment to admire the work you've just accomplished.

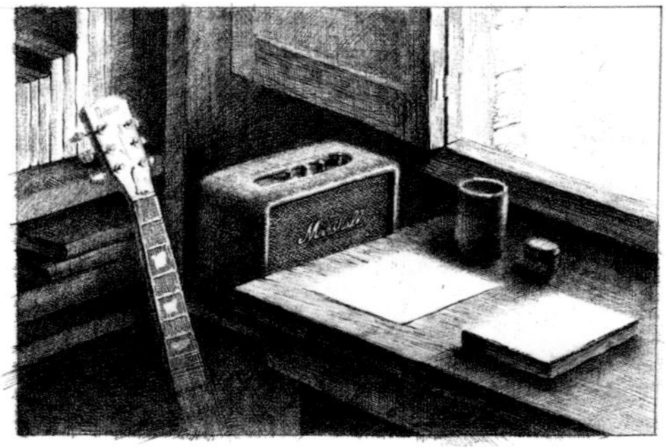

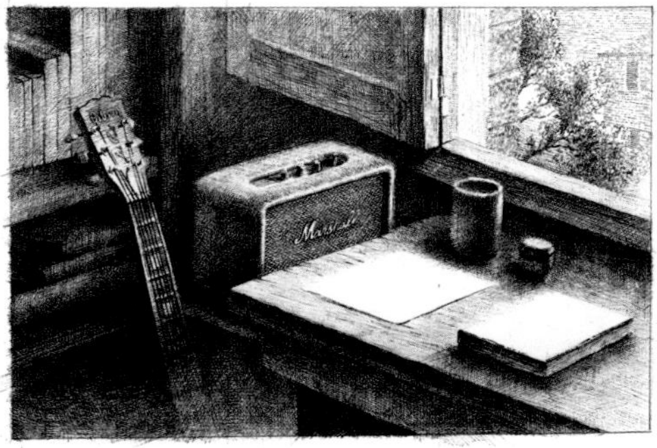

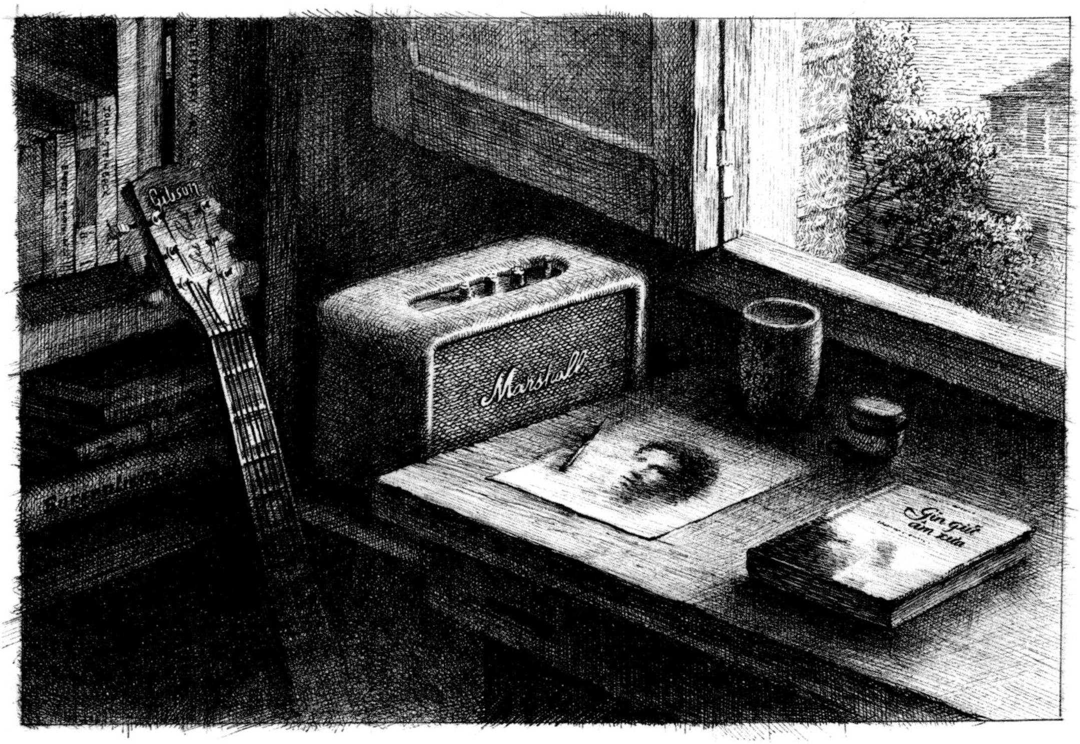

Let's Go Outside!

No matter where you are—busy city streets, peaceful countryside, or a vast beach—grab your materials and let's capture a moment of the world around you with a pen-and-ink drawing.

Defining the Composition: Start with outlining the perspective lines to establish the overall composition of your drawing. This could include the horizon line, a road, city skyscrapers, a hillside, or the coastline—any lines that define the context of your scene. This helps you get a sense of the space and makes it easier to add other details in later stages.

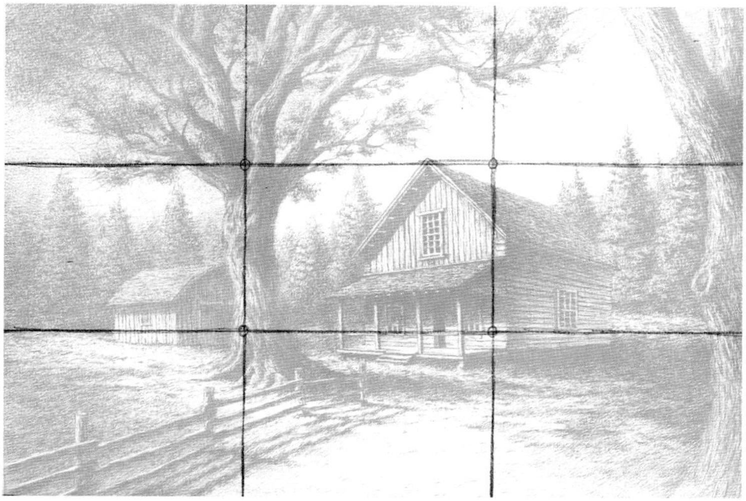

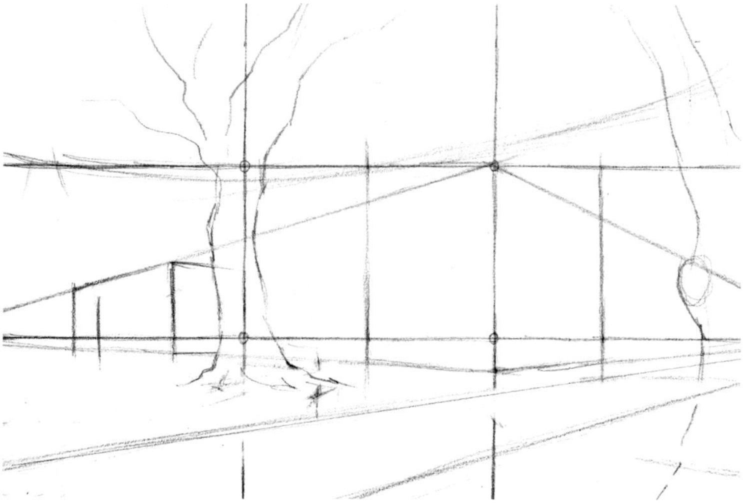

Scaling Subjects: Use simplified forms and constructive drawing methods to sketch larger to smaller subjects, similar to how we did with the indoor space drawing. This will help you create connections between subjects and the space around them. If you're in a bustling city, start with buildings, houses, and roads, then move on to buses, cars, and pedestrians. In a natural setting, sketch distant mountains and clouds first, then the ground, rocks, trees, and animals. In this drawing, I used triangular shapes to depict the trees in the distance, basic geometric shapes to simplify the structure of the house, and straight lines based on linear perspective to draw the fence.

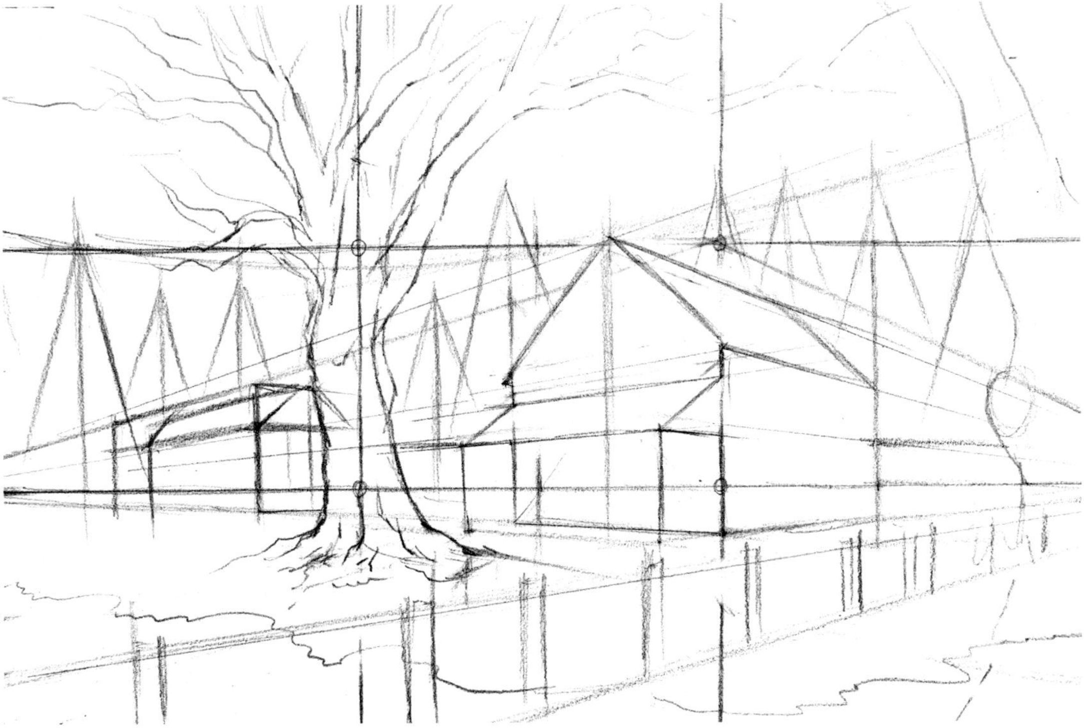

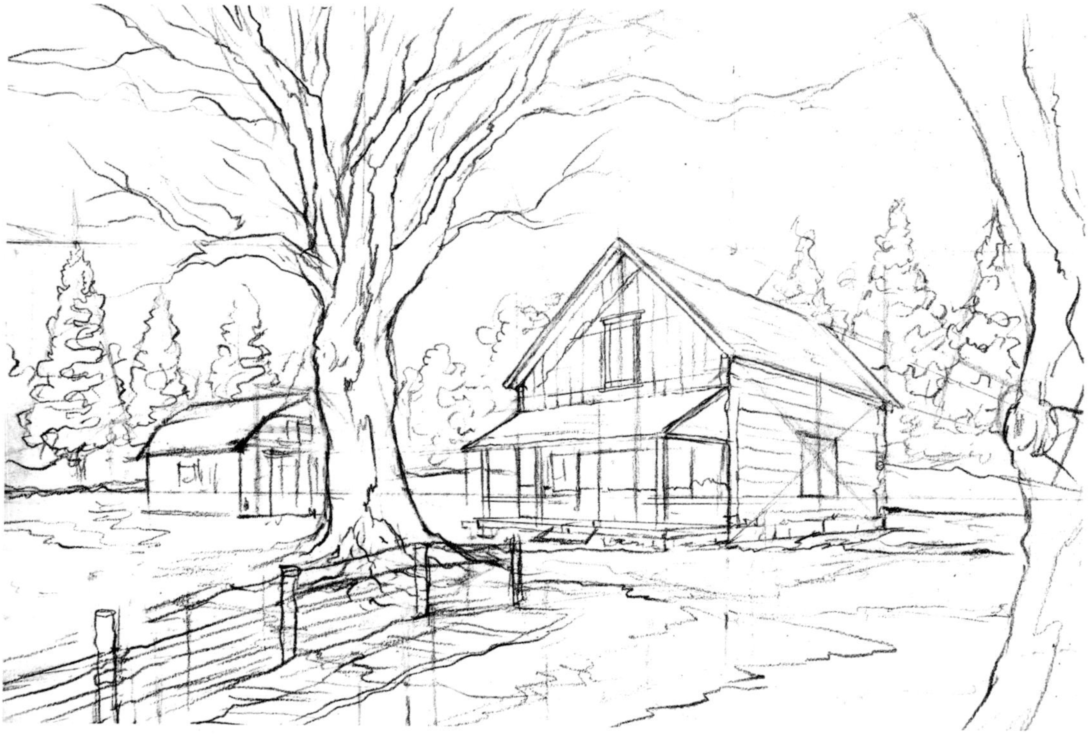

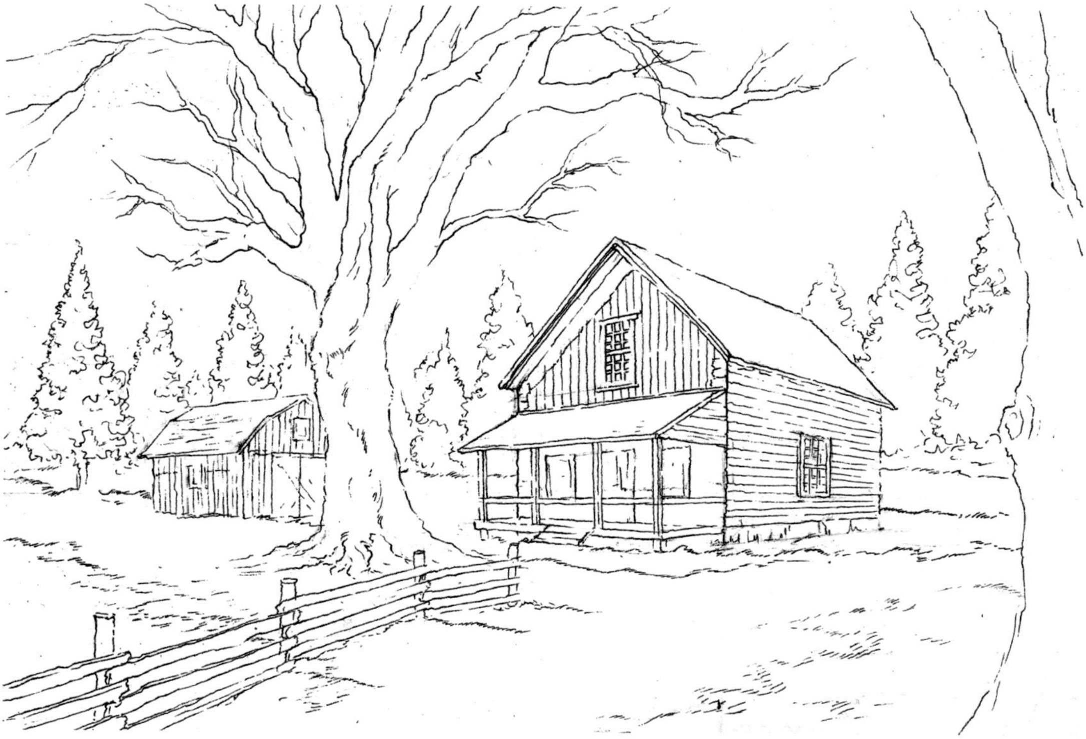

Key Shading Components: As we usually do, use a pencil to define the positions of some important key shading components, such as the core shadow and cast shadow. As you can see in this illustration, I have applied light shading just enough to establish the core shadow on the edges of the house and the middle section of the tree trunk, as well as shading the cast shadows of the house and the fence. Focus more on the larger elements like tall buildings or a hillside before diving into smaller details like tree branches.

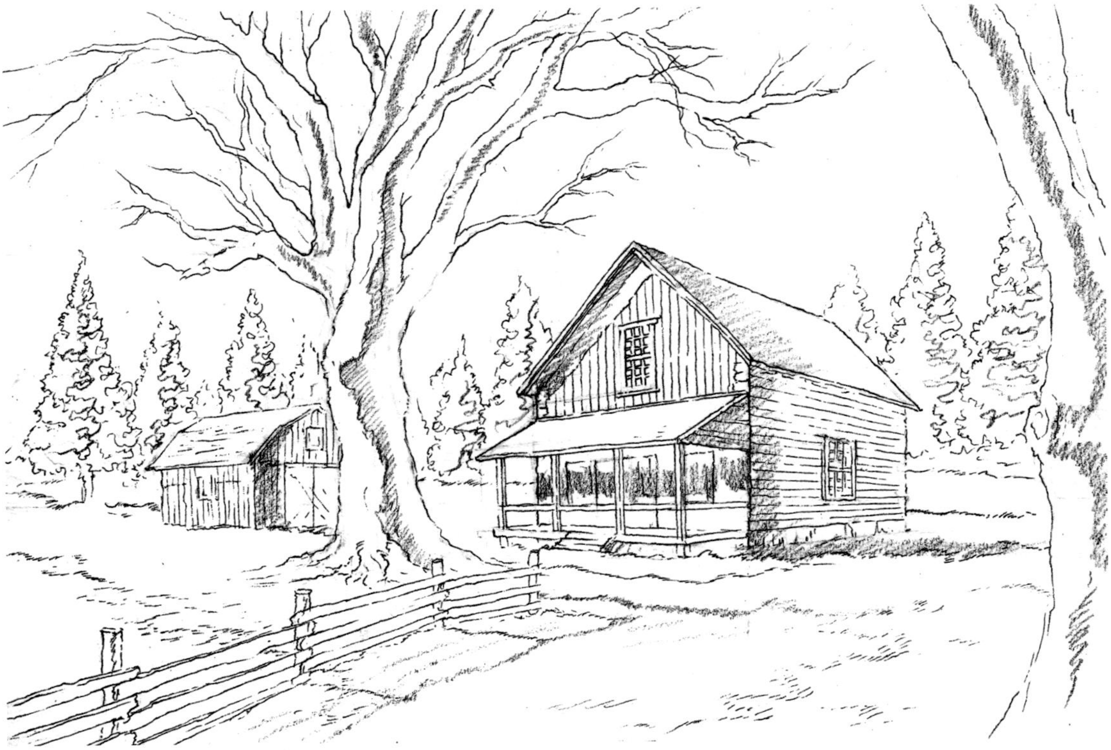

Overall Shading with Pen and Ink: Based on the shading components you've identified, start applying overall value with pen and ink. You can start anywhere you like on the drawing. However, in my experience, controlling values is easier if you begin with the focal areas, the most attractive points in your drawing. This way, the less prominent or lower-contrast areas will be easier to balance harmoniously. I use hatching to establish the overall value, creating a light layer of shading in the darker areas. Specifically, for the house, the hatching lines are on the right side of the house, as the light source comes from the left. Additionally, I shade the shadow cast off the roof onto the front of the house, and the shadow of the house cast onto the ground. For the tree trunk, similar to the tree drawing exercise (page 116), I apply hatching in the direction of the tree's growth, focusing on the right half of the trunk. For the ground, you can use short hatching strokes to depict the texture of the soil and natural grass. Pay attention to the cast shadows of objects in the scene, such as the house, tree trunk, and fence, as they interact with the ground.

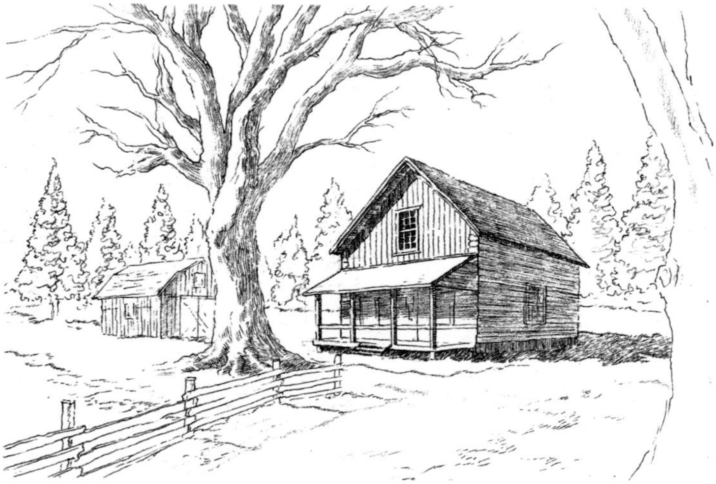

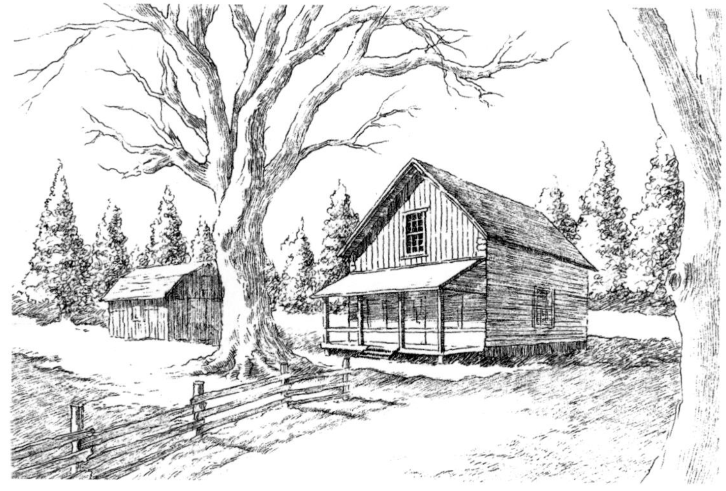

Core Shadow Is the Key: Shade the dark areas on the drawing including the core shadow and the cast shadow, particularly in the focal areas. Additionally, you can identify some very dark (almost black) areas in the scene and shade those spots. In a street scene, the darkest points might be the windows, car wheels, or pedestrian clothes. In a natural landscape, the darkest areas are often found under tree canopies where light is blocked or in the shaded areas of rocks.

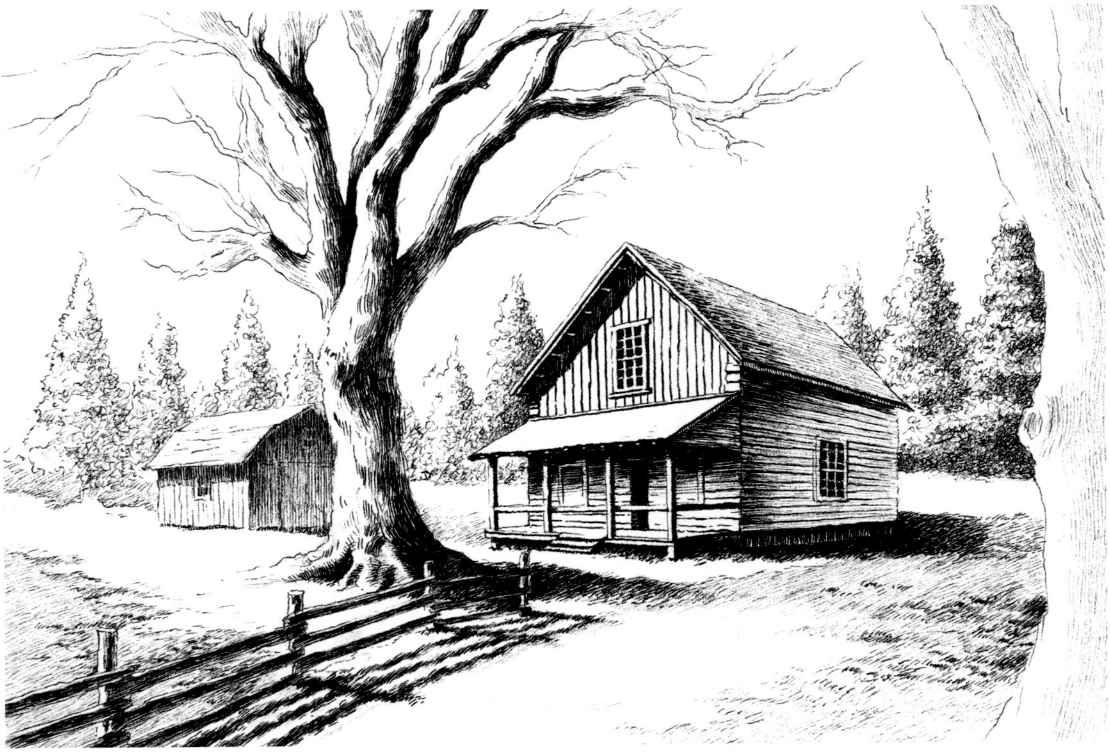

Shading Components: Based on the black points and core shadows, continue shading the mid-tones to blend the value, balancing light and dark, and highlighting direct light and bright areas. The best way to create depth in a drawing is to build value gradually, layer by layer. I will focus on the tree and house first, as they are the focal points of the composition. For the house, I add layers of hatching in the darker areas, define the reflected light on the right corner, and add shading details to the smaller structural elements. For the tree trunk, I use a combination of hatching and crosshatching to balance the contrast. Once the focal points are completed, I use them as a reference to shade the rest of the scene, ensuring that the focal points remain the most contrasting and attention-grabbing areas. The distant trees, house, sky, and grassy ground are all shaded but kept within a balanced value range (not too dark or too bright) to reduce contrast. In these areas, I also use crosshatching to gradually build up the shading layers.

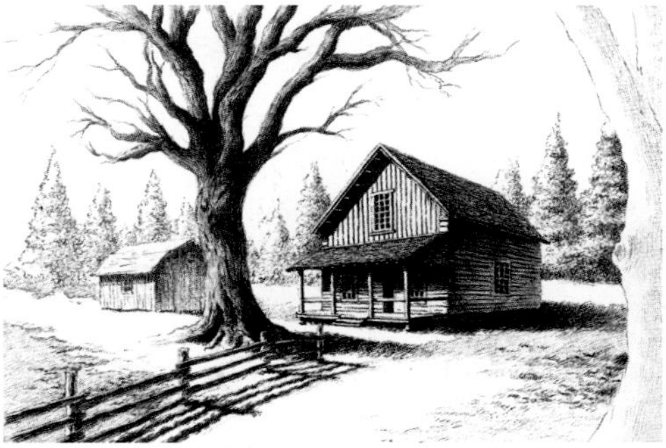

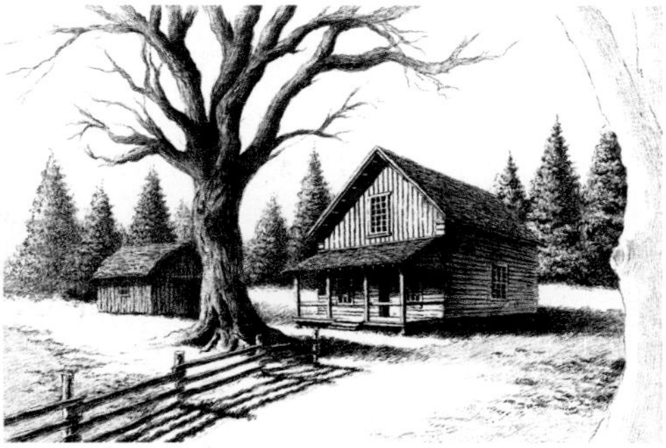

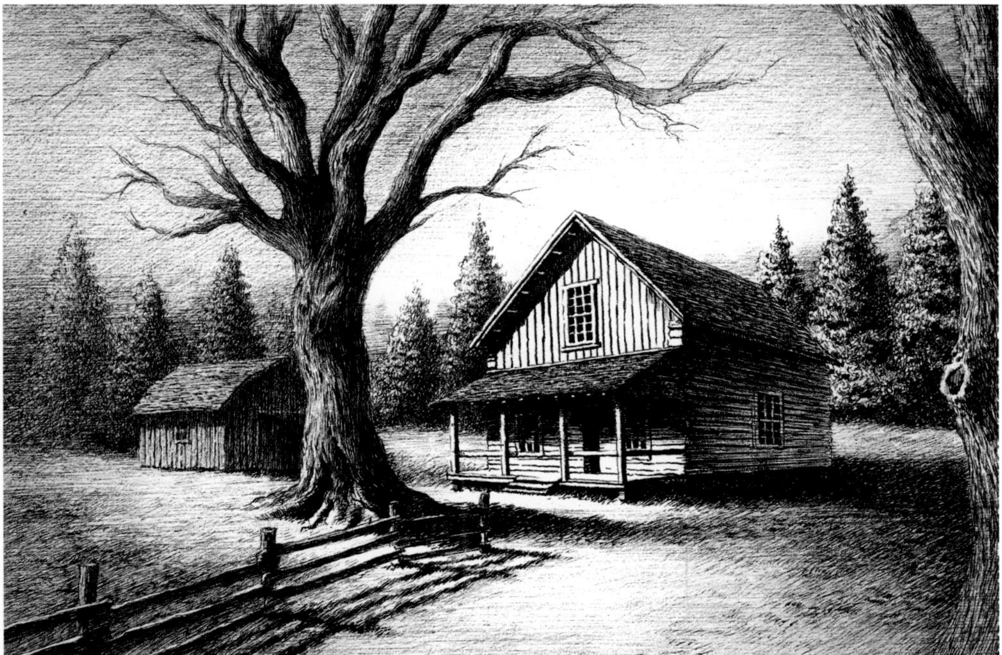

Refinement & Details: Finally, take a break, observe, modify, and add fine details to your drawing, such as the texture of a tree, the rough surface of the mountain in a nature landscape, the restaurant's sign, or the clothes of pedestrians in an urban-scape. And that's it! You've finished an open-space drawing.

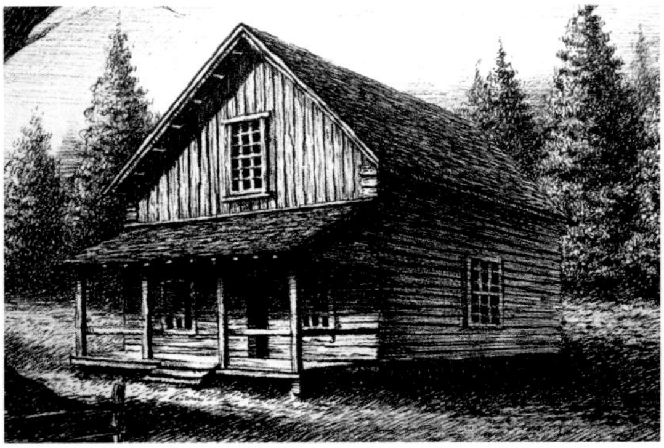

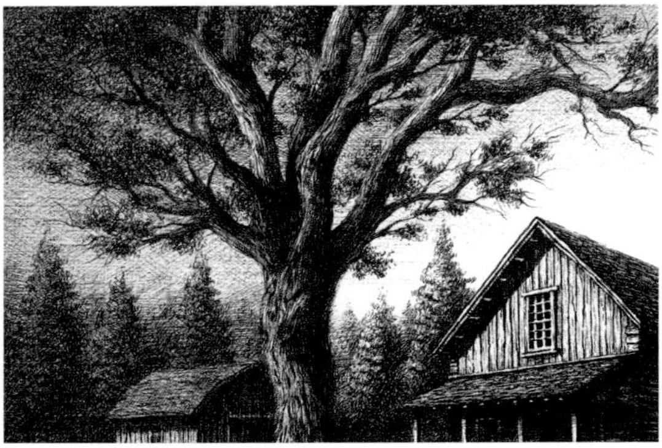

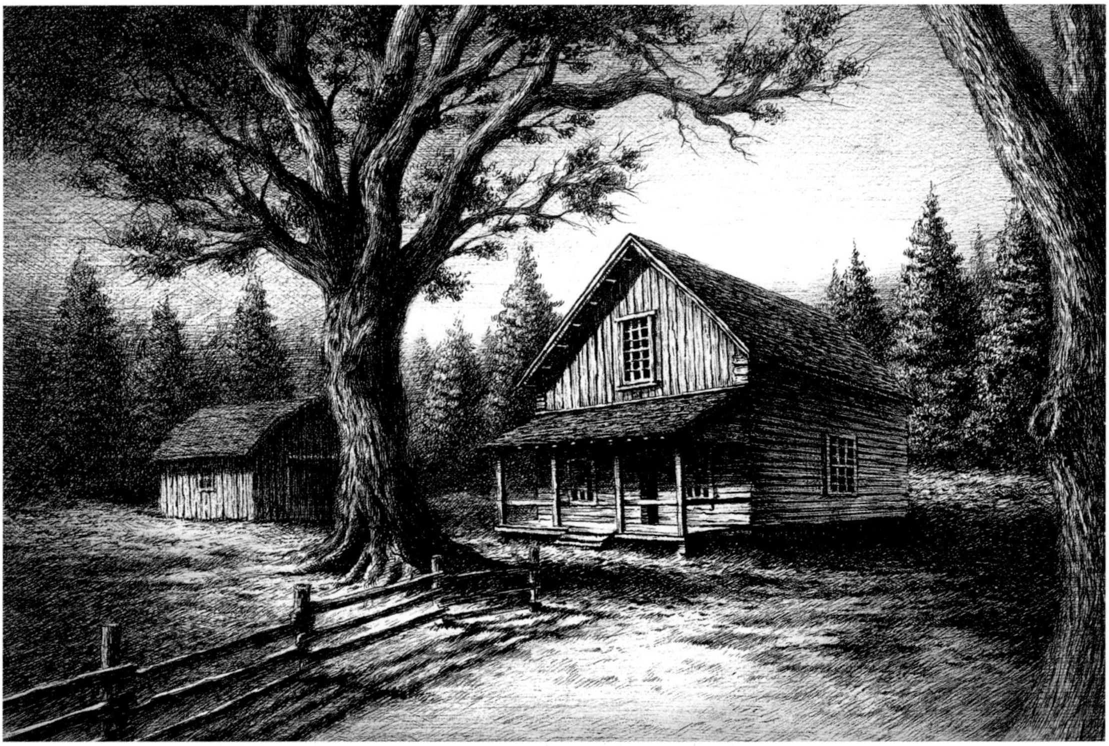

DRAW A PORTRAIT

Portraits are a great source of inspiration for those who love art and creativity. In this section, let's draw a portrait using pen and ink. Every person has unique features and personality traits on their face, so there isn't a precise standard for facial proportions. However, we can rely on some basic, relative proportions as a starting point. From there, you can easily adjust to capture the distinctive characteristics of the person you're drawing. Let's practice the basic facial proportions with the following guidelines. We will begin with an initial sketch and then move on to applying shading techniques to complete the portrait.

Sketching the Portrait

In this demonstration, I'll be drawing a portrait using traditional, classic lighting and perspective setup. The face will be slightly turned to one side, allowing us to capture both the front and side of the portrait. Soft lighting will come from above, covering about three-quarters of the face. This setup is known as three-quarter lighting.

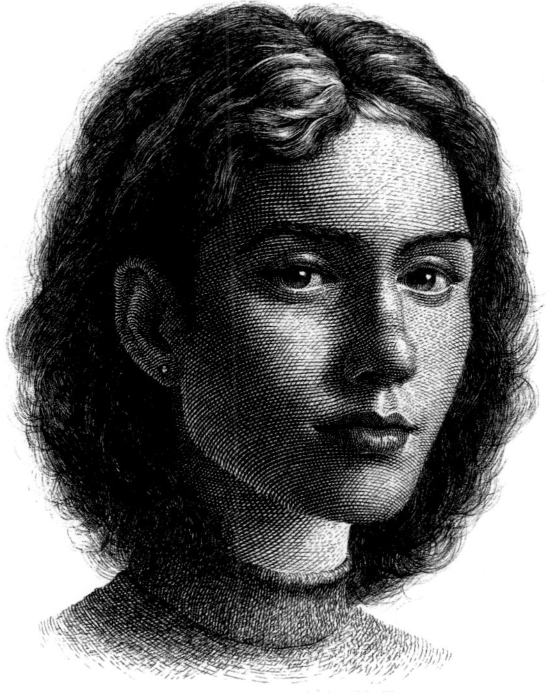

Step 1: To sketch the portrait, one of the most widely used methods by illustrators and artists is the Loomis method. Start by sketching a sphere with an H or HB pencil to represent the top of the head.

Step 2: Imagine flattening the sides of the sphere. If viewed from a half-profile perspective, the flattened part will resemble a smaller circle, concentric with the larger circle from the previous step. The diameter of this smaller circle is about two-thirds of the larger one. Now, draw two oval shapes to represent the flattened surface, adjusting them according to the correct perspective. Also, draw a slightly curved line from the top of the head down to the chin to represent the vertical axis of the face.

With the basic proportions, the distance between the hairline, eyebrows, bottom of the nose, and chin are all equal. The horizontal line that passes through the center marks where the eyebrows will be placed. The radius of this flattened surface (half of its height) will correspond to the distance from the eyebrows to the hairline and from the eyebrows down to the bottom of the nose. You can now figure out the distance from the bottom of the nose to the chin (which is the same as the distance from the bottom of the nose to the eyebrows).

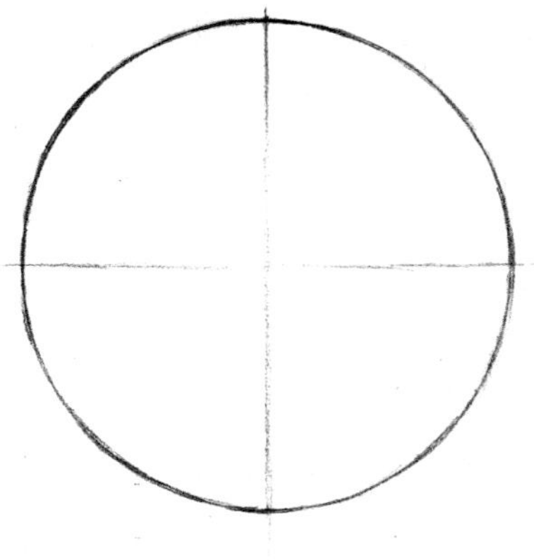

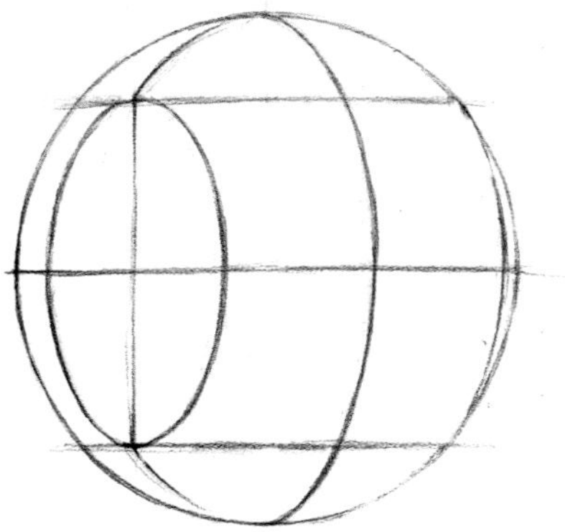

Step 3: Based on the flattened sides of the head, draw a curved line connecting the oval shapes to the chin. This will show the division between the front surface of the face and the sides of the head.

Step 4: Draw an angled line from the chin intersect with a vertical line to form the center of the oval shape to define the jawline. The line indicating the jaw also marks the position of the ear. The height of the ear should be between the eyebrow and the bottom of the nose. And with that, you've completed a simplified sketch of the head structure!

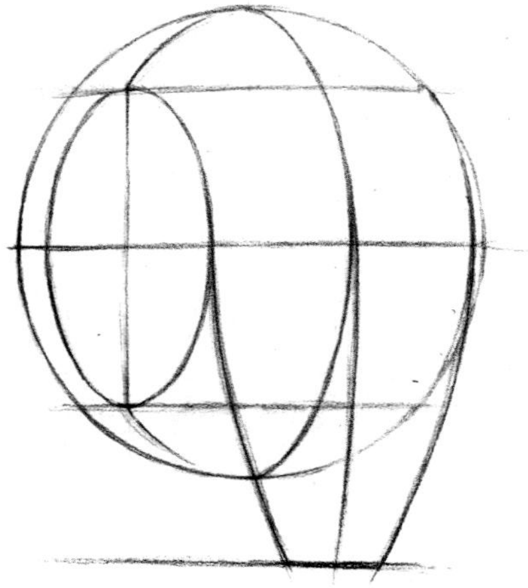

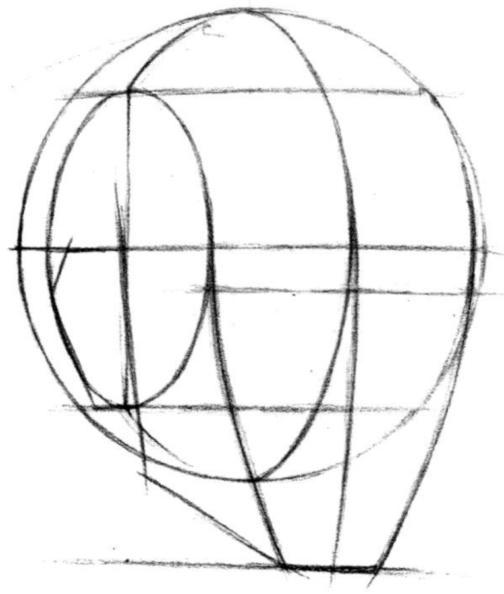

Step 5: Let's start by sketching simplified forms of the facial features:

- *Eyes:* The eyeball has the structure of a sphere, with the eyelids wrapping around it to create the shape of the eye. The iris is a small circle with a diameter about one-third of the eyeball's diameter.
- *Nose:* The nose is formed from a shape like a cube, with a central plane representing the top of the nose, two side planes for the sides of the nose, and a bottom plane for the underside. The tip of the nose can be simplified into a small sphere.
- *Mouth & Lips:* From the nose to the chin, the mouth and lips are simplified into a series of connected planes that change direction continuously.

Step 6: Once you have the positions and simplified structures of the facial features and the entire head, use a 2B pencil to sketch the actual shapes and details of the portrait. At this stage, observe and compare with your reference to achieve accurate outlines. To draw hair, create random wavy strokes that follow the direction of hair growth. As you can see, human hair grows around the head. Imagine the direction in which the hair grows and draw along those lines to capture the natural strands.

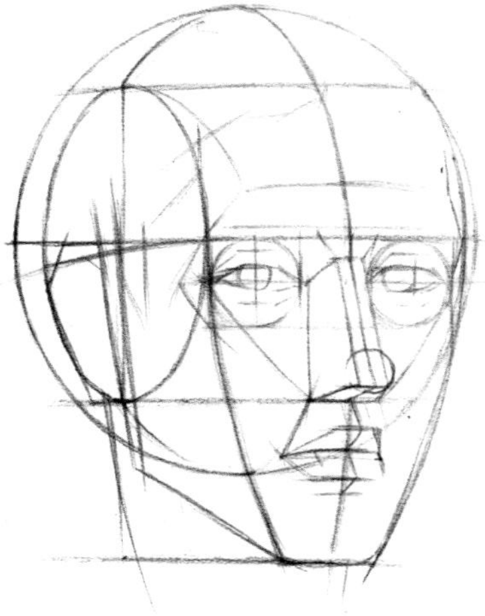

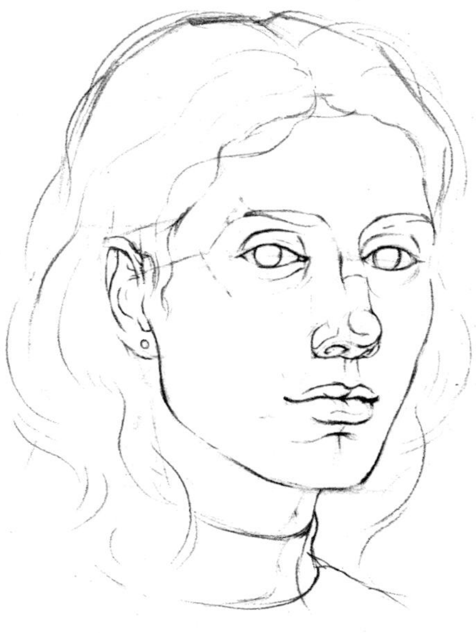

Apply Shading to the Portrait

After completing the sketch, let's move on to shading the portrait using pen and ink. In this demonstration, I'll be applying cross-contour and line thickness techniques to create a portrait that resembles a classic engraving. However, you can draw using any pen-and-ink shading technique you prefer. The most important thing, regardless of the technique, is that the process of shading and representing value remains the same. This is what we need to focus on the most. Let's get started!

Step 7 (Applying Cross-Contour): For an engraving-like technique and style, there's an extra step before beginning shading: cross-contour. You can skip this step if you're using other shading techniques that don't require cross-contour, such as hatching or crosshatching. Use a light pencil to sketch nearly parallel lines across the surface structure, and follow the form of the portrait.

Step 8: To easily identify the values, lightly mark the areas of shading components on the face using a pencil. With the three-quarter lighting setup, the core shadow usually falls on areas opposite the light source and on well-defined structures like the cheekbones, the edge of the forehead, under the nose, below the lips, and under the chin. Highlights will appear on raised parts of the face, such as the tip of the nose, above the eyebrows, the lower lip, the chin, and the eyelids.

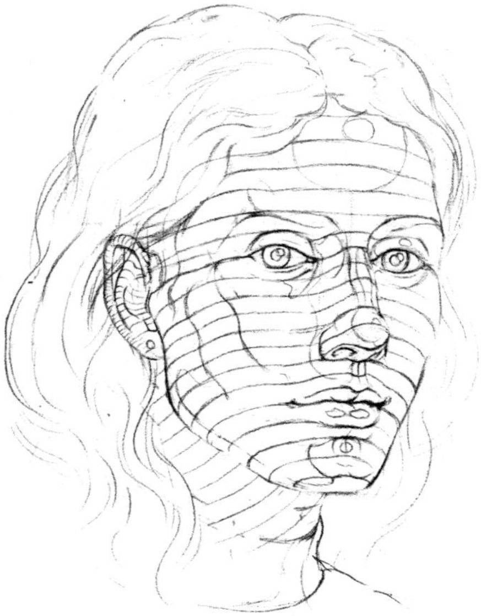

Step 9: With the cross-contour and line thickness techniques I'm using, the overall value will be represented by solid and broken lines drawn parallel to each other, spaced about 1 mm apart. Use a 005 or 01 pen to establish the overall value for the portrait. By combining solid continuous lines and broken/dashed lines, you can depict different areas of light and shadow. For darker areas, use the solid lines; for lighter areas, use broken lines; and for highlights, you can either use dots or leave the very bright areas of the portrait blank.

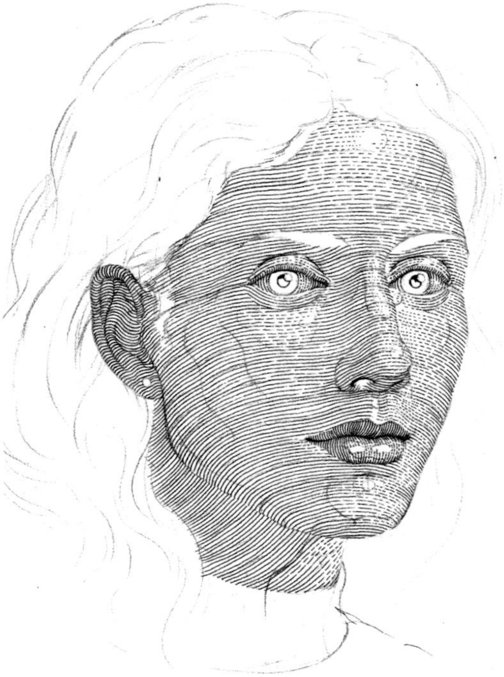

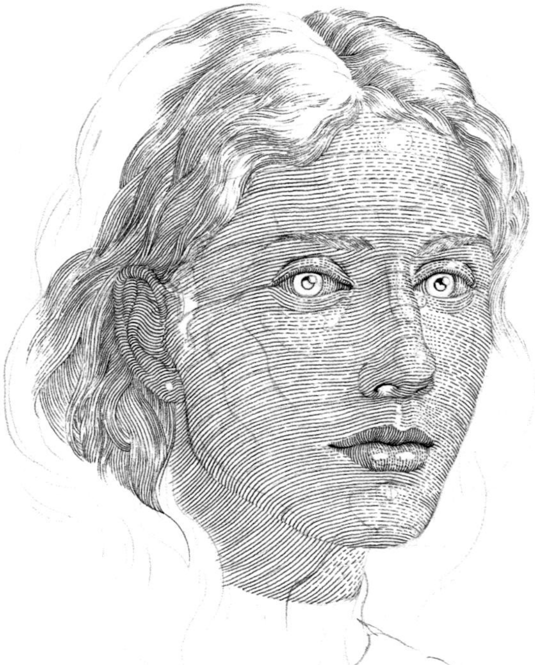

Step 10: Define the darkest spots on the portrait, which are usually under the eyelids, the pupil in the iris, the nostrils, the corners of the mouth, the eyebrows, or the hair (depending on the specific hair color of the person you're drawing). Use a fineliner to shade these areas, which are very dark (almost black). At the same time, slightly shade the core shadow areas like the cheek, the side of the nose, or under the lower lip. This step will help you establish a key value, making it easier to represent the in-between values in the following steps.

Tips for Shading the Eyes: To capture the beauty of the eyes, pay close attention to the contrast between the pupil (in the iris) and the highlight reflected from the light source. Next, shade the iris (the area surrounding the pupil); this part is usually darker around the outer edge and under the upper eyelid, and slightly lighter as it gets closer to the pupil. Finally, shade the eyeball and eyelids to balance and harmonize the values across the entire eye.

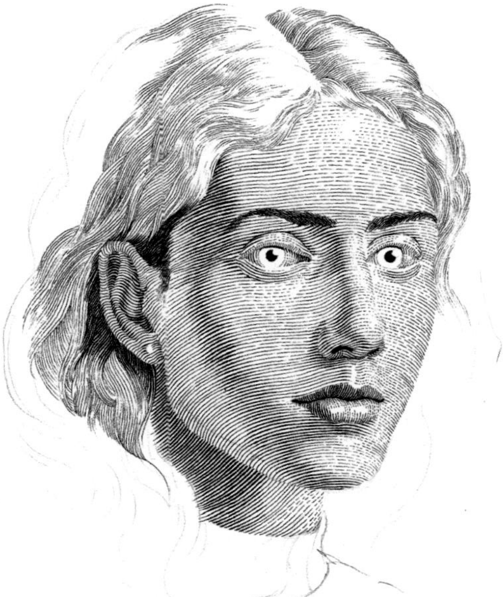

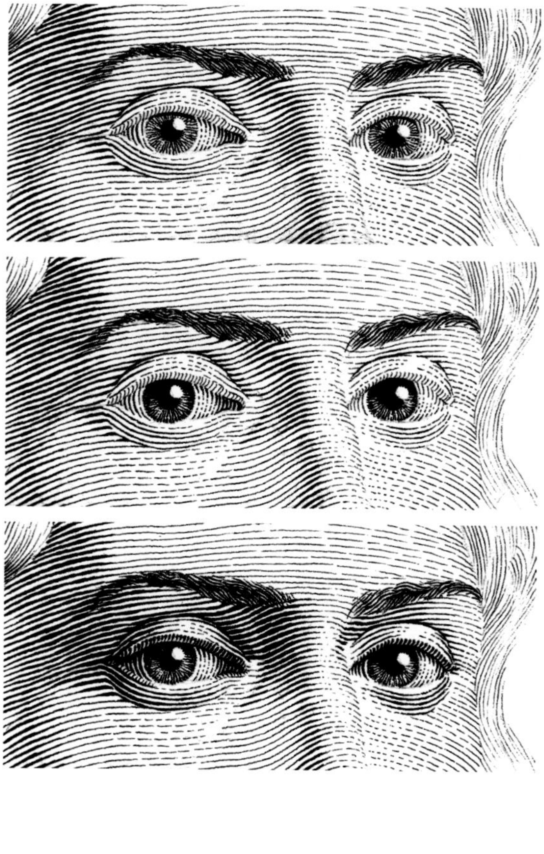

Step 11: Begin focusing on shading the dark areas of the portrait, including the core shadow, cast shadow, and reflected light. These shadows will be on one side of the face, hair, and nose. For now, we'll hold off on shading the light areas of the portrait. With the line thickness technique, carefully adjust the thickness of the lines to darken these areas.

Tips for Drawing Hair: Similar to how we approached animal fur on page 133, human hair also has specific growth directions and volume. Follow these directions to create hatching lines that cover the dark areas of the hair. The direction of hair growth can vary depending on the hairstyle you're drawing, so feel free to reflect this variation.

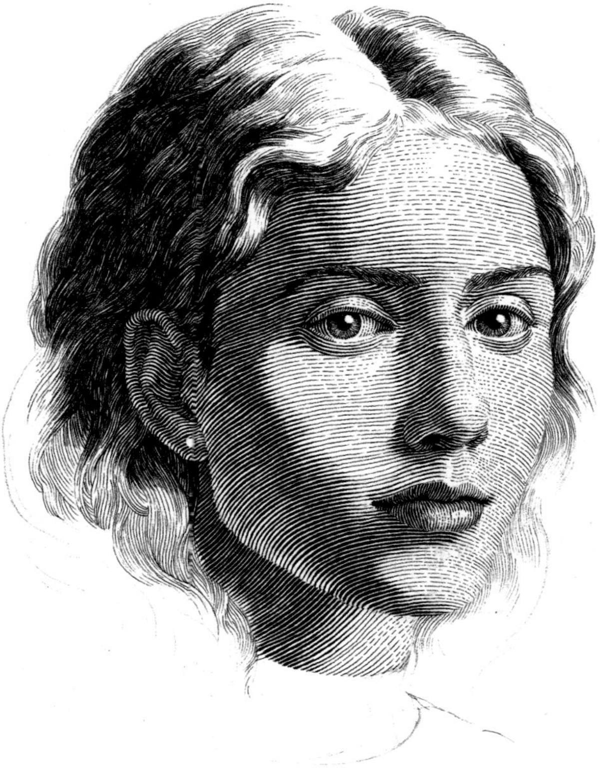

Step 12: In this step, you can start shading the mid-tone and direct light areas, and emphasize the highlights. Highlights are areas where light directly hits, typically found on raised parts of the face. They often appear on the tip of the nose, cheekbones, philtrum, chin, forehead, and highly reflective areas like the eyes and lips. Direct light surrounds these highlight areas and transitions into the mid-tones, which serve as the bridge between direct light and the core shadows established in the previous step. Pay attention to the natural harmony of the face, and shade the light areas gently.

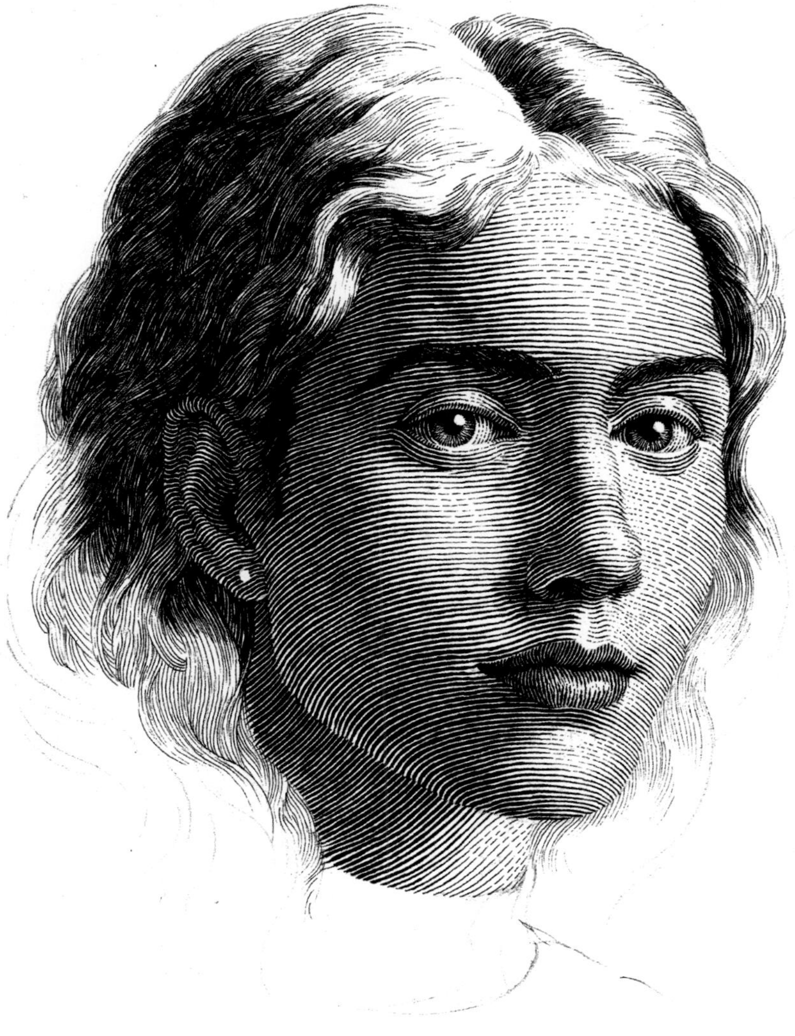

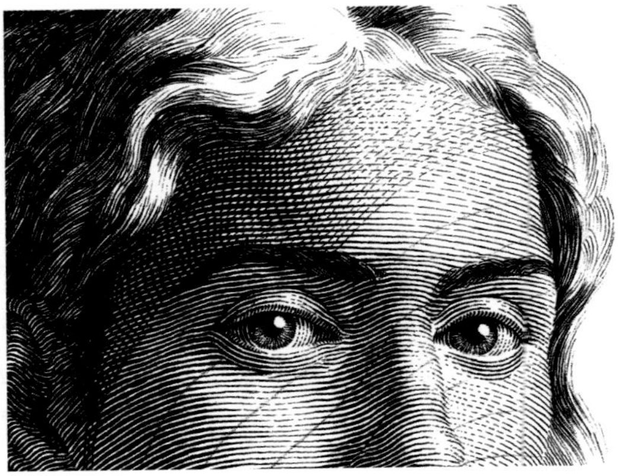

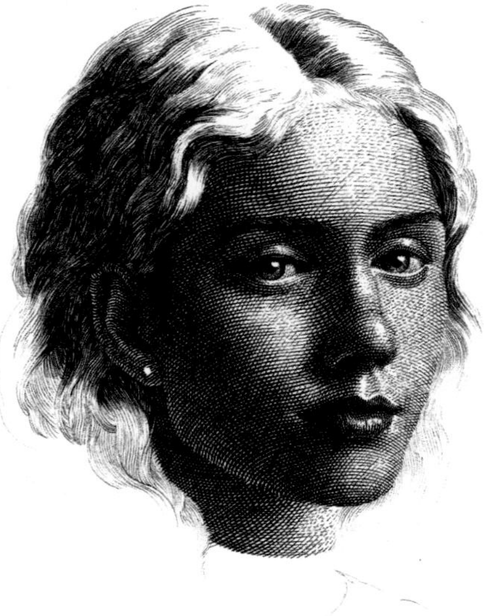

Step 13: Based on the values drawn in the previous step, continue balancing and harmonizing the values by adding more depth and contrast. In this step, try to make the value as close to the reference as possible to emphasize the portrait structure and lighting. In this demonstration, the crosshatching technique can be applied using parallel cross-contour lines in a 30-degree direction to the first hatching layer.

Step 14: Shade the hair by darkening areas that fall in shadow (you can also use a brush pen to shade large sections that are very dark, almost black). For the lighter and highlighted areas of the hair, use a 005 fineliner to create gentle, fine lines that give a textured feel to each strand.

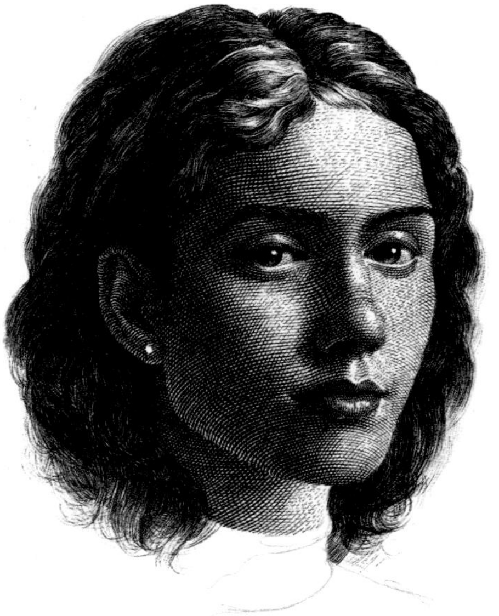

Step 15: Observe, evaluate, and modify the values while adding smaller details such as reflections in the eyes, eyelashes, or any special textures on the face that you want to include in the drawing. I added a turtleneck sweater by combining cross-contour, hatching, and crosshatching techniques to create texture. Additionally, I included an earring to introduce an interesting detail. You've completed a portrait drawing using pen and ink! You can practice more by drawing for friends or family or by gathering other references to improve your portrait skills.

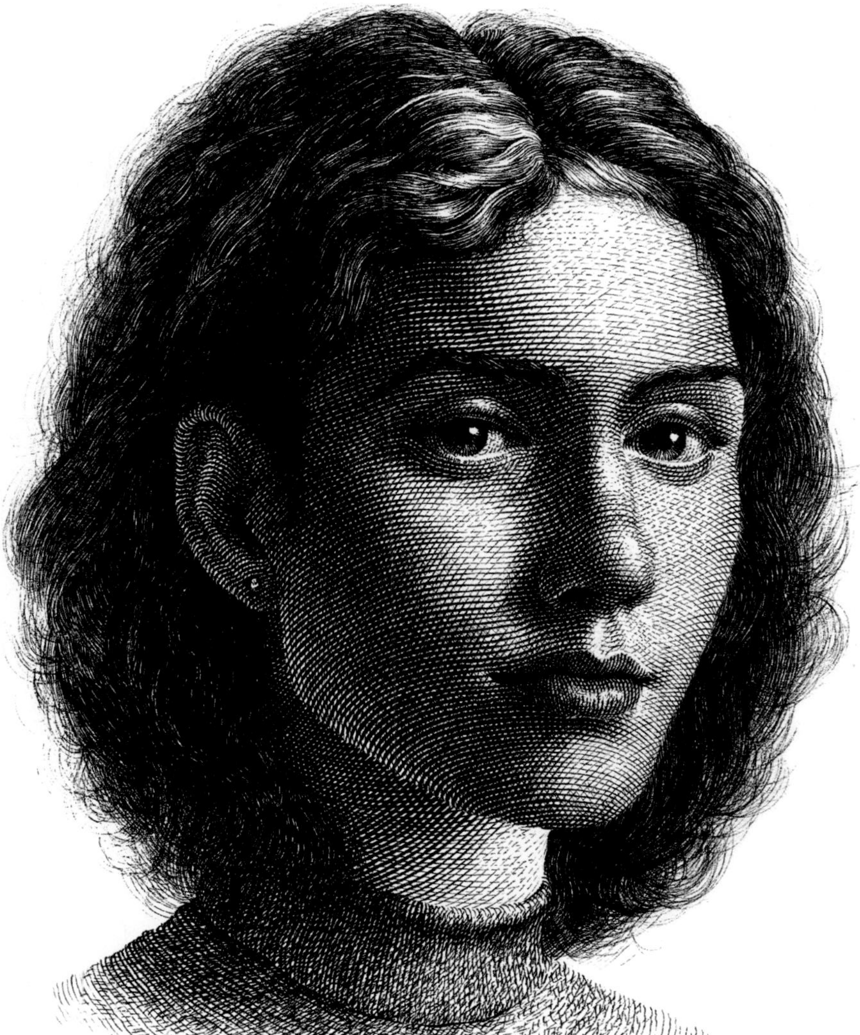

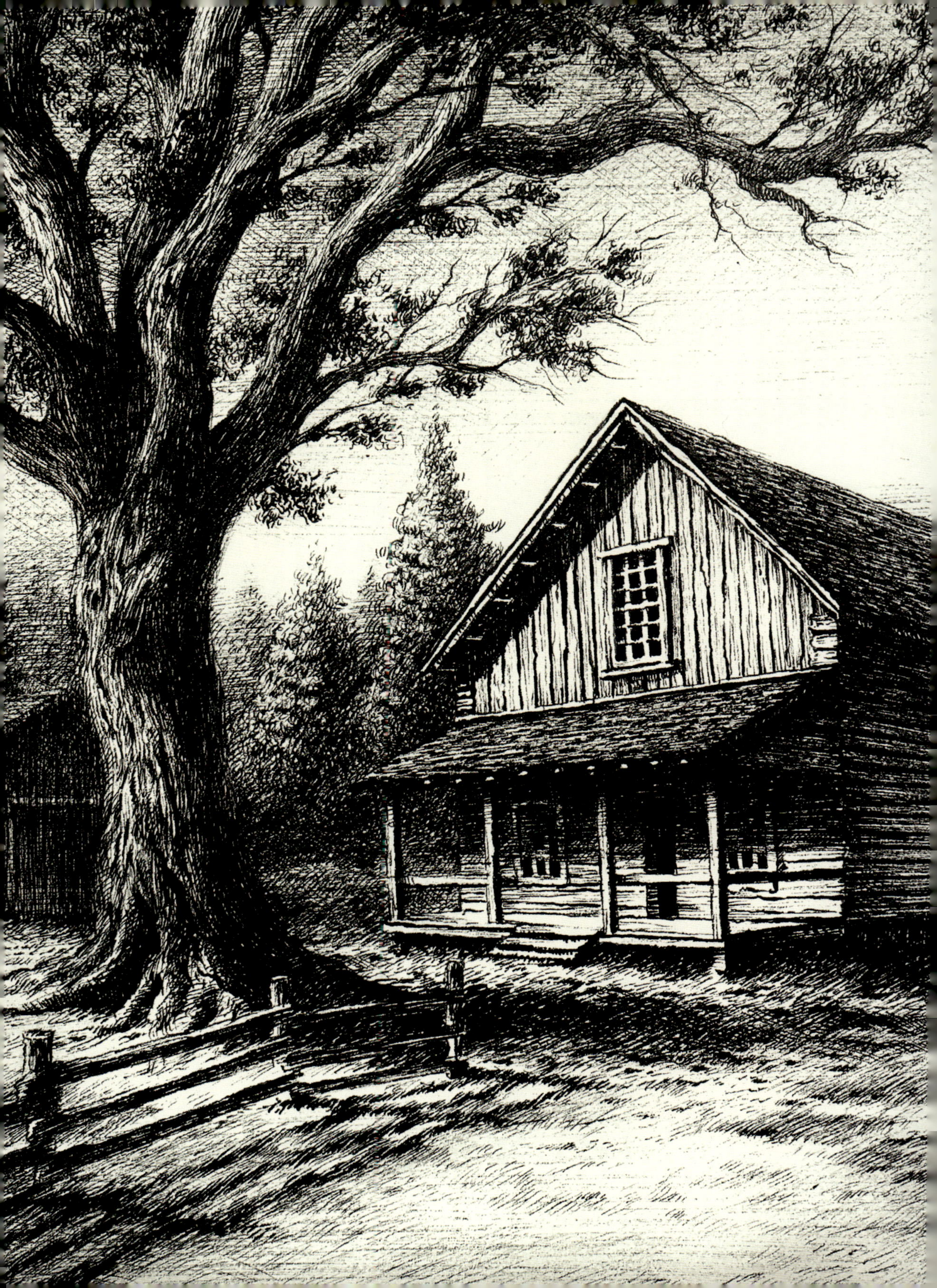

ACKNOWLEDGMENTS

This book is not only a significant milestone in my journey of sharing art but also a great source of motivation and inspiration for me to keep learning, improving, and contributing more to the artistic community. I am deeply grateful to and appreciative of everyone who helped me bring this book to life in the best way possible throughout its development.

To my parents, brother, wife, and friends—thank you for your unwavering support and sincere love, no matter the challenges. My family and friends have always encouraged me to grow and improve myself.

To my editors and the teams at Page Street, who have been incredibly supportive and kind, and who guided me through the process to ensure this book reached its full potential. I have learned so much from all of you to make this book the best it can be.

To my students—past, present, and future—you are the reason I continue to contribute and share my artistic experiences. It's been an honor to witness your learning process, discovery, and creativity along your journey.

And to the art-loving community—thank you all for always keeping art alive and holding a special place for it, and for filling our spirits, souls, and hearts with beauty.

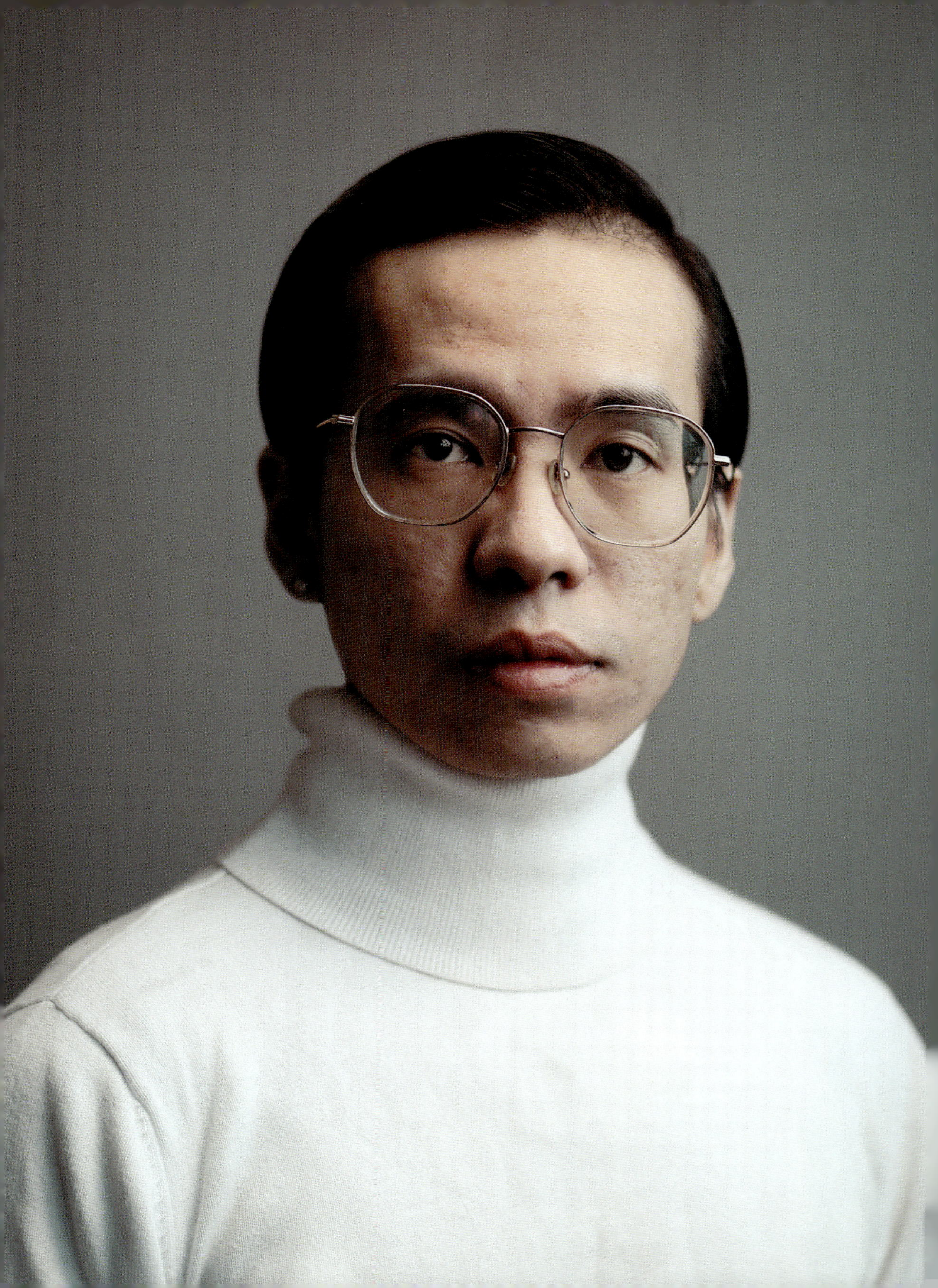

About the Author

Tri Le is an independent artist and art instructor based in Toronto, Canada. His works often emphasize visual and artistic storytelling, conveyed through classic pen-and-ink techniques. With nearly ten years of experience as an art instructor and extensive expertise in pen-and-ink mediums, Tri has developed a unique style that blends technical precision with emotional depth.

His artworks not only showcase meticulous detail but also create visual worlds for viewers to explore and enjoy. As an art instructor, Tri compiles comprehensive, accessible course materials that cover a wide range of mediums and techniques. He also leads both in-person and online workshops, sharing his deep knowledge and experience in the art world.

Beyond his passion for drawing and art, Tri enjoys photography and playing musical instruments. These hobbies not only enrich his artistic soul but also serve as emotional inspiration, fueling his personal growth and creativity in his art practice.

Website: trileart.com

Instagram: @tri.shiba

YouTube: youtube.com/@trileartist

INDEX

T

U

V

W